TIME & SPACE VISUALISER

TIME & SPACE VISUALISER

The story and history of **Doctor Who** as data visualisations

Designed & written by

PAUL SMITH

Published in the UK in 2013 by Paul Smith/Wonderful Books
14 St George's Court, Garden Row, London SE1 6HD
www.wonderfulbook.co.uk

Printed on demand through CreateSpace

ISBN: 978-0-9576062-0-3

With thanks to David J Howe, Jon Preddle, Paul Scoones and Tony Smith

About the author

Paul Smith is a graphic designer and production editor with more than 20 years' experience in the business press. Much of his work has involved presenting technical information and data in a clear fashion for easy understanding by the readership, but this is the first time he has applied those techniques to the facts and fiction of the BBC television series *Doctor Who*. His devotion to the programme goes back to childhood and has frequently sought a creative outlet. In his teens he edited the fiction fanzine *The Black Pyramid*, began designing alternative covers for the *Doctor Who* DVD range in 2001 (ongoing at www.velvet-jacket.com), and in 2011 he wrote, illustrated and produced *The Wonderful Book of Dr Who 1965*, a tongue-in-cheek pastiche of BBC Books' *Brilliant Book of Doctor Who*. It was followed this year by a light-hearted update of the 1973 *Radio Times Doctor Who 10th Anniversary Special* to celebrate the modern series.

CONTENTS

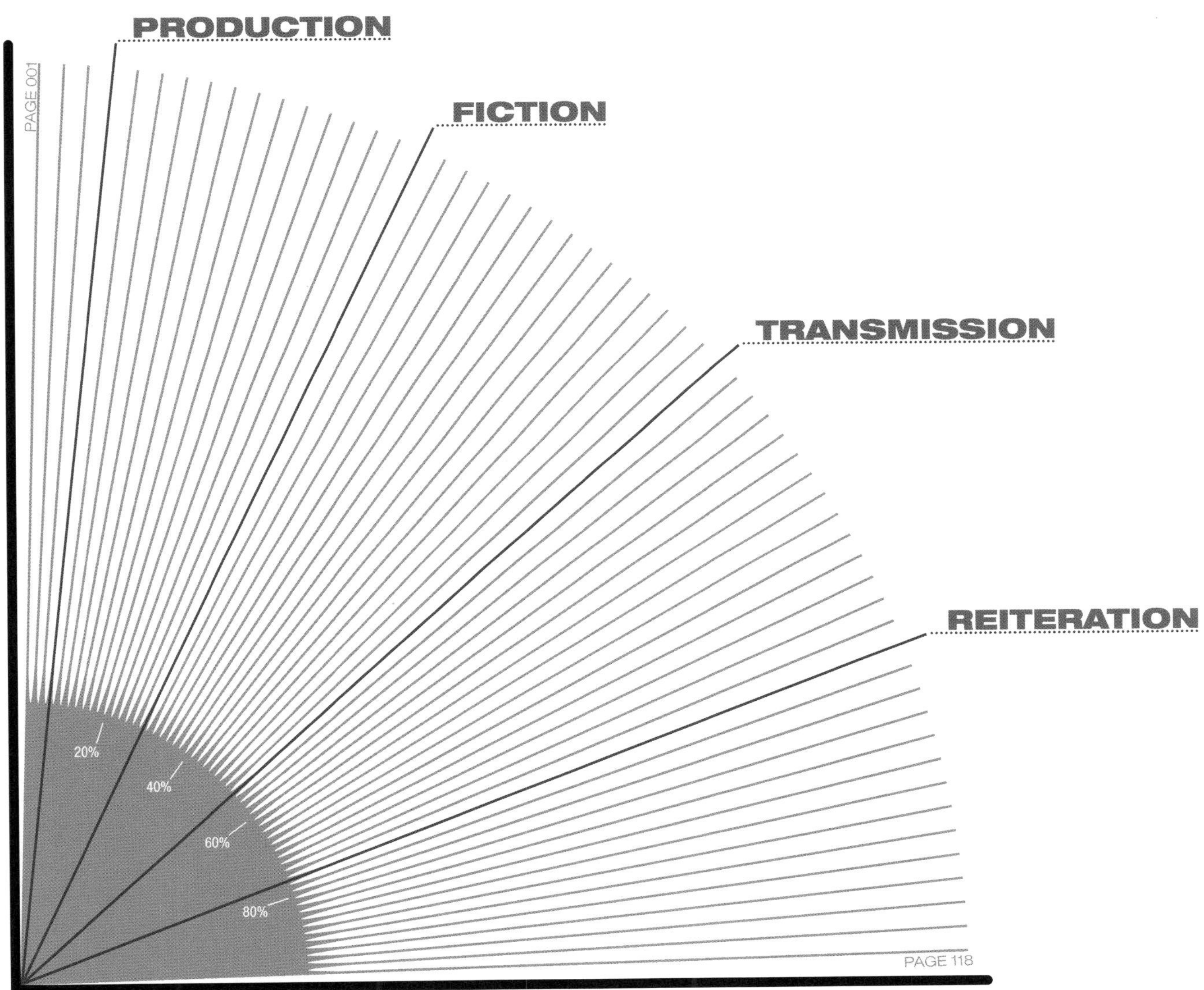

PRODUCTION
FICTION
TRANSMISSION
REITERATION
PAGE 001
PAGE 118
20%
40%
60%
80%

INTRODUCTION

The world is full of information

It may seem that our lives are dominated by information now more than ever, particularly since the digital revolution, but they have always been so. From knowing where and what time of year mammoths are easiest to hunt, to finding which supermarket has the lowest price for frozen beefburgers, information is a product of the way humans codify the world around us. But how we categorise, interpret and represent that information is crucial to its utility and value. Knowing that mammoth herds head south as winter approaches is of little use if you don't know which direction 'south' is or can relate 'winter' to increasing coldness. And now, when our every online action produces reams of data about our likes and habits, what we buy, where we go on holiday and who our friends are, companies are battling to collate all this information to better target their wares at a more receptive audience.

Much of that information is in the form of numbers (and I don't just mean ones and zeroes): how many people do this, the number of times they watch that, how much someone spends on those. But to most people raw numbers are a difficult form to grasp. We can tell if a given quantity of something is bigger or smaller than the equivalent at an earlier point in time, but understanding the relative difference or the rate at which it's changing is harder just from looking at the numbers. We're much better at dealing with visual forms of information. Tell someone they eat 8,000 calories too much each day and they probably won't be able to relate to the fact, but show them exactly how much food that represents and they'll immediately understand the need to cut down. From the first people who translated measurements of distance and direction into maps and atlases, to Dr John Snow taking the tallies of cholera victims and plotting them on a street map of London to pinpoint the source of the disease, and Harry Beck rendering the route of the London Underground based on electrical diagrams, presenting data visually makes it easier to comprehend, interpret and apply.

One particular source of a surprising amount of information is the television series *Doctor Who*. While it may not be knowledge that's of much interest or use to most people, even those who enjoy watching an episode on a Saturday evening, there is a lot of it. With the programme approaching its 50th anniversary — an incredible achievement for any TV show (and even during the years when it wasn't on television it continued in the form of books, videos, magazines, plays, comedy acts, computer games and more) — there is a wealth of data not only about the places, people and monsters the Doctor has encountered on screen, but also how the episodes were produced, who starred in them, why particular creative decisions were made, where filming took place and what made it such a popular, iconic and enduring programme. And to a certain type of devotee of *Doctor Who* (I know because I'm one of them), this information is something to be accumulated, memorised (or at least held in books and magazines) and comprehended. By knowing as much factual detail about the show as we can, perhaps we can come to understand what it is that makes it speak so deeply to us.

But as we've seen, people aren't very good at understanding numerical and textual data. We prefer to picture it in a way that we can more readily relate to and appreciate any connections and correlations. That is what I've attempted to do in this book. I have taken facts from the full history of *Doctor Who* and visualised them in ways that are, I hope, informative, enlightening, unusual or simply eye-catching. Whether you're a follower of the Doctor's adventures or not, the aim is to show that data needn't be just numbers and tables, but can be treated more pictorially, and that by doing so we can more easily see what that information means and what conclusions can be drawn.

How big is the 'Whoniverse'?

Doctor Who is more than just a television programme. It may have begun that way but it has since spread into pretty much every other form of media, adapting and expanding as it goes. Within two years of the first episode's broadcast, the series appeared in book form. Three early serials were adapted into novels, one in particular recasting large parts of the original screenplay to detail events that were never seen on television. Shortly afterwards the first annual appeared, telling completely new tales about the Doctor. By then there were also two regular comic strips in production, one featuring the Doctor and the other presenting a history of the Daleks. In the mid-1960s the concept was translated to the cinema as two movies starring Peter Cushing as a human Doctor who has invented his own TARDIS. There were stage plays in the 1960s, 1970s and 1980s, ever more sophisticated computer games as the technology has advanced over the last three decades, and when the programme was no longer being made by the BBC for television, fans produced their own video and audio adventures. And throughout the series' history, there have been books and, latterly, websites cataloguing and analysing these myriad narratives.

This book, however, focuses on information solely from the television series as first shown on the BBC from 1963 to 1989 and 2005 onwards (up to "The Angels Take Manhattan" in 2012), in order to be accessible to the widest audience. While the Doctor's escapades in other media have been successful in their own right, the television series is the core output that is seen by the largest number of people, and the only one whose 'authenticity' is accepted by all. Not all information detailed is applicable to all eras of the series, so where reference is made to the 'original' or 'Classic' series, this refers to the initial 26-year run, while the 'revived' or 'New' series refers to *Doctor Who*'s 21st Century comeback, which has been explicitly presented as a continuation of the original rather than a separate reinterpretation or reboot of the concept. For those readers less familiar with the televised history of *Doctor Who*, the graphical guide at the start of the first section of this book will fill you in on the basics.

Visualising Time and Space

The book is divided into four sections. The first, **Production**, deals with information about the making of *Doctor Who* as a television programme, looking at details of its recording and the contributions made by the various production teams. The **Fiction** section examines data from within the narrative of the show, such as what planets the Doctor has visited, the lives of the companions he travelled with, and the plans of the villains and monsters they encountered. **Transmission** investigates the patterns in the way the programme was broadcast, its episodic structure and whether those who were watching liked what they saw. Lastly, **Reiteration** looks at how *Doctor Who* has lived on beyond its initial airing, from UK repeats to showings overseas, and from book adaptations to archival releases on video and DVD.

Every graphic should tell a story by itself, particularly to those ardent fans who have the underlying information already stored in their brains. For people who aren't quite so informed, each chart is accompanied by notes detailing the background and context of the subject under consideration, an explanation of how the data was compiled and discussion of the results and what they may reveal. Some highlight previously unconsidered relations between factors, some overturn long-held assumptions among fans, and some simply provide a new way of interpreting known facts. My primary goal has been to find as many different ways of visualising data as I could to show there are lots of options beyond lists and tables.

In compiling the data used in this book much has come from my own knowledge as a follower of *Doctor Who* for more than 30 years, as well as new research and viewings of the episodes themselves. But inevitably many of the facts about the programme, particularly such things as transmission information and releases in other media, are sourced from or corroborated using some of the innumerable reference books and websites about the series. Mostly these were general programme guides, but where I have relied on specific sources for a chart these are acknowledged in the text.

All collation, application, analysis and interpretation of the data is my own, however, including responsibility for verification and any errors arising from my calculations. I trust that the information presented here is true and accurate, but if you do spot any mistakes please contact me via the website given at the front of this book so it can be corrected for any future editions. Similarly, in some cases subjective decisions have been required when categorising certain aspects of the programme, and I welcome any discussion and debate of my choices.

Seeing the whole picture

Doctor Who is probably the most researched and analysed television series ever, having as it does an almost unique power to captivate a core portion of its audience and inspire them not only to imagine but to want to know all about this incredible programme. The amount of information already recorded and still being discovered is staggering, but the more we learn the harder it becomes to see what, if anything, it all means. I hope this book shows there are ways to present this knowledge that make it easier to digest, simpler to understand and more intuitive to engage with. And that goes beyond the specifics of one media property: all information on any subject can be depicted in a way that makes it more attractive and applicable.

The volume of data in the world can only increase, and as more of our personal and working lives rely on the digital realm much of this data is being gathered and stored for the first time. Rather than let it sit ignored on numerous servers, we can use this data to better understand our interactions and impact on each other and the world around us. But to avoid being overwhelmed, we need to represent the information in a way that allows us to envisage what it means to us. There is a growing field of data visualisation and infographics that seeks to find new ways of appreciating all forms of information — a quick search online will lead you to numerous examples. My area of appreciation is *Doctor Who* — what's yours?

PRODUCTION

ALL OF TIME AND SPACE

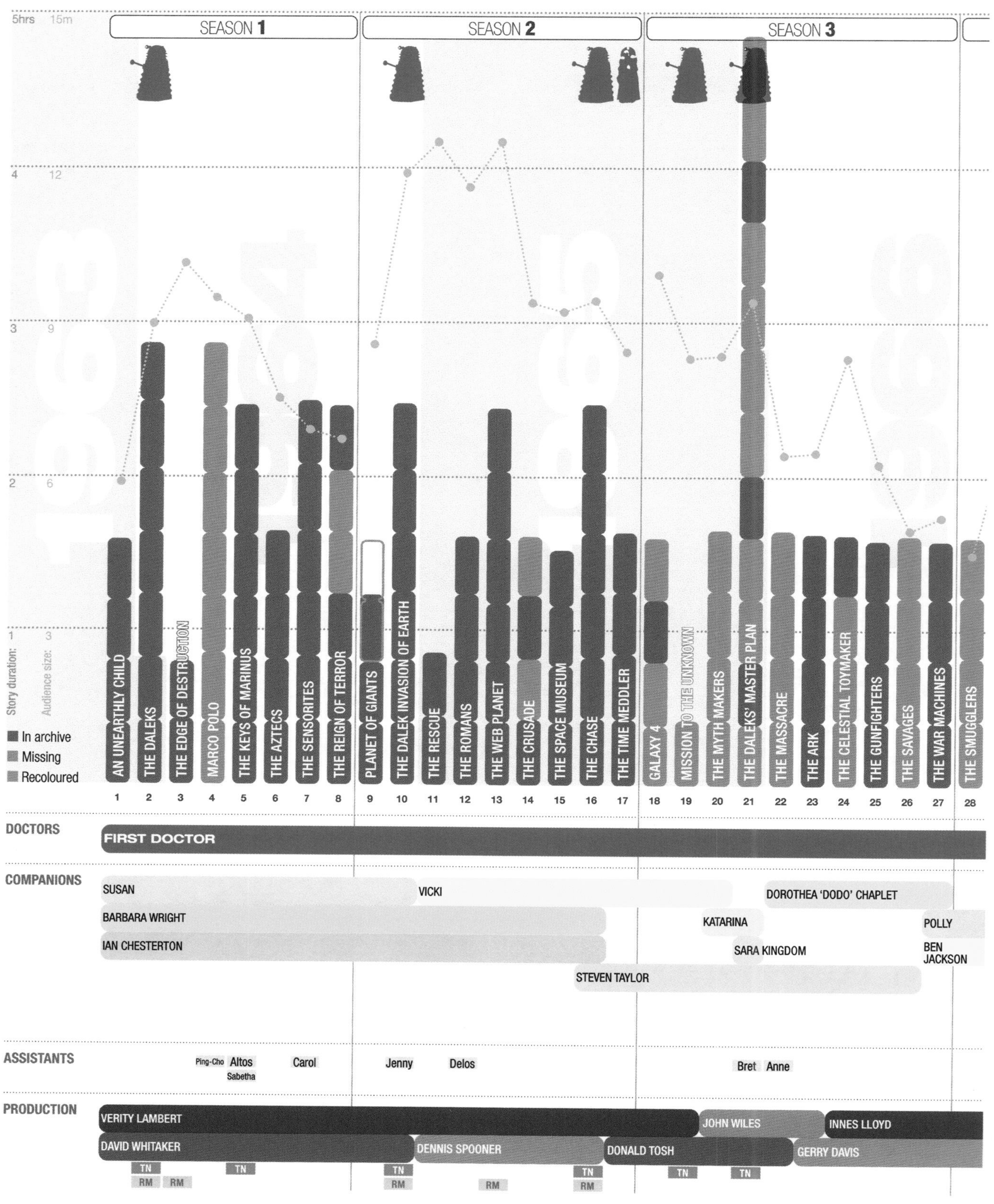

Everywhere and anywhere. Everything that happened or ever will. Where do you want to start?

While this book isn't a typical guide to *Doctor Who*, it may be handy to know a little about what stories were shown when, who was in them, and which production teams made them. So starting as we mean to go on, here is that data presented visually, rather than in the commonly seen tables or lists.

Stories are in transmission order (which sometimes differs slightly from the order they were made). The vertical scale in beige is time, with each block being one episode, scaled to its duration. The colour of the blocks shows each episode's state in the archive: surviving, missing or recoloured by combining black-and-white film prints with colour from off-air video recordings or other non-broadcast-quality sources. [continued on next page]

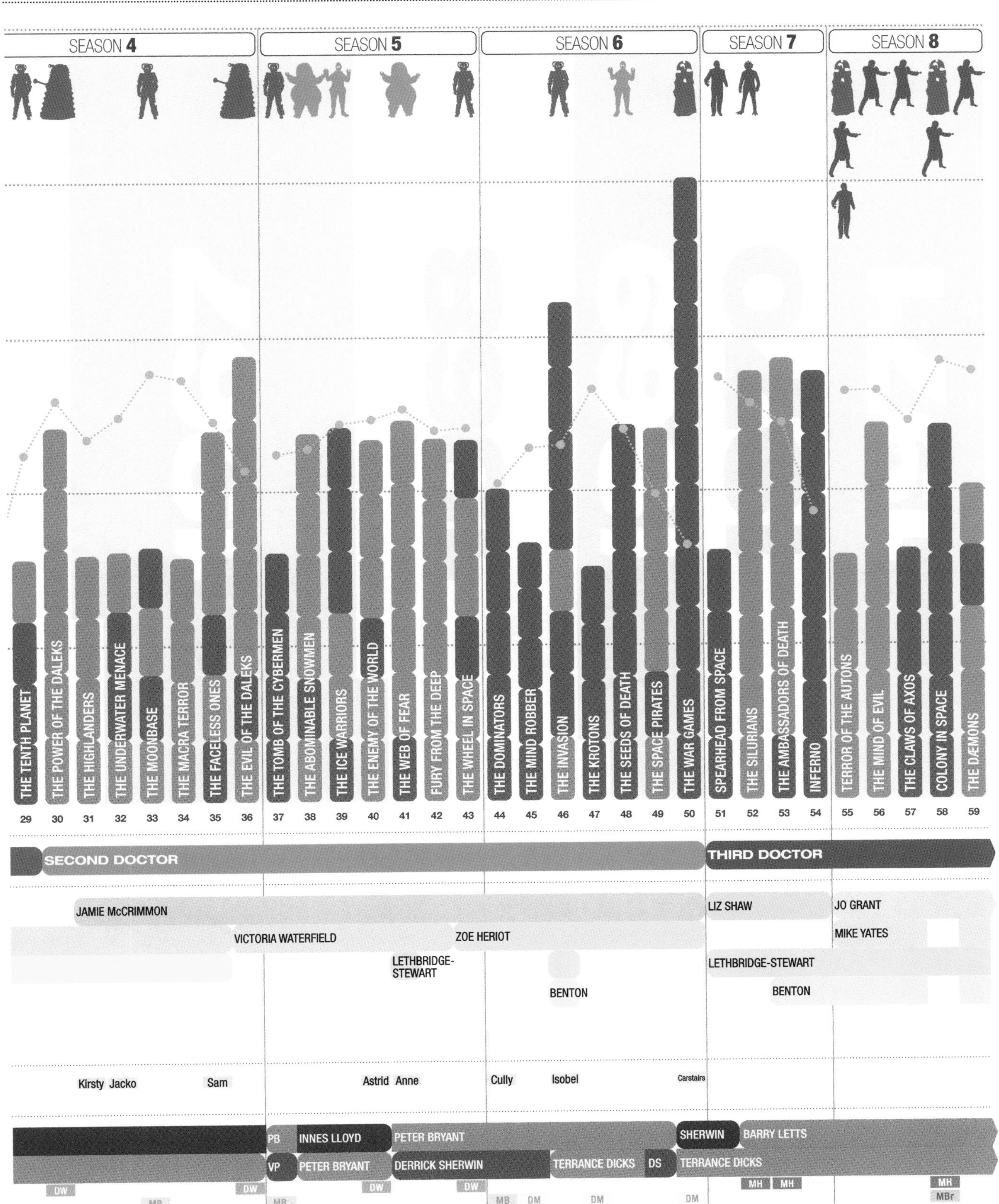

"Planet of Giants" was written and recorded as four episodes but the last two were cut into one for transmission. "Shada" was to be the concluding six-parter of Season 17 but strike action at the BBC prevented its completion. "The Five Doctors" was produced as part of Season 20 but not shown until eight months later for the show's 20th anniversary. "Resurrection of the Daleks" was made (and shown abroad) as four parts but re-edited into two longer episodes for first UK transmission to avoid a break during the Winter Olympics. Season 23 comprised one 14-part story, "The Trial of a Time Lord", and is numbered as such. But it was produced in three separate sections covering four linked stories, which are listed individually here to make the changes in companions and production personnel clearer. The only televised outing for the Eighth Doctor didn't have a story title on screen other than "Doctor Who" but is commonly called "The TV Movie". "The End of Time" is the only New Series two-episode story to have one overall title shown as parts one and two.

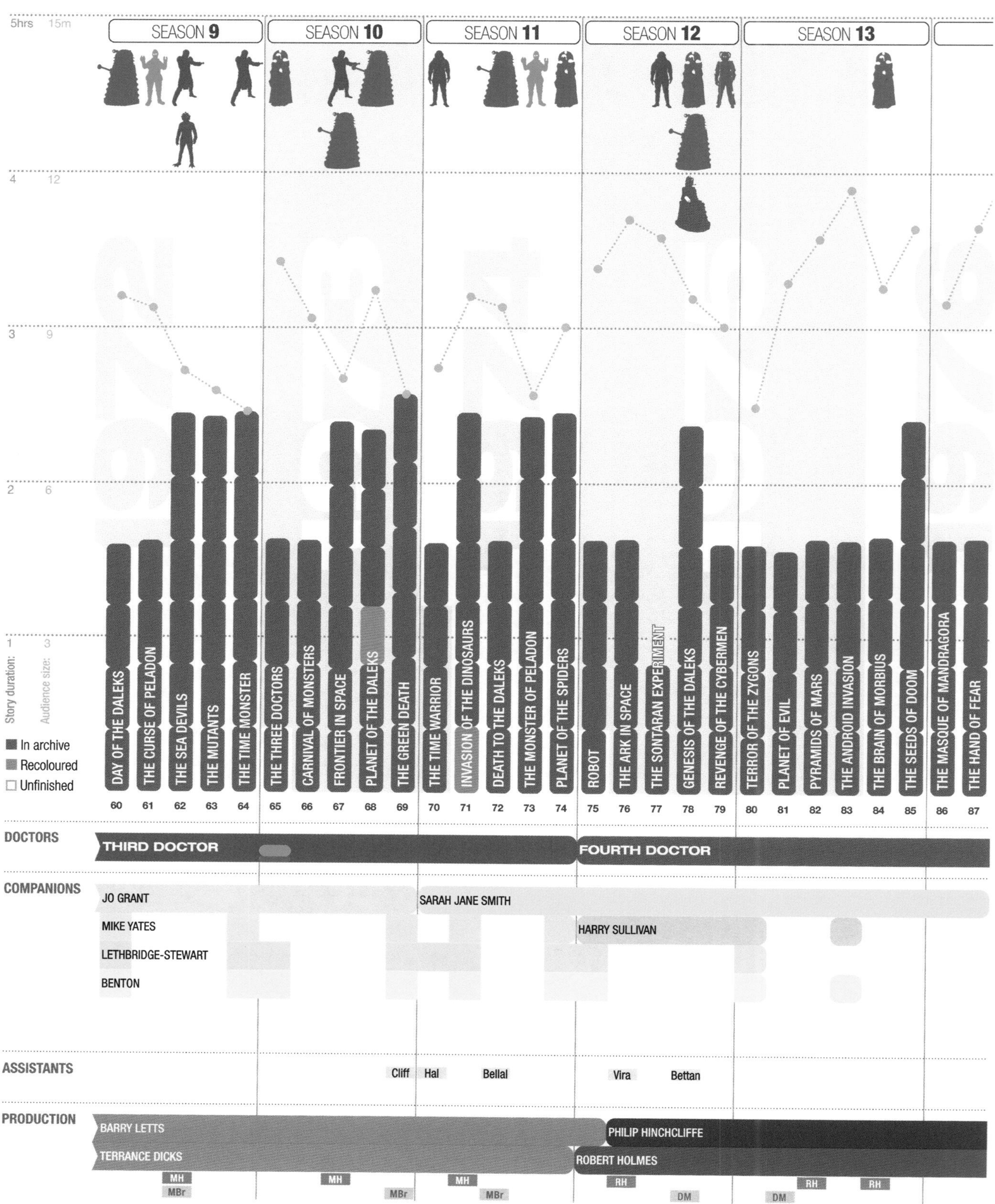

- Overlaid in light blue are the **viewing figures** for each story (vertical scale on the left in blue). These are the average of the figures for each episode of a story, based on the officially recorded figures, which in recent years include time-shifted viewing within a week of first broadcast but not online catch-up.
- **Enemies** appearing more than twice are shown at the top, coloured according to the Doctor against whom they first battled. These are, in order of appearance: **FIRST DOCTOR** Daleks, Time Lords (excluding the Doctor, Romana and the Master), Cybermen; **SECOND DOCTOR** Yeti, Ice Warriors; **THIRD DOCTOR** Autons, Homo Reptilia (Silurians/Sea Devils), the Master, Sontarans; **FOURTH DOCTOR** Davros; **TENTH DOCTOR** Ood, Judoon, Weeping Angels; **ELEVENTH DOCTOR** The Silents. No enemies first encountered by the Fifth, Sixth, Seventh or Ninth Doctors made more than one further appearance.

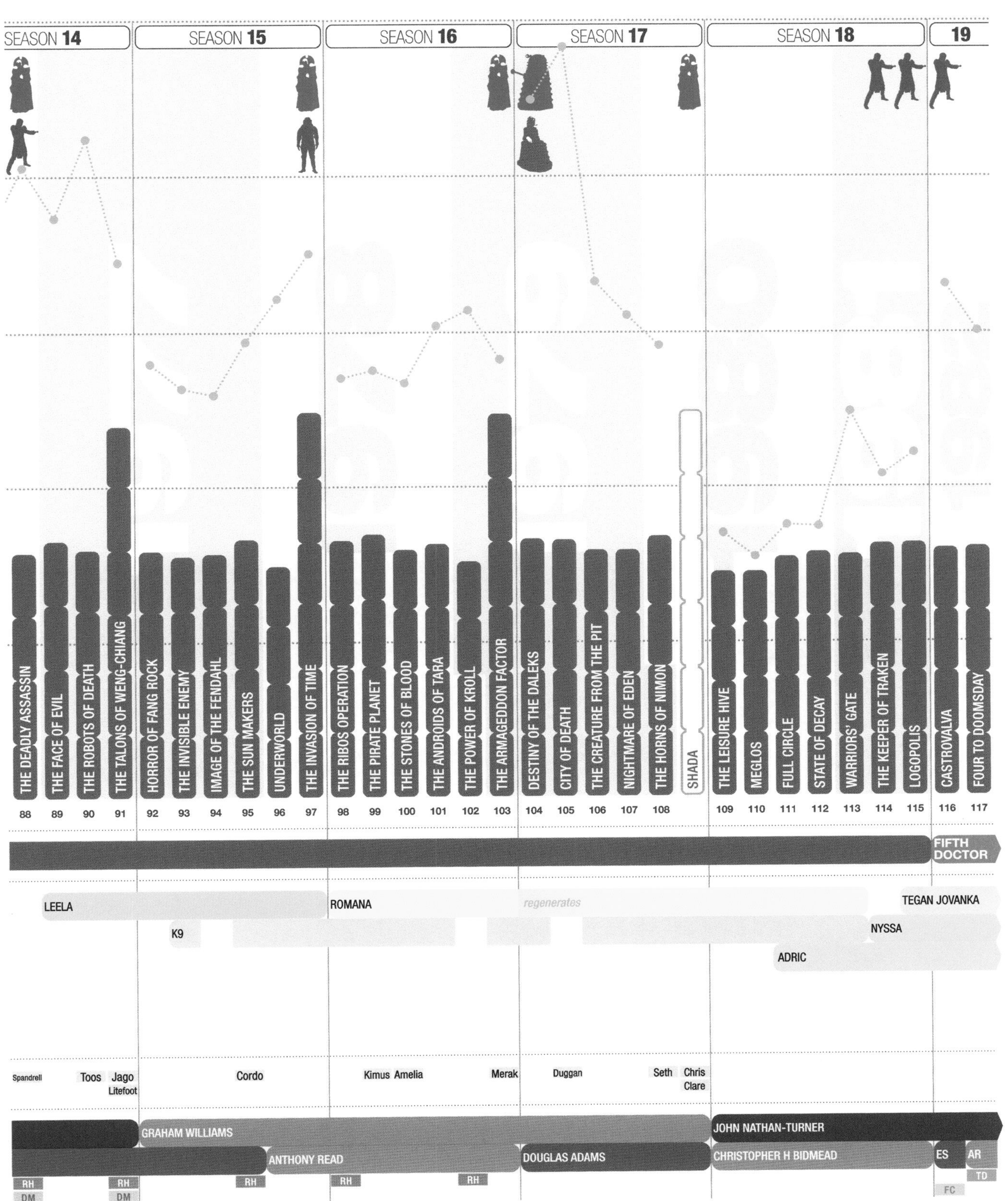

The colour coding for each **Doctor**'s era is used throughout the rest of this book for easy reference. Later appearances by past Doctors are indicated by their respective colours. The Seventh Doctor initially featured in the TV Movie before regenerating into the Eighth — the two didn't appear together.

Companions lists the generally accepted companions of the Doctor, so the likes of Katarina, Sara Kingdom, UNIT's Captain Yates and Sergeant Benton, Kamelion, Grace and Wilf are included, even though some never travelled with the Doctor. Curved corners on the bars indicate the start and end of their ongoing time with the Doctor, with later return appearances shown separately. Square corners indicate a temporary absence during their regular run. One-scene cameos are not included, even if they had lines, such as the phantom companions in "The Five Doctors" or Rose in Series 4 before "Turn Left".

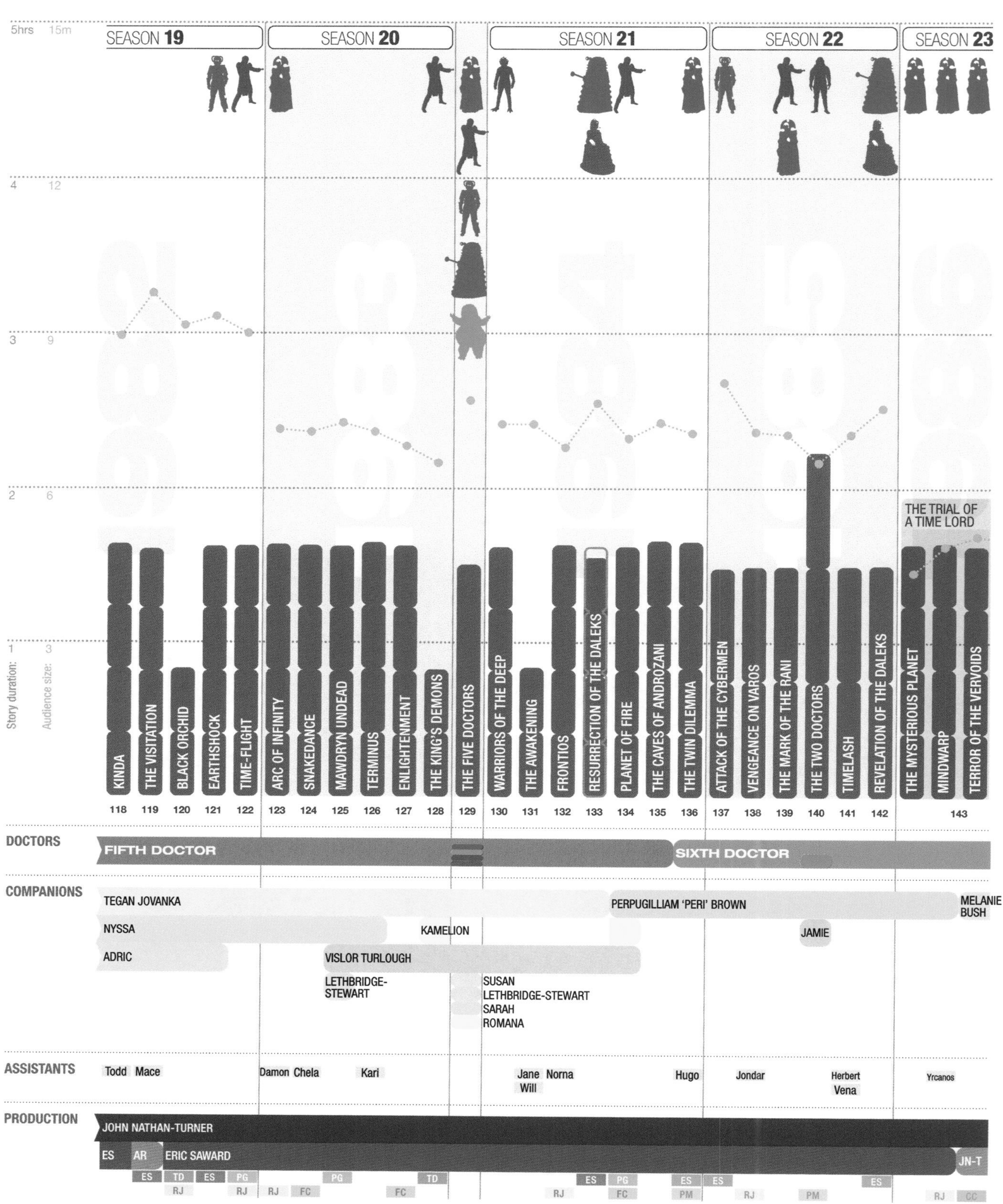

Assistants indicates people who helped out for a significant proportion of a story, often performing a companion-type role alongside either the Doctor or one of his regular companions. Obviously there are many characters who assist the Doctor during his adventures, but these are the ones who feel like they could have gone on to become regular companions if the producers had so chosen or, in the case of the revived series, those relatives of regular companions who appear whenever the Doctor returns to modern-day Earth.

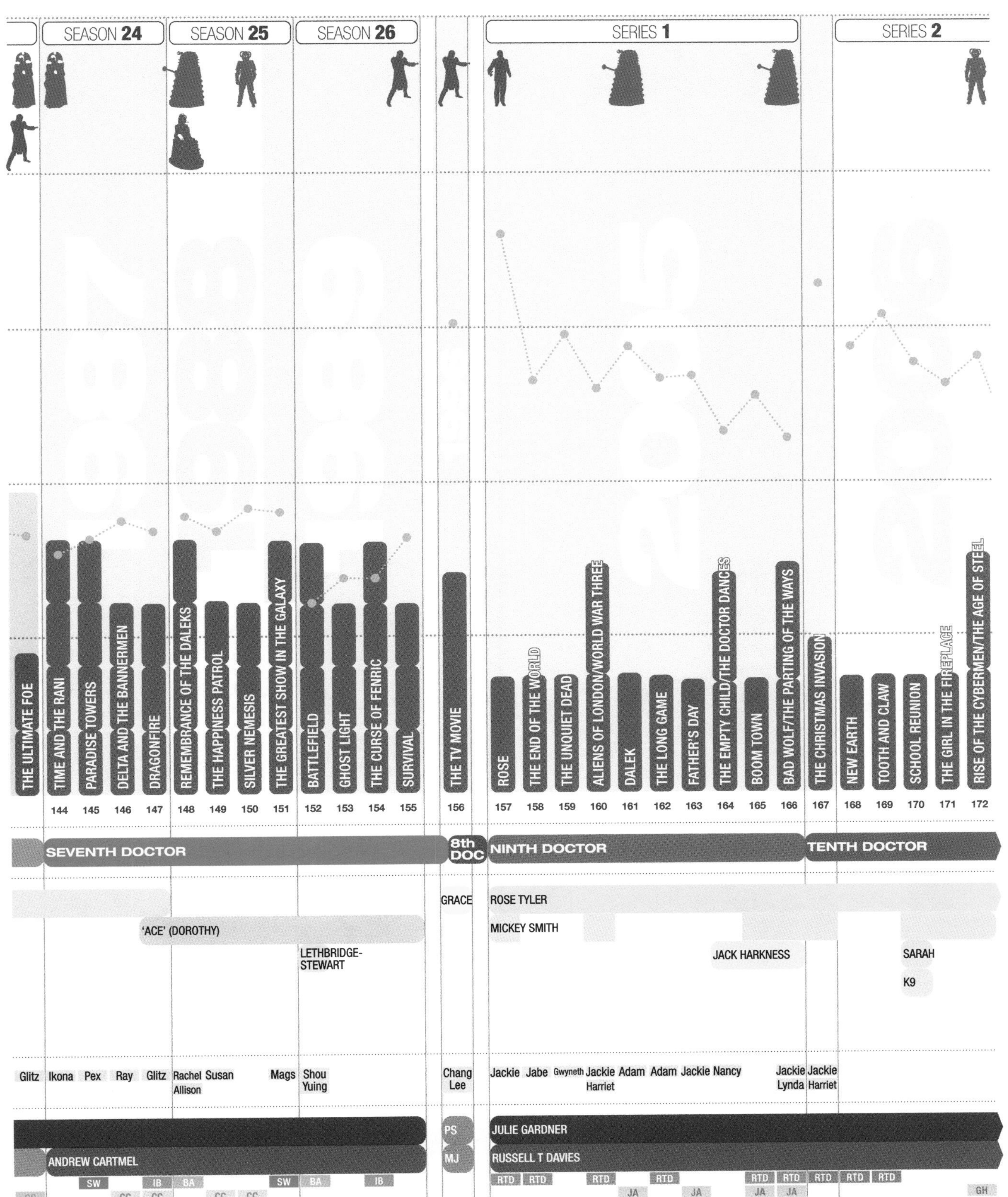

The **Production** section shows the tenures of the programme's producers and script editors. For the duration of the original series, these two roles were the prime creators of the programme at the BBC, commissioning the writers and selecting the directors and designers to make the show. Modern television production no longer follows this structure and the revived *Doctor Who* is overseen by a string of contracted and freelance executive producers, line producers, directors and supervisors. To simplify things for comparison purposes, under the New Series episodes are listed the two executive producers with key responsibility for the whole production and the scripting side respectively. This is not to ignore their other roles or to belittle the rest of the production teams, but to indicate who was arguably the closest equivalents of the old-style producer and script editor roles. Most abbreviations are expanded nearby except VP=Victor Pemberton, AR=Antony Root, PS=Philip Segal and MJ=Matthew Jacobs.

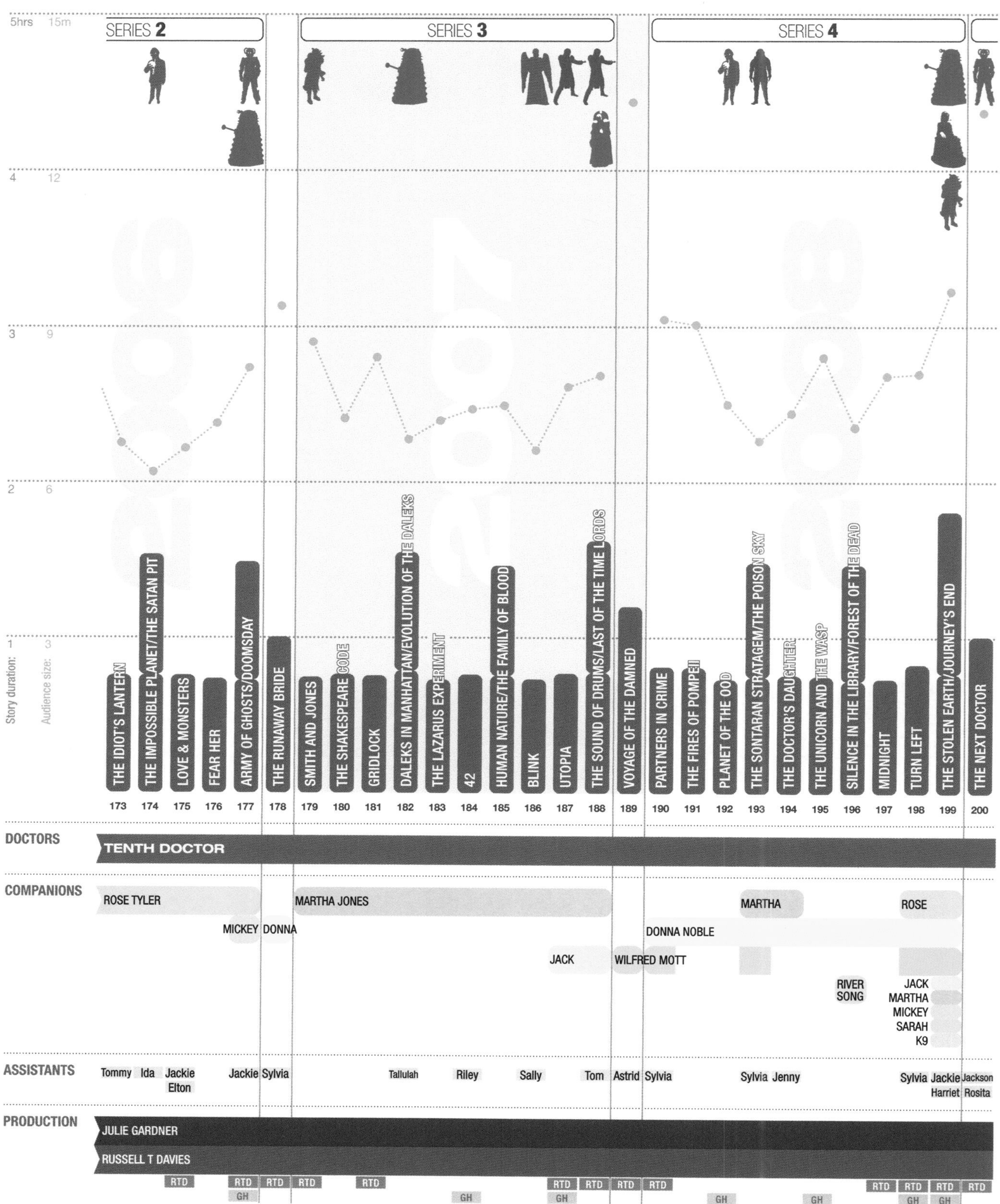

The bottom two lines of the **Production** section respectively show which stories were by the most prolific writers and directors during each Doctor's era. These are: **FIRST DOCTOR** Terry Nation (writer), Richard Martin (director); **SECOND DOCTOR** David Whitaker (writer), Morris Barry and David Maloney (directors); **THIRD DOCTOR** Malcolm Hulke (writer), Michael Briant (director); **FOURTH DOCTOR** Robert Holmes (writer), David Maloney (director); **FIFTH DOCTOR** Terence Dudley, Eric Saward and Peter Grimwade (writers), Fiona Cumming and Ron Jones (directors); **SIXTH DOCTOR** Eric Saward (writer), Peter Moffatt, Ron Jones and Chris Clough (directors); **SEVENTH DOCTOR** Stephen Wyatt, Ian Briggs and Ben Aaronovitch (writers), Chris Clough (director); **NINTH DOCTOR** Russell T Davies (writer), Joe Aherne (director); **TENTH DOCTOR** Russell T Davies (writer), Graeme Harper (director); **ELEVENTH DOCTOR** Steven Moffat (writer), Nick Hurran (director)

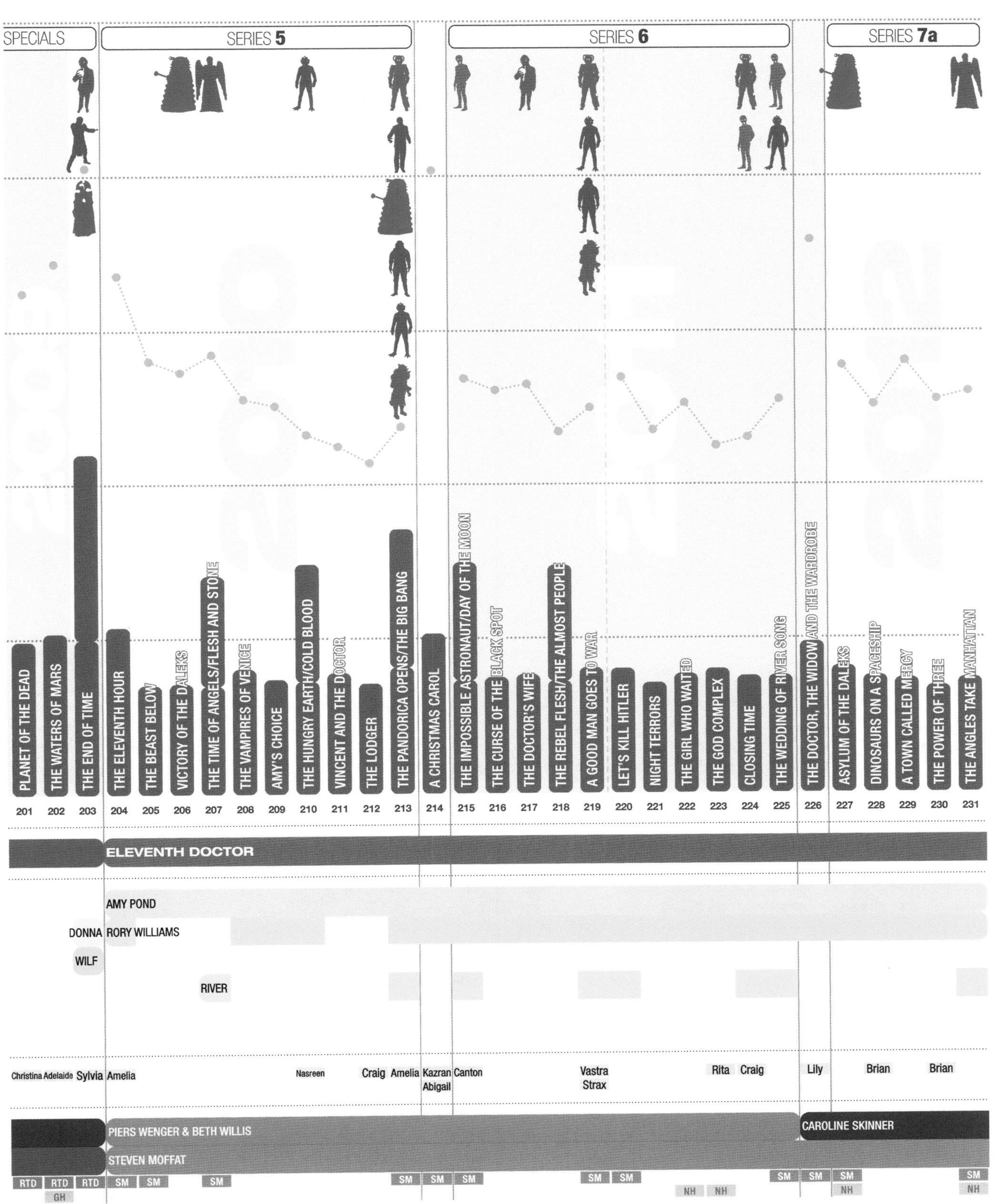

THE BEAST BELOW

The prevalence of story titles beginning with 'The', and other popular forms

It's probably not surprising that the word 'the' crops up a lot in the titles of *Doctor Who* stories — it is the most common word in the English language, after all. And given that most episodes are named with reference to a person, creature, place or concept within the story, it's standard to address that with the definite article. In fact, out of 359 *Doctor Who* titles — all on-screen titles, including the individual episode titles from the first 25 stories as well as their later assigned overall titles, plus "Shada" — 197 (54.9%) begin with 'The', 232 (64.6%) contain a 'the', and there are 247 instances of 'the' altogether, accounting for 22.7% of all words used in *Doctor Who* titles. In contrast only ten stories begin with the indefinite article, from the opening episode "An Unearthly Child" to 2012's "A Town Called Mercy".

Most story titles beginning 'The' follow one of three forms: 'The [noun(s)]', 'The [adjective] [noun]' or 'The [noun] [preposition] [noun]'. Only a handful take different structures. Some use lists of nouns, such as "The Unicorn and the Wasp" or "The Doctor, the Widow and the Wardrobe". Others drop the preposition by taking a possessive form: "The Daleks' Master Plan", "The King's Demons", "The Idiot's Lantern", "The Doctor's Daughter" and "The Doctor's Wife". Only four beginning with 'The' include a verb: "The Nightmare Begins" (the first episode of "The Daleks' Master Plan"), "The Pandorica Opens", "The Girl Who Waited" and "The Angels Take Manhattan".

Most of the titles that don't begin with 'The' or 'A' follow the same grammatical forms but simply drop the article. The fact that the Target novelisations of the television stories could comfortably prefix most titles with 'Doctor Who and the…' shows any original lack of the definite article was an affectation. It was only in the 1980s when more single-word titles were used — generally the name of a character or place — that this convention became tricky. There had been a few one-word titles before then, particularly among the individual episode titles of the early serials, but for overall titles only "Inferno", "Underworld" and the unfinished "Shada" preceded the rise of the form under John Nathan-Turner's producership. Of the nine seasons he produced only two didn't have a story with a one-word title, and in both cases that was down to last-minute changes. Throughout production of Season 23, the second segment was called "Mindwarp" until it was decided to show the whole season under the umbrella title "The Trial of a Time Lord". And Season 25's "Silver Nemesis" was simply "Nemesis" until late in the day when the adjective was added to highlight its anniversary nature.

Another reason for occasionally dropping an otherwise likely leading article was when the '[noun] [preposition] [noun]' form used a proper noun at the end. While a few Second Doctor stories had been happy to repeat the definite article — "The Power of the Daleks", "The Tomb of the Cybermen", "The Enemy of the World" — during the 1970s it became common to pick one or the other, thus "Invasion of the Dinosaurs", "Genesis of the Daleks", "Image of the Fendahl" and so on. This has persisted into the revived series, such as "Rise of the Cybermen" and "Last of the Time Lords".

There are some further noun combinations among those titles without a leading 'The', namely "Time and the Rani", "Delta and the Bannermen", "Tooth and Claw", "Love & Monsters" (we'll come back to that ampersand), "Smith and Jones", "Flesh and Stone" and "Vincent and the Doctor". Plus a few more verbs: "All Roads Lead to Rome" (episode two of "The Romans"), "Don't Shoot the Pianist" (episode two of "The Gunfighters"), "Fear Her" (the only title to use a pronoun instead of a noun), "Blink" (the only verbal one-word title), "Turn Left", "A Good Man Goes to War" and "Let's Kill Hitler". Other less common forms include "Small Prophet, Quick Return" (episode two of "The Myth Makers"), "Death to the Daleks" and "Mawdryn Undead".

Punctuation is rare in story titles. Apostrophes are most common — usually in those possessive forms plus the two contractions mentioned above — but even so there are only 13 in all 359 titles (3.6%). As well as the lone ampersand and comma we've already mentioned, there are just two hyphens: in "Rider from Shang-tu" (episode five of "Marco Polo") and "The Talons of Weng-Chiang". There have also been only two titles with numerals: "Galaxy 4" (while that's a later-applied umbrella title for the serial it seems always to have been written with the numeral) and "42". At two characters, the latter is the shortest ever title, while the longest, in both characters and words, is "The Doctor, the Widow and the Wardrobe".

The data

The on-screen titles of each episode and story, plus the generally accepted overall titles for the first 25 stories, were grouped by the number of words they contain. "Shada" was included despite not being broadcast, but not the individual segment titles of "The Trial of a Time Lord". "42" was counted as one word, "Galaxy 4" as two. Contracted words were counted as one but hyphenated words as two. The groups were then divided between those that began with 'The' and those that didn't.

Obviously there are no one-word titles beginning with 'The'. "Kidnap", episode five of "The Sensorites" (1964), was the earliest, but the first single-word story title wasn't until 1970's "Inferno" (also the name of episode four of "The Romans"). The last was 2008's "Midnight". Similarly, the earliest two-word title not beginning with 'The' was episode three of "The Sensorites", "Hidden Danger". The fourth serial is collectively known as "Marco Polo", making that the earliest two-word story title although it was never used on screen; for that we had to wait for 1980's "Full Circle". Two-word titles beginning with 'The' are common, starting with the fourth ever episode, "The Firemaker"; the second ever story, "The Daleks"; or, for an on-screen story title, 1966's "The Savages", which was the first serial not to use individual episode titles.

The most common title length is three words, making up 34.5% of all titles, 62.9% of which begin with 'The'. The four-letter titles include many of the form 'The *x* of *y*' or '*x* of the *y*' — 89.7% of those beginning with 'The' and 54.3% of others — while most (85.7%) of the five-letter titles beginning with 'The' extend this to 'The *x* of the *y*'. The sole example in the non-The group is "Last of the Time Lords". Only four titles have reached six words — "The Trial of a Time Lord", "The Greatest Show in the Galaxy", "The Curse of the Black Spot" and "A Good Man Goes to War" — beaten only by the seven-word title of the 2011 Christmas Special.

Number of stories
40
30
20
10
0
10
20
30
40
50
60
70
Number of words in title
one
two
three
four
five
six
seven
Stories titled
'x of the y'
Stories titled
'The x of y'
Titles not beginning 'The...'
Titles beginning 'The...'

THE DOMINATORS

The BBC hierarchy of people in charge of *Doctor Who*, 1963-1989

While fans will often know off by heart the names of the producers and script editors who made *Doctor Who*, they're less likely to know those people's department heads within the BBC, who will have had just as much influence over the changes in the programme through the years. The names Sydney Newman and Donald Wilson will be familiar as the two men credited with creating the concept of *Doctor Who* in the first place, but what of their replacements? Who were the people who supervised the day-to-day production teams' work, and did their career movements influence the show?

This chart lists those BBC employees in the management chain with direct responsibility for *Doctor Who*. While the title for each level may not be the precise job title for everyone — for example, the Drama Department was reorganised several times, particularly in the 1980s, with *Doctor Who* falling under the remit of the Head of Serials, Series or the two combined at various times — they indicate an equivalence of seniority. Assistant Script Editor was an occasionally filled position which here includes those periods when an incoming script editor was shadowing his predecessor to learn the ropes. Similarly, the steps in the Producer level indicate where incoming and outgoing producers overlapped as their tasks were handed over. Note also that Peter Bryant's brief stint as Associate Producer was not really an overseeing role, as Mervyn Pinfield's and Barry Letts' were, more a deputy position to producer Innes Lloyd as Bryant was assessed for promotion. However, he is included in the upper level for simplicity.

A number of higher management changes coincided with recastings of the Doctor. It's notable that while producer John Wiles' suggestions for replacing William Hartnell were vetoed by his Head of Serials Gerald Savory, it was only after Shaun Sutton had succeeded him that moves to remove Hartnell were approved. Patrick Troughton had decided to relinquish the role a few months before Ronnie Marsh became Head of Serials, and by then Head of Drama Shaun Sutton was more directly involved in persuading Jon Pertwee to take the part, whose tenure was secure under Marsh. But once Bill Slater took over as Head of Serials it seems the department was more willing to replace Pertwee than agree to his salary demands, and Slater was instrumental in the casting of Tom Baker.

Doctor Who could also have an effect on its departmental managers. In the mid-1970s the show was increasingly a target for the ire of Mary Whitehouse and her National Viewers' and Listeners' Association. This reached a climax after the broadcast of "The Deadly Assassin" in November 1976, when Whitehouse complained that the cliffhanger to episode three — in which the Doctor appeared to have drowned — breached the BBC's own guidelines. This not only resulted in Bill Slater instructing incoming producer Graham Williams to cut down the violence in the programme, but Director General Sir Charles Curran issued a public apology admitting a misjudgement had been made. While it would be going too far to suggest this in itself was instrumental in Graeme McDonald taking over from Slater as Head of Serials a month later, it's no coincidence that McDonald took a much closer interest in *Doctor Who*'s scripts from then on to ensure they didn't cross the line again.

Higher management's involvement in the programme usually involved issues of scheduling. While the show was a popular BBC1 Saturday evening hit, there was little to concern them, but by 1981, when Alan Hart became Controller of BBC1, *Doctor Who*'s viewing figures were in decline in the face of a concerted move by ITV to schedule *Buck Rogers in the 25th Century* in the same timeslot across its regions. It was Hart who moved *Doctor Who* from its traditional Saturday and ran it twice a week in mid-week early evening slots, both to try to regain its audience and as part of a wider experiment to see how a twice-weekly soap opera might fare. This had some success and *Doctor Who* was well supported by new Head of Series and Serials David Reid, culminating in the BBC organising a major event at Longleat in April 1983 to celebrate the show's upcoming 20th anniversary and the agreement to an out-of-season special to be shown near the anniversary itself. This would change under Reid's successor, Jonathan Powell, especially after he was promoted to Head of Drama when, with newly appointed Controller of BBC1 Michael Grade, he was party to the cancellation of *Doctor Who*. Only a fan outcry saved the series, but from then on it was considered something of an albatross around the neck of management. Powell and Grade later ordered the sacking of Sixth Doctor Colin Baker (whose casting had been approved by Reid in the very last weeks of his tenure as Head of Series and Serials), and it was under Powell's controllership of BBC1 that the show went into indefinite suspension.

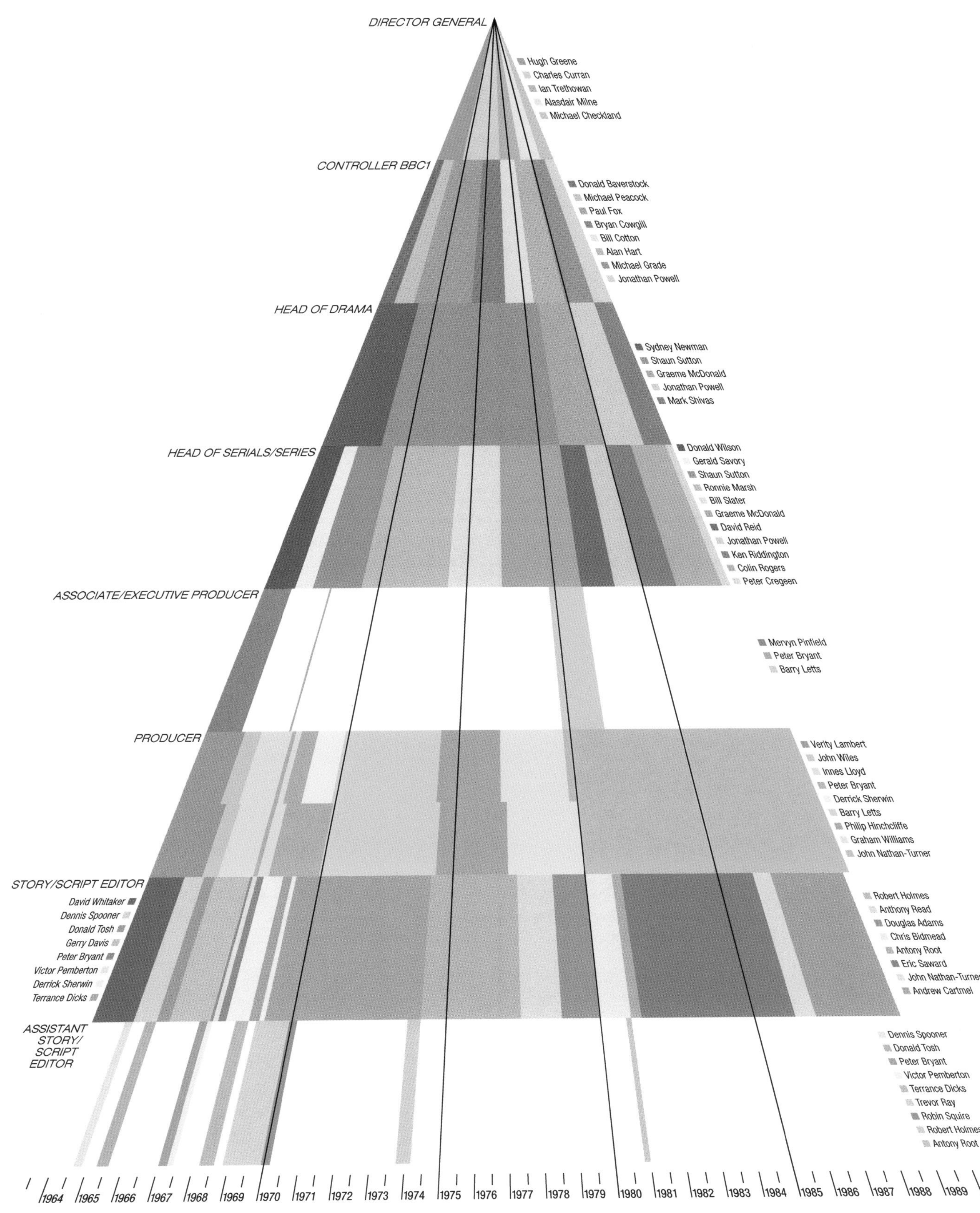
DIRECTOR GENERAL
Hugh Greene
Charles Curran
Ian Trethowan
Alasdair Milne
Michael Checkland
CONTROLLER BBC1
Donald Baverstock
Michael Peacock
Paul Fox
Bryan Cowgill
Bill Cotton
Alan Hart
Michael Grade
Jonathan Powell
HEAD OF DRAMA
Sydney Newman
Shaun Sutton
Graeme McDonald
Jonathan Powell
Mark Shivas
HEAD OF SERIALS/SERIES
Donald Wilson
Gerald Savory
Shaun Sutton
Ronnie Marsh
Bill Slater
Graeme McDonald
David Reid
Jonathan Powell
Ken Riddington
Colin Rogers
Peter Cregeen
ASSOCIATE/EXECUTIVE PRODUCER
Mervyn Pinfield
Peter Bryant
Barry Letts
PRODUCER
Verity Lambert
John Wiles
Innes Lloyd
Peter Bryant
Derrick Sherwin
Barry Letts
Philip Hinchcliffe
Graham Williams
John Nathan-Turner
STORY/SCRIPT EDITOR
David Whitaker
Dennis Spooner
Donald Tosh
Gerry Davis
Peter Bryant
Victor Pemberton
Derrick Sherwin
Terrance Dicks
Robert Holmes
Anthony Read
Douglas Adams
Chris Bidmead
Antony Root
Eric Saward
John Nathan-Turner
Andrew Cartmel
ASSISTANT STORY/ SCRIPT EDITOR
Dennis Spooner
Donald Tosh
Peter Bryant
Victor Pemberton
Terrance Dicks
Trevor Ray
Robin Squire
Robert Holmes
Antony Root
1964
1965
1966
1967
1968
1969
1970
1971
1972
1973
1974
1975
1976
1977
1978
1979
1980
1981
1982
1983
1984
1985
1986
1987
1988
1989

THE BRINK OF DISASTER

Number of weeks between studio recording and transmission of 1960s episodes

Today each *Doctor Who* story is recorded like a small movie. Scenes set in the same environment are shot together, either on location or in a studio, usually several times to capture them from multiple points of view. There are then several weeks of editing, to pick the best-looking scenes and compile them in the right order, and post production to add effects shots, background sounds and music. When *Doctor Who* began in the 1960s, however, the process of television production was very different. Still coming off the back of an era when all programmes were broadcast as they were being performed, each episode would be structured so that it could be recorded almost continuously from start to finish. Actors moved between sets while the cameras were shooting an intermediate scene, music was played into the studio and recorded onto the soundtrack alongside the actors' dialogue, and visual effects were mixed in from the studio gallery to be recorded onto videotape at the same time as the cameras' output.

As such, each episode was a weekly production, with the actors rehearsing usually from Monday to Thursday while sets were being built. Then on a Friday the sets would be erected in a studio, the actors and cameramen would practise their final movements, and in the evening the episode would be recorded pretty much straight through. Editing videotape in those days was a costly business to be avoided, so apart from planned breaks when the tape would simply be stopped and started again, the episodes were recorded in almost one go, occasionally with minor mistakes left in.

If a particular scene was too complicated to do in the television studio, or required special equipment, it could be filmed ahead of the recording session. Initially this was done at the BBC's film studios in Ealing, but over the years shooting some scenes on location became more affordable. These would be filmed a few weeks ahead of the studio recording, often taking the regular cast away from rehearsals for other episodes, then edited on film so the required scenes could be recorded onto videotape in the appropriate places during the studio session. Once the episode was on video and its technical quality approved, it was ready for broadcast on the scheduled Saturday.

How far ahead of broadcast each episode was able to be recorded varied, however, and at times 1960s *Doctor Who* was produced surprisingly close to its transmission. Any delay in the weekly process, such as for Christmas or owing to technical problems, moved the production one week closer to its showing time, and there were periods when episodes were recorded just one week ahead of broadcast.

This chart shows the changing lead times for 1960s episodes, with each spool of video representing a week (rounded) between recording and transmission. Initially the programme was recorded a comfortable five weeks ahead of broadcast, the first episode proper going before the cameras on Friday 18 October 1963 for transmission on Saturday 23 November. Very soon this was eaten into, however, when the recording of the opening episode of "The Daleks", made on 15 November, was deemed unfit for broadcast because talk among the production crew had been picked up on the soundtrack. This episode had to be re-recorded on 6 December, just two weeks ahead of its transmission slot, bumping part 4 and all subsequent episodes back a week. A week off for Christmas shortly after meant the series was being recorded just three weeks ahead of broadcast.

It clawed back a week in June 1964 when episode 3 of "The Sensorites" was delayed owing to coverage of Wimbledon, and although the first season closed on television with the final part of "The Reign of Terror", production continued on the next two stories, giving them a solid lead time of ten weeks (although the decision to edit parts 3 and 4 of "Planet of Giants" into one cut this down to nine weeks). Once the production team were back from their break following recording of "The Dalek Invasion of Earth", by which time the new season had begun on BBC1, they were just four weeks ahead again, and only three following Christmas. This pattern repeated for the break between Seasons 2 and 3, although an extra week's filming at Ealing for the epic "The Daleks' Master Plan" meant that after Christmas 1965 the programme was recorded two weeks ahead of broadcast.

This remained the case until the end of the season, although recording continued with "The Smugglers". When production resumed for "The Tenth Planet", the weekly recording sessions moved to Saturdays, so now the programme was taped exactly three weeks before transmission. A week's break before Patrick Troughton's debut story, followed shortly by another due to last-minute script changes, meant the remainder of Season 4 was recorded just one week ahead of broadcast. Although the actors were used to live performances, this was a tight schedule and stressful for all.

"The Tomb of the Cybermen" was recorded at the end of Season 4's block of stories, and when production resumed on "The Abominable Snowmen" the first two episodes were taped on successive days, Friday 15 and Saturday 16 September 1967, to gain an extra week's lead. That year Christmas fell mid-week, allowing for recordings on 23 and 30 December, enabling the programme to hold on to its three-week lead. Season 6 started well, with the most number of episodes on tape ahead of time to date. Even with a two-week gap between broadcast of "The Mind Robber" and "The Invasion" for Wimbledon coverage, the latter was being recorded six weeks ahead of transmission (by this time back to Friday evening recording sessions). However, problems throughout that year rapidly cut down this lead. Actors missing rehearsals to film location scenes for later stories was proving a problem, and was particularly disliked by Patrick Troughton. Producer Peter Bryant therefore planned a week's gap between stories' studio sessions to allow for location filming. Problems with scripts also meant those that did finally go ahead had to be completed fast and left little time for pre-production work. By the time the team embarked on the season's final story, the 10-part "The War Games", the programme was back to a single week's lead time. Troughton had already decided to leave the show the previous year, in part because of stress from the tight production schedule, but sadly this was a particularly tiring end to his time as the Doctor.

When *Doctor Who* returned in colour in 1970, production methods were changing. Videotape editing was becoming easier and cheaper, and incoming producer Barry Letts instigated a schedule whereby two episodes were recorded on successive days each fortnight, instead of one a week. This allowed for more efficient use of sets, but also meant rehearsals and location filming could be scheduled more conveniently. Over the following few years the programme moved to recording out of sequence, putting the days of as-live production firmly in the past.

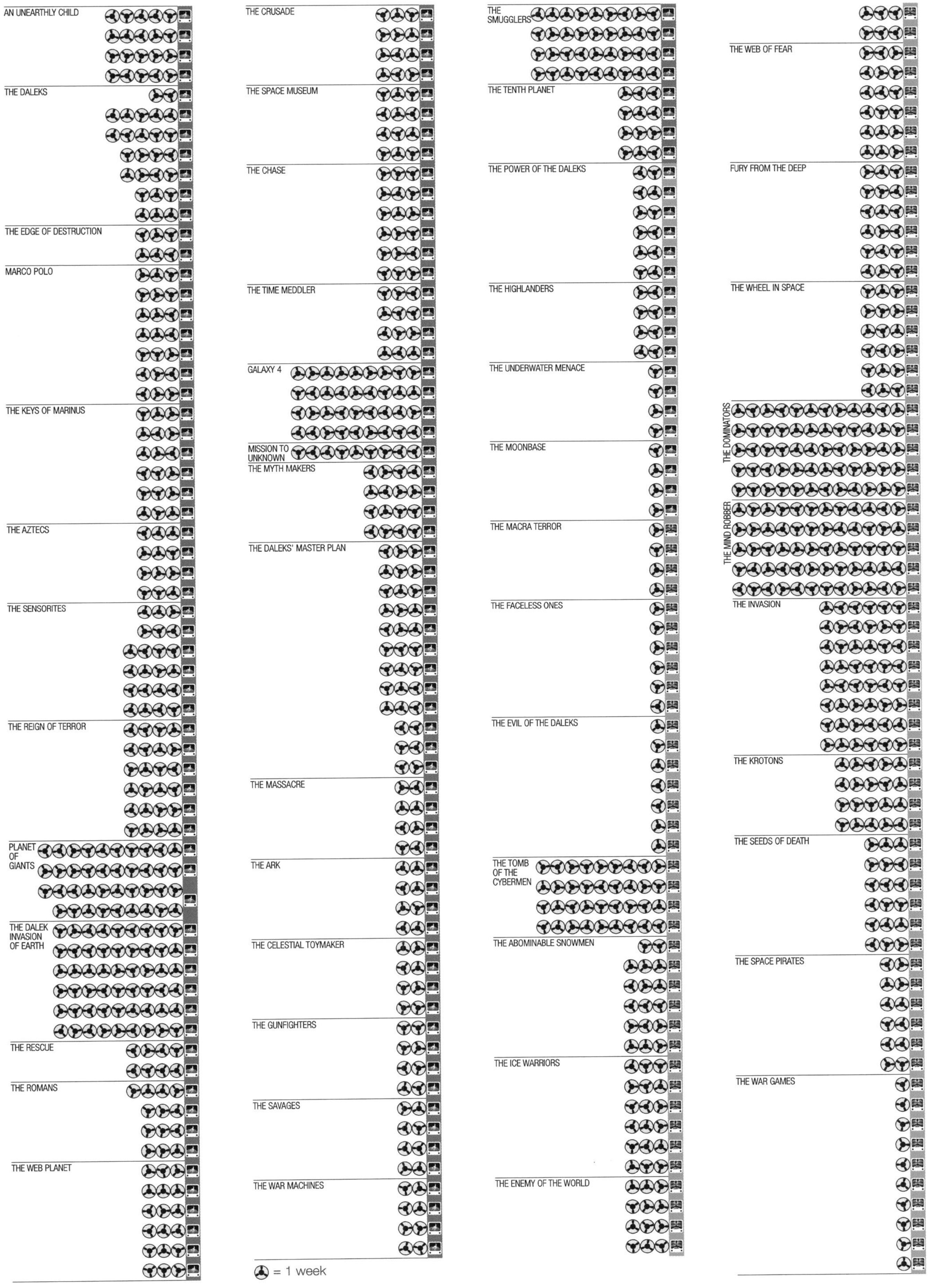

AN UNEARTHLY CHILD

THE DALEKS

THE EDGE OF DESTRUCTION

MARCO POLO

THE KEYS OF MARINUS

THE AZTECS

THE SENSORITES

THE REIGN OF TERROR

PLANET OF GIANTS

THE DALEK INVASION OF EARTH

THE RESCUE

THE ROMANS

THE WEB PLANET

THE CRUSADE

THE SPACE MUSEUM

THE CHASE

THE TIME MEDDLER

GALAXY 4

MISSION TO UNKNOWN

THE MYTH MAKERS

THE DALEKS' MASTER PLAN

THE MASSACRE

THE ARK

THE CELESTIAL TOYMAKER

THE GUNFIGHTERS

THE SAVAGES

THE WAR MACHINES

= 1 week

THE SMUGGLERS

THE TENTH PLANET

THE POWER OF THE DALEKS

THE HIGHLANDERS

THE UNDERWATER MENACE

THE MOONBASE

THE MACRA TERROR

THE FACELESS ONES

THE EVIL OF THE DALEKS

THE TOMB OF THE CYBERMEN

THE ABOMINABLE SNOWMEN

THE ICE WARRIORS

THE ENEMY OF THE WORLD

THE WEB OF FEAR

FURY FROM THE DEEP

THE WHEEL IN SPACE

THE DOMINATORS

THE MIND ROBBER

THE INVASION

THE KROTONS

THE SEEDS OF DEATH

THE SPACE PIRATES

THE WAR GAMES

BBC studios used for recording 1960s episodes

Television Centre on Wood Lane in Shepherd's Bush, West London, has been the symbol of the BBC for 50 years since it opened as the broadcaster's first purpose-built television studios in June 1960. The BBC's initial television broadcasts famously came from Alexandra Palace in North London, which had been built as a public space for the Arts in the 1870s and was partly leased to the BBC from 1935. Its establishment there included the erection of the 67m transmission mast which is still in use today (and featured in the 2006 episode "The Idiot's Lantern"). When programme production resumed after the Second World War, it was becoming clear the two studios at Alexandra Palace would not be enough to supply a full television service.

In 1949 it was announced the BBC would build its own complex with eight studios in White City, and in the meantime it bought the nearby Lime Grove Studios as a temporary facility — one it ended up using for 40 years. These had been built by the Gaumont Film Company in 1915, expanded and redeveloped in 1932, and bought by the Rank Organisation in 1941. The BBC spent six months converting the film stages into four main studios for television production: Studios D, E, G and H, supplementing Studios A and B at Alexandra Palace (the letter C was skipped to avoid potential confusion with the Central Control Room, known as CCR, while Studio F was only ever used as a scenery store). While construction began on TV Centre in 1951, financing problems delayed the project, so in 1954 the BBC acquired Riverside Studios beside the Thames in Hammersmith. These buildings had been converted from industrial use into film studios by Triumph Films in 1933, and the BBC renamed its two studios R1 and R2. TV Centre finally came into use in 1960, first with Studio 3 (TC3) in June, followed by Studios 2, 4 and 5 over the following year.

When *Doctor Who* was being planned over the summer of 1963, the question of where to record it was high on the agenda. The production team naturally wanted to use the new, state-of-the-art facilities at TV Centre. Lime Grove was still the prime production hub, however, even though the equipment there, particularly the lighting rigs, was over ten years old by then and the studios were not considered suitable for a highly technical show like *Doctor Who*. Nonetheless, Lime Grove Studio D was allocated and the first ever episode, the unbroadcast 'pilot', was recorded there on Friday 27 September 1963. Even after the series went into regular production with the restaging of "An Unearthly Child" on 18 October, concerns about the studios continued, with the limited technical equipment and unpleasant working conditions — largely due to the heat of the lights — making life difficult for cast and crew alike. A move to Studio G wasn't a viable solution as it didn't solve the technical problems and, although slightly larger than Studio D, had a more oblong floor space, too narrow for *Doctor Who*'s set requirements. Even so, the first four episodes of "The Reign of Terror" were recorded in Studio G during July 1964, after which production moved to TC4 while Lime Grove D had its sound equipment updated. This move had been decided earlier in the year to avoid the programme having to record under Studio D's hot lights in the high summer months, and may have been a factor in getting "Planet of Giants" made at all. A story in which the TARDIS crew were shrunk had been mooted from the very beginning of the show but CE Webber's original scripts were dropped when it was clear they couldn't be adequately produced with Studio D's facilities. The idea stayed on the schedules, however, moving down the running order until an appropriate studio could be assured. Story Editor David Whitaker didn't formally commission a new storyline from Louis Marks until late March 1964, by which time the summer studio allocation would have been decided. Or it may be that the production team's continued desire to make such a story finally persuaded the studio planners to give it the space it required in TV Centre.

After its first year's struggle, *Doctor Who* settled into Riverside 1 as its main home for the next two and a half years (possibly because series creator Sydney Newman threatened to abandon the return of the popular Daleks if suitable facilities weren't provided). R1 was almost the same size as TC3 and TC4, and better equipped than Lime Grove. The programme was allocated occasional stints at TV Centre — most notably for the 12-week production of "The Daleks' Master Plan" — but was mainly recorded in R1 until the end of February 1967, when it abruptly returned to Lime Grove D for the majority of the remainder of the 1960s. The main reason for this was that, with TV Centre up and running with six studios (and two more opening in 1967), the BBC was winding down its use of Riverside Studios and had ceased all production there by 1970. Why *Doctor Who* wasn't transferred to TV Centre may have been to do with the introduction of colour television around that time. BBC2 had begun broadcasting in 1964 and from July 1967 was showing programmes in colour. TC6 and TC8 opened that year as full colour studios, with TC1 and TC7 equipped for colour in 1968, TC3 in 1969 and TC4 in 1970 (TC5 wasn't updated until 1973 and TC2 was never fitted for colour production). The restricted use of TV Centre's studios because of this work must have required many programmes to continue being made at Lime Grove, including *Doctor Who* (the long-term future of which, let alone a switch to colour, was constantly in doubt during this period).

Another impact of TV Centre's move to colour seems to have been on *Doctor Who*'s switch to the higher-definition 625-line picture system. Although Lime Grove's cameras had been upgraded to 625-line-capable EMI 203 models in 1964, when the series returned there in 1967 it was still recorded in the old 405-line format. It didn't switch to 625 lines until episode three of "The Enemy of the World", recorded in December 1967, around the time BBC2 became a full-colour service. That channel had been broadcasting in 625 since it launched, so did its move to colour in the latter half of 1967 mean black-and-white 625-line-capable video recording desks were freed up for installation in Lime Grove?

The programme returned briefly to TV Centre for the end of the 1967/68 recording block (which ran to the end of "The Mind Robber"), with a final visit to Riverside during "The Wheel in Space". Interestingly, the two episodes recorded there were both captured onto 35mm film rather than video — R1's video recording equipment may have been removed by then. *Doctor Who* returned to TV Centre for good for the Second Doctor's swan song. Curiously some episodes were recorded in TC6 and TC8, both colour studios. It's tantalising to think these episodes were tests for recording the show in colour, as by then the next season had been commissioned, but the videotape catalogue numbers for them indicate they were monochrome.

The pie chart opposite shows the relative use of each studio. Despite successive production teams' unhappiness with it, Lime Grove had the most often used studios during the 1960s, although overall most episodes were produced in the larger studios at Riverside and TV Centre.

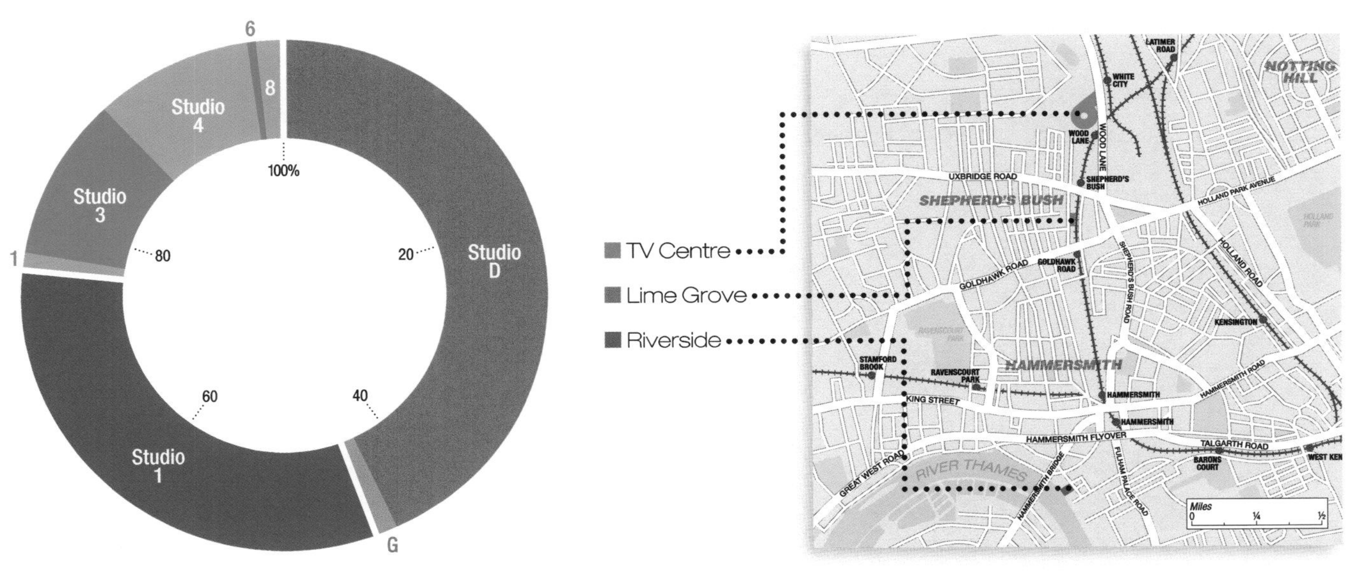

SEASON 1

AN UNEARTHLY CHILD | THE DALEKS | THE EDGE OF DESTRUCTION | MARCO POLO | THE KEYS OF MARINUS | THE AZTECS | THE SENSORITES | THE REIGN OF TERROR

SEASON 2

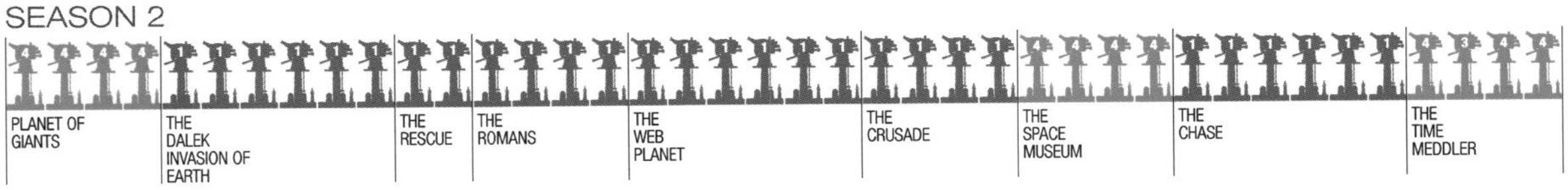

PLANET OF GIANTS | THE DALEK INVASION OF EARTH | THE RESCUE | THE ROMANS | THE WEB PLANET | THE CRUSADE | THE SPACE MUSEUM | THE CHASE | THE TIME MEDDLER

SEASON 3

GALAXY 4 | MISSION TO UNKNOWN | THE MYTH MAKERS | THE DALEKS' MASTER PLAN | THE MASSACRE | THE ARK | THE CELESTIAL TOYMAKER | THE GUNFIGHTERS | THE SAVAGES | THE WAR MACHINES

SEASON 4

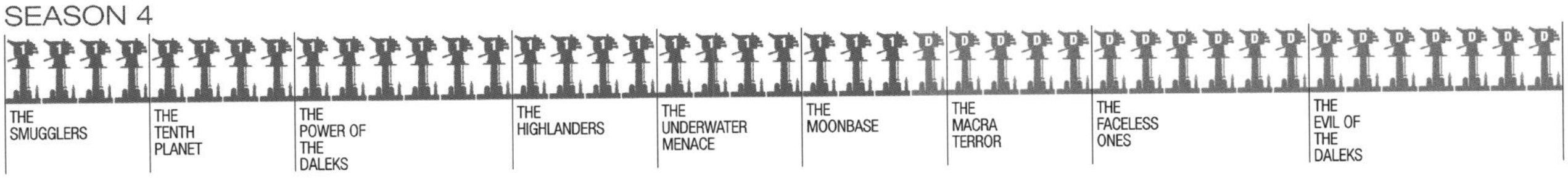

THE SMUGGLERS | THE TENTH PLANET | THE POWER OF THE DALEKS | THE HIGHLANDERS | THE UNDERWATER MENACE | THE MOONBASE | THE MACRA TERROR | THE FACELESS ONES | THE EVIL OF THE DALEKS

SEASON 5

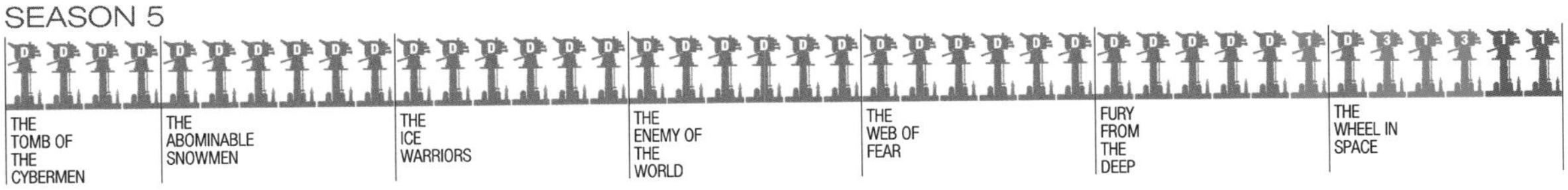

THE TOMB OF THE CYBERMEN | THE ABOMINABLE SNOWMEN | THE ICE WARRIORS | THE ENEMY OF THE WORLD | THE WEB OF FEAR | FURY FROM THE DEEP | THE WHEEL IN SPACE

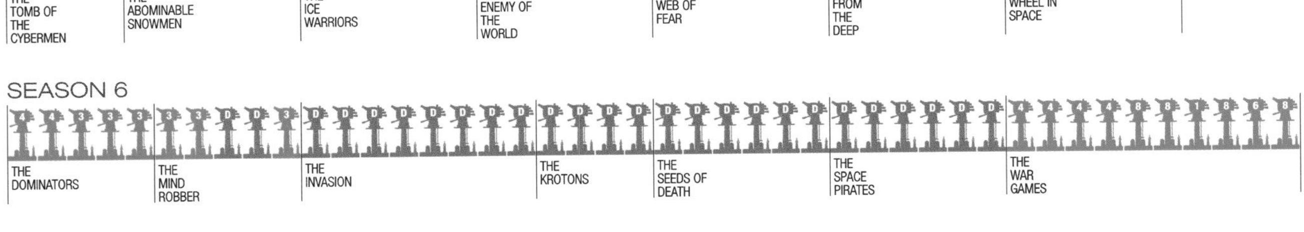

THE MYTH MAKERS

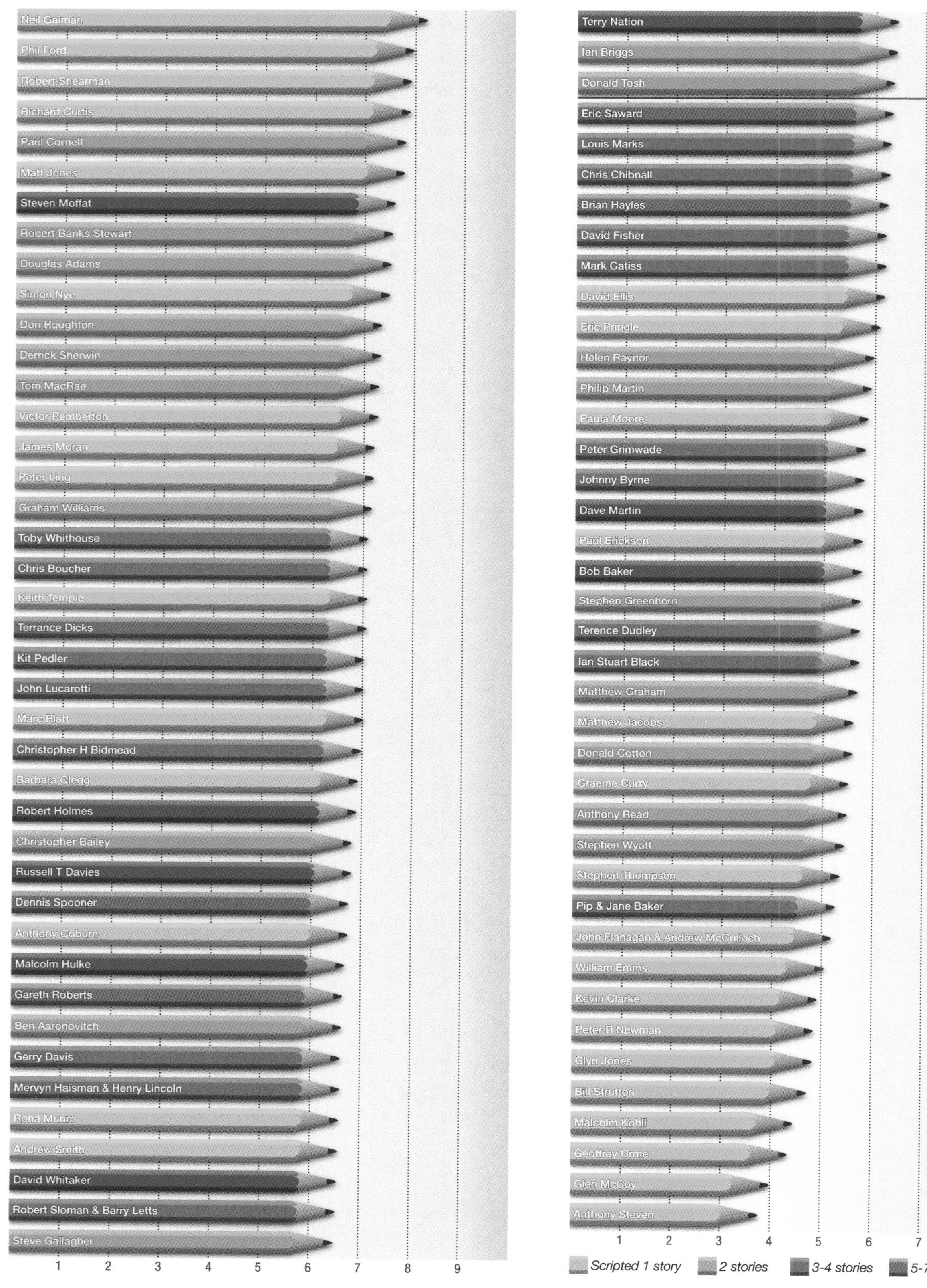

Neil Gaiman
Phil Ford
Robert Shearman
Richard Curtis
Paul Cornell
Matt Jones
Steven Moffat
Robert Banks Stewart
Douglas Adams
Simon Nye
Don Houghton
Derrick Sherwin
Tom MacRae
Victor Pemberton
James Moran
Peter Ling
Graham Williams
Toby Whithouse
Chris Boucher
Keith Temple
Terrance Dicks
Kit Pedler
John Lucarotti
Marc Platt
Christopher H Bidmead
Barbara Clegg
Robert Holmes
Christopher Bailey
Russell T Davies
Dennis Spooner
Anthony Coburn
Malcolm Hulke
Gareth Roberts
Ben Aaronovitch
Gerry Davis
Mervyn Haisman & Henry Lincoln
Rona Munro
Andrew Smith
David Whitaker
Robert Sloman & Barry Letts
Steve Gallagher
1 2 3 4 5 6 7 8 9
Terry Nation
Ian Briggs
Donald Tosh
Above average
Below average
Eric Saward
Louis Marks
Chris Chibnall
Brian Hayles
David Fisher
Mark Gatiss
David Ellis
Eric Pringle
Helen Raynor
Philip Martin
Paula Moore
Peter Grimwade
Johnny Byrne
Dave Martin
Paul Erickson
Bob Baker
Stephen Greenhorn
Terence Dudley
Ian Stuart Black
Matthew Graham
Matthew Jacobs
Donald Cotton
Graeme Curry
Anthony Read
Stephen Wyatt
Stephen Thompson
Pip & Jane Baker
John Flanagan & Andrew McCulloch
William Emms
Kevin Clarke
Peter R Newman
Glyn Jones
Bill Strutton
Malcolm Kohll
Geoffrey Orme
Glen McCoy
Anthony Steven
1 2 3 4 5 6 7 8 9
Scripted 1 story
2 stories
3-4 stories
5-7 stories
8+ stories

Writers and directors ranked according to popularity of their stories among fans

Using the results from the Doctor Who Dynamic Rankings website (dewhurstdesigns.co.uk/dynamic), an ongoing survey of fans' favourite stories with more than 7,300 voters to date, the writers (left) and directors (below) of each story are ranked according to the average score out of ten of all stories they worked on. So as to slightly benefit those who have made more than one contribution, the figures are calculated as the square root of the mean of the squares of the individual stories' scores. This boosts those with more stories to their name, as well as those with a wider spread of individual scores. Where writers have always contributed as a pair, they are listed together, but separately if they ever wrote alone. Where a pseudonym was used the true writers are counted here, as are those uncredited writers known to have made a significant contribution to a script. Similarly, where another director has taken over from the credited director on a story, that serial's score is counted for both directors.

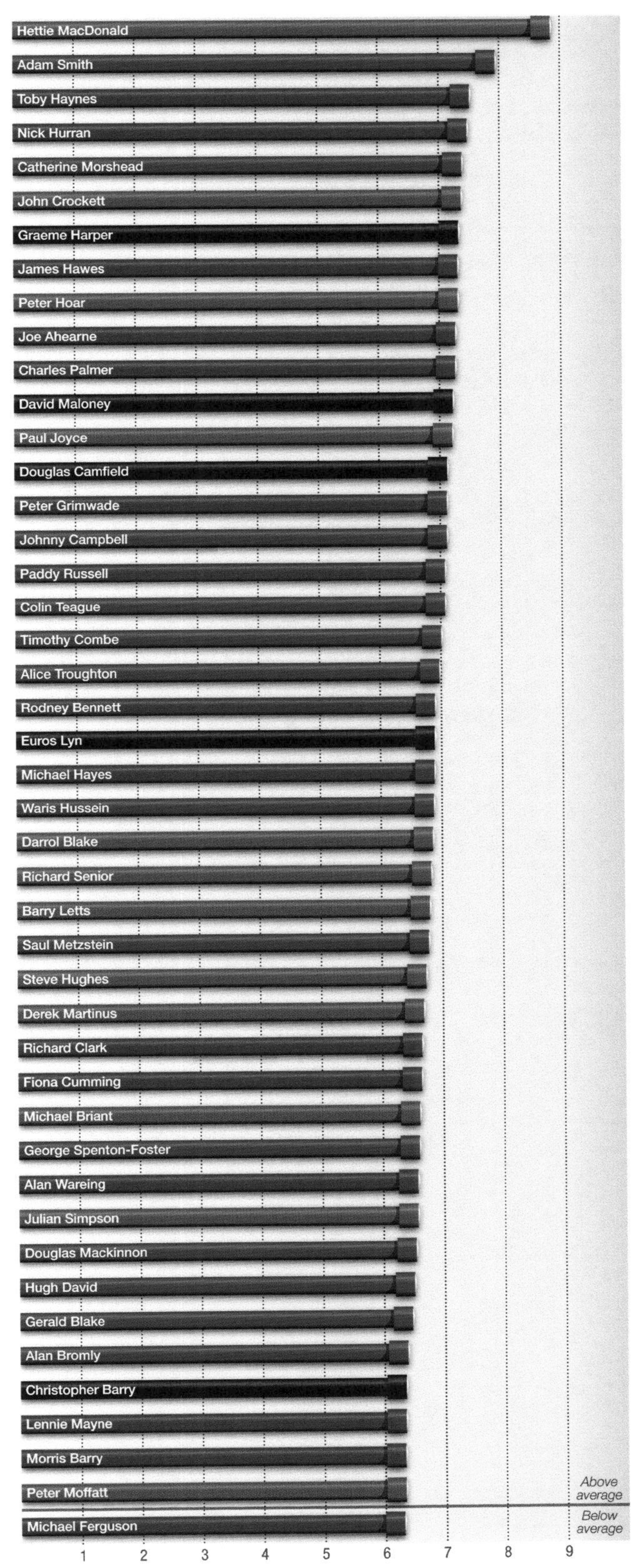

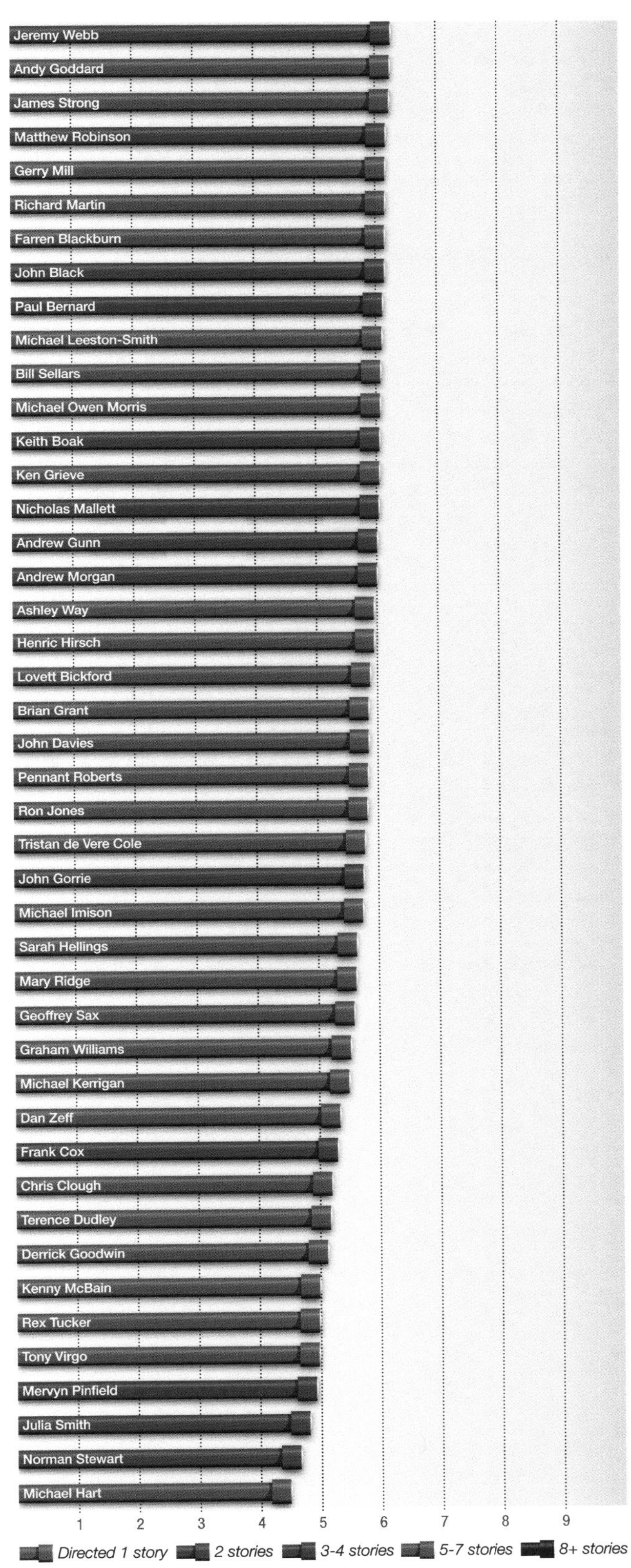

GENESIS OF THE DALEKS

Relative contributions of the people who brought *Doctor Who*'s most iconic enemy to life

When discussing the creation of the Daleks, it's common for many sources to credit writer Terry Nation and stop there. Among *Doctor Who* fans the more acclaimed contributor is designer Raymond Cusick, who devised the unique look of the creatures that arguably made them into the icon they remain to this day. But even that overlooks those who worked to develop the distinctive croaking voice of a Dalek — just as memorable an aspect — and also the tireless actors who risked wearing their legs to stumps while pedalling the deadly dustbins around studios and cobbled streets.

There have been 22 Dalek stories, plus they have waved their sink plungers in another five (not counting silent cameos in "The Waters of Mars" and "The Wedding of River Song"). This chart tallies all the designers, voice artists, writers, directors and actors who have helped the universe's most evil creations in their ongoing attempt to destroy all life. While the sizes of the four separate body parts are not related to the number of contributions (well, I couldn't mess with the classic proportions of a Dalek), the shaded banding within them represents the share of each person's involvement.

DESIGNERS In recognition of his genius in creating the distinctive Dalek shape and features, Raymond Cusick is credited here for all 27 stories in which Daleks appear. Other designers are counted if they made a significant addition to the creatures' appearance. Ed Thomas was production designer for the revived series and led the team that updated the look of the Daleks without betraying the classic form, before leading a more radical (and controversial) redesign for "Victory of the Daleks". Peter McKinstry is a concept artist on the modern series and developed the Supreme Dalek for "The Stolen Earth/Journey's End" and the New Paradigm Daleks. Other designers who worked on only one Dalek story are: John Brace, who created new Dalek casings with a more upright shape for "Revelation of the Daleks", plus the glass Dalek seen in that story; Stuart Brisdon, the visual effects designer on "Remembrance of the Daleks" who produced the sleeker look of the Imperials; Spencer Chapman, designer on "The Dalek Invasion of Earth", who modified the original Daleks with a larger base and power dish; and Matthew Savage, the concept artist who developed the design of the New Series Daleks. The other notable contributor to the look of the Daleks is Bill Roberts, whose company Shawcraft Models built the original props and who worked closely with Raymond Cusick on refining their form.

VOICES Original voice artist Peter Hawkins, who with David Graham first provided the monotone Dalek speech, ties with the New Series' Nicholas Briggs for number of stories on which they have worked. Roy Skelton, who was the voice of the Daleks throughout *Doctor Who*'s 1970s heyday, comes one story behind. Michael Wisher is better known for his role as Davros, the Daleks' fictional creator, but also provided Dalek voices for four stories. One-off users of ring modulators were: Oliver Gilbert and Peter Messaline for "Day of the Daleks" and David Gooderson in "Destiny of the Daleks", in which he primarily played Davros but also provided some Dalek voices alongside Skelton. Also deserving a mention is BBC Radiophonic Workshop member Brian Hodgson whose idea it was to feed the Dalek speech through a ring modulator to give it that grating, staccato quality.

WRITERS/DIRECTORS A lot of the Daleks' appeal is in their look and sound, but where would they be without the writers to give them new dastardly plans to attempt and the directors to make them frighten us each time they appear? Unsurprisingly, the man who created the metal meanies in the first place, Terry Nation, has written more of their adventures than anyone else, penning two-fifths of Dalek stories. New Series showrunner Russell T Davies comes a distant second with three stories. Directors have been less prolific, Graeme Harper and Richard Martin leading the pack with three stories each — the former distinguished by his being the only one to direct the Daleks in both the original and current series. The one-time writers for Daleks are: Ben Aaronovitch, Terrance Dicks, Mark Gatiss, Louis Marks, Helen Raynor and Robert Shearman; directors are: Paul Bernard, Michael Briant, Douglas Camfield, Ken Grieve, Andrew Gunn, Toby Haynes, Nick Hurran, Peter Moffatt, Andrew Morgan, Matthew Robinson and James Strong.

OPERATORS The Daleks' lack of legs and gliding movement were key elements of their initial appeal, but rather than clever mechanics their real motive power is the men inside who pedal along through the open base (sorry to dash any illusions). Yet it has always been trained actors, rather than stuntmen or props handlers, who have operated the Daleks, as their movement is a key part of their character and performance. Renowned as the man inside many *Doctor Who* monsters, John Scott Martin almost made a career out of playing Daleks, donning the armour for more than 50% of their appearances. The first man inside a New Series Dalek who had to rediscover the required skills, Barnaby Edwards, now matches original series stalwarts Robert Jewell, Peter Murphy Grumbar and Cy Town. Those who never got the chance to be a Dalek more than once are: Keith Ashley, Norman Bacon, Dan Barratt, Stuart Crossman, Mathew Doman, Nick Evans, David Harrison, Jeremy Harvey, Ian Hilditch, Gethin Jones, Mike Mungarvan, Ricky Newby, Sean Saye, Hugh Spight, Michael Summerton, Ken Tyllsen, Joe White and Nigel Wild.

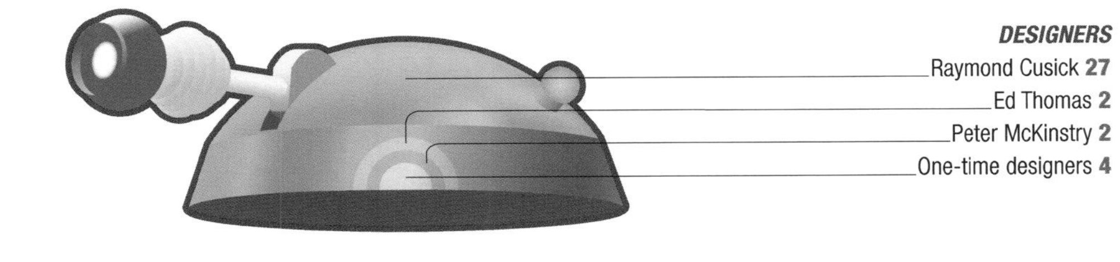

DESIGNERS
Raymond Cusick 27
Ed Thomas 2
Peter McKinstry 2
One-time designers 4

VOICES
Nicholas Briggs 8
Peter Hawkins 8
Roy Skelton 7
David Graham 5
Michael Wisher 4
Royce Mills 3
Brian Miller 2
One-time voices 3

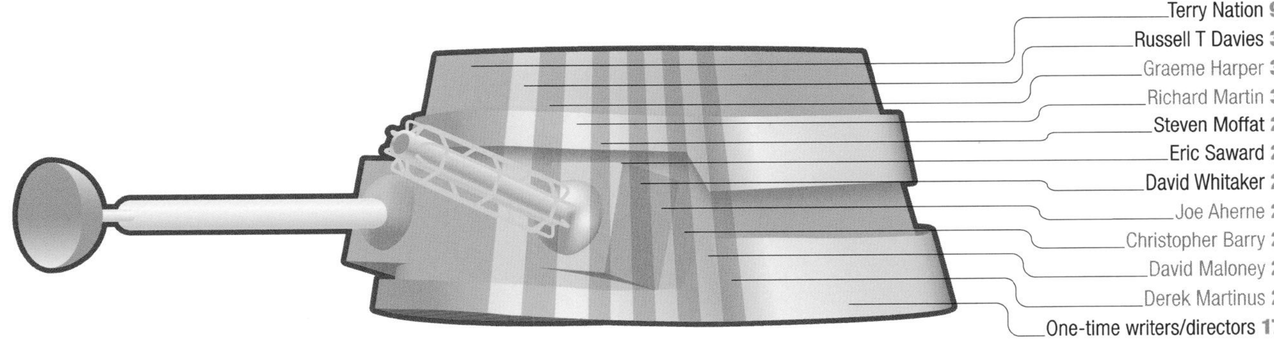

WRITERS & DIRECTORS
Terry Nation 9
Russell T Davies 3
Graeme Harper 3
Richard Martin 3
Steven Moffat 2
Eric Saward 2
David Whitaker 2
Joe Aherne 2
Christopher Barry 2
David Maloney 2
Derek Martinus 2
One-time writers/directors 17

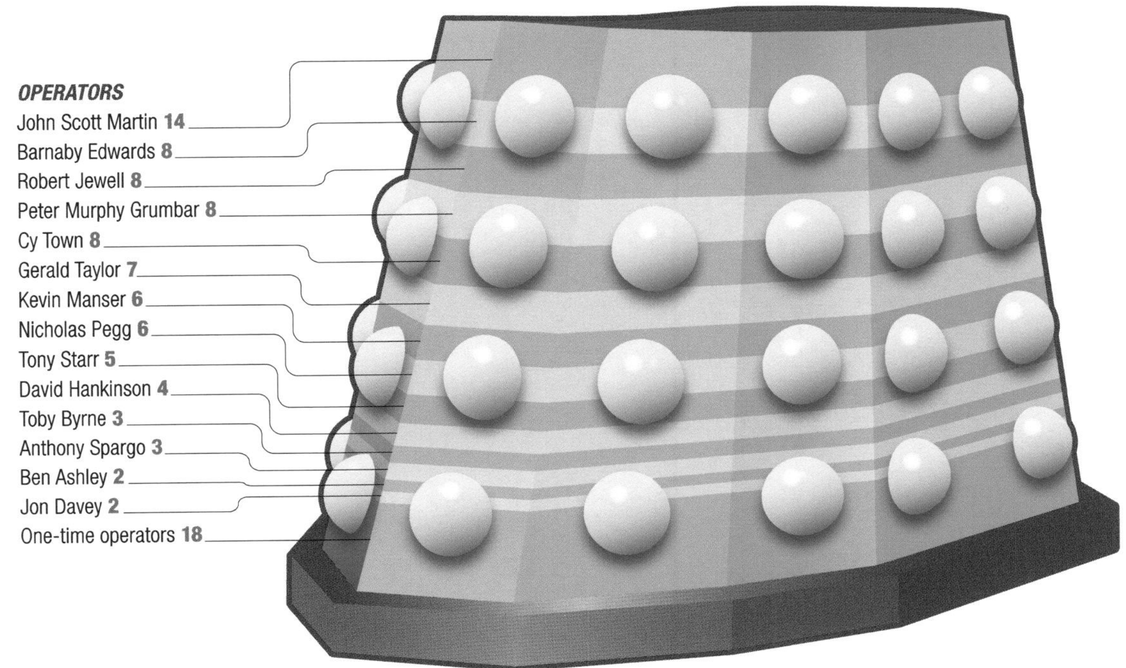

OPERATORS
John Scott Martin 14
Barnaby Edwards 8
Robert Jewell 8
Peter Murphy Grumbar 8
Cy Town 8
Gerald Taylor 7
Kevin Manser 6
Nicholas Pegg 6
Tony Starr 5
David Hankinson 4
Toby Byrne 3
Anthony Spargo 3
Ben Ashley 2
Jon Davey 2
One-time operators 18

THE SOUND OF DRUMS

Share of stories by composer of incidental music

Paying a composer to write and record incidental music was something of a luxury for television dramas in the 1960s, especially for a tightly budgeted show like *Doctor Who*. When the series was establishing itself it was one worth paying for, with all but one story of Season 1 (the two-part filler "The Edge of Destruction") receiving a specially composed score. This wasn't written after recording to fit the pictures, as is the norm today, but general mood pieces would be recorded beforehand and played into studio at the appropriate points as the episodes were shot. Thus the composer might score 15-20 minutes of music to be used throughout a story irrespective of its length. By Season 2 money was being saved by using stock library music for some stories, or even that from earlier *Doctor Who* stories: "The Rescue" features cues originally written for "The Daleks".

This trend increased throughout the 1960s, with only half of Second Doctor stories having original scores written for them, the rest using stock pieces or even no music at all to really save money. By the 1970s, though, drama without incidental music was unusual and *Doctor Who*'s shorter seasons made paying a composer more affordable. Dudley Simpson, who had been writing occasional scores for the programme since 1964's "Planet of Giants", became the regular composer and by far the most prolific of the original series, scoring all but a handful of stories between 1970 and 1979. In 1980, however, incoming producer John Nathan-Turner felt a new style was needed alongside his other changes to the show and he turned to the BBC's Radiophonic Workshop to provide the scores. It had been creating sound effects for *Doctor Who* since its inception, most famously the TARDIS take-off sound, and in the cases of 1968's "The Wheel in Space" and 1969's "The Krotons", Workshop composer Brian Hodgson's extensive soundscapes were essentially the incidental scores for otherwise music-less serials. But by the 1980s the Workshop had proven itself a pioneer in electronic music, not just a maker of unusual sounds, and nearly all of its team of composers contributed to *Doctor Who*. Even when from 1986 the show returned to using freelance composers they were solo musicians producing their soundtracks electronically in their own studios.

Since the series returned in 2005 the music has been composed entirely by Murray Gold, who (as of "A Good Man Goes to War" in 2011) has now overtaken Simpson for the number of individual stories scored. Initially he recorded the music himself but from Series 2 was afforded the services of the BBC National Orchestra of Wales conducted by Ben Foster. Gold has even written several songs for the programme: 'Song for Ten' sung by Tim Phillips, which featured in the Tenth Doctor's debut "The Christmas Invasion"; 'Love Don't Roam' sung by Neil Hannon in "The Runaway Bride"; 'My Angel Put the Devil in Me' sung by Miranda Raison in "Daleks in Manhattan"; 'The Stowaway' sung by Yamit Mamo in "Voyage of the Damned"; 'Vale Decem' sung by Mark Chambers in "The End of Time"; and 'Abigail's Song' sung by Katherine Jenkins in "A Christmas Carol".

The data

COMPOSER	NUMBER OF STORIES	SHARE OF STORIES
Murray Gold	75	34.56%
Dudley Simpson	62	28.57%
Peter Howell	10	4.61%
Tristram Cary	8	3.69%
Paddy Kingsland	8	3.69%
Roger Limb	8	3.69%
Malcolm Clarke	7	3.23%
Keff McCulloch	6	2.76%
Dominic Glynn	5	2.30%
Jonathan Gibbs	4	1.84%
Mark Ayres	3	1.38%
Carey Blyton	3	1.38%
Norman Kay	3	1.38%
Geoffrey Burgon	2	0.92%
Brian Hodgson	2	0.92%
Raymond Jones	2	0.92%
Richard Rodney Bennett	1	0.46%
Charles Botterill	1	0.46%
Francis Chagrin	1	0.46%
John Debney & co	1	0.46%
Don Harper	1	0.46%
Richard Hartley	1	0.46%
Stanley Myers	1	0.46%
Elizabeth Parker	1	0.46%
Humphrey Searle	1	0.46%

Simpson and Gold stand head and shoulders above all other composers on the series, between them accounting for almost two-thirds of scores. Even taken together, the Radiophonic Workshop composers — Malcolm Clarke, Jonathan Gibbs, Brian Hodgson, Peter Howell, Paddy Kingsland, Roger Limb and Elizabeth Parker — provided music for only 18% of stories, leaving just 18.5% (40 stories) to other musicians.

Those who were chosen to provide new arrangements of the *Doctor Who* theme tune bear no relation to prevalence, more a case of being in the right place at the right time. While Gold has produced three distinct arrangements of the theme during his time as sole composer on the series (and a few remixes of each), Simpson never had the opportunity to give us his interpretation. Ironically, the creator of the original, Delia Derbyshire, never composed incidental music specifically for the show, although tracks by her were used as stock music in 1970's "Inferno".

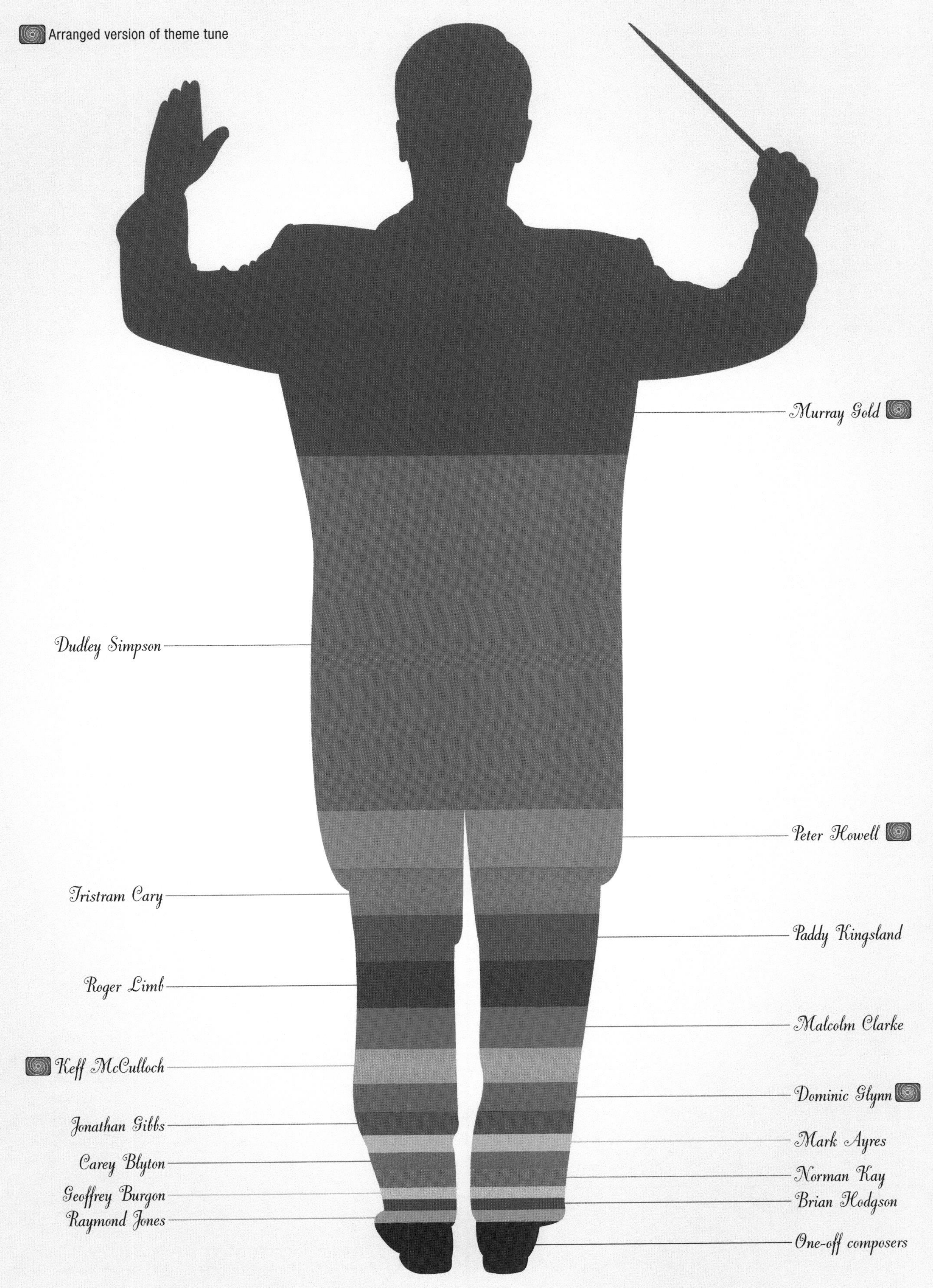

Arranged version of theme tune
Murray Gold
Dudley Simpson
Peter Howell
Tristram Cary
Paddy Kingsland
Roger Limb
Malcolm Clarke
Keff McCulloch
Dominic Glynn
Jonathan Gibbs
Mark Ayres
Carey Blyton
Norman Kay
Geoffrey Burgon
Brian Hodgson
Raymond Jones
One-off composers

THE PANDORICA OPENS

Opening title sequences by number of episodes they fronted

While *Doctor Who* undeniably has one of the most recognisable theme tunes ever composed, its opening title graphics have frequently been equally as engaging and groundbreaking. The combination of eerie electronic music and spooky swirling images quickly became the signature of the programme.

The first sequence was created by BBC graphic designer Bernard Lodge using a technique called 'howl-around', whereby two video cameras were linked to a single monitor. The first was fed with an image, such as a caption card or a flash of light, while the second was pointed at the monitor. The image would appear on the screen, be picked up by the second camera, then fed back to the screen. The resulting electronic feedback would gradually deteriorate until the starting image was reduced to a dwindling series of amorphous shapes. Lodge and his assistant Norman Taylor filmed hours of material, some incorporating a title card showing the 'Doctor Who' logo, from which the final sequence was edited together.

Shortly after Patrick Troughton had taken over the role of the Doctor in 1966, the production team decided to redo the titles. Lodge was again assigned to create new howl-around footage, but this time the Doctor's face would be incorporated. This was an idea that had been tried in the original sessions but deemed too scary. However, Lodge had found that using a pattern to begin a feedback sequence, rather than a light, gave him some control over the result, so he was able to include a face by feeding in a photograph of Troughton. When *Doctor Who* went into colour a new title sequence was needed, but Lodge found using the howl-around technique with a colour monitor didn't produce the same effect. So he reshot some black-and-white feedback, this time based on a diamond pattern as well as a photo of Jon Pertwee, with coloured lighting gels between the camera and the screen.

The fourth sequence, introduced for what turned out to be Pertwee's final season, adapted the 'slit-scan' technique seen in Stanley Kubrick's 1968 film *2001: A Space Odyssey*. A rostrum camera locked to expose one frame of film was moved towards a slit in a black card, behind which a sheet of plastic under a polarised light was moved sideways. This produced a patterned streak from the centre to the edge of the frame, either a flat 'wall' if the slit was vertical or a tunnel effect if the slit was a ring. The film was then wound on by one frame, the background shifted to a slightly different starting position, and a second frame was exposed. Thus a sequence was built up in which the viewer appeared to be moving forwards past the patterned wall. Lodge even used a slit in the shape of the Doctor's outline to produce a Doctor-shaped tunnel. It was a long-winded process that took three months to complete, but when Tom Baker replaced Pertwee a year later, Lodge had to recreate the sequence, this time also incorporating the TARDIS.

In 1980, incoming producer John Nathan-Turner wanted new opening graphics and designer Sid Sutton was assigned. He wanted to keep the forward motion of the previous sequence, but to open it out from an enclosed tunnel by setting it in space. A rostrum camera was moved towards a sheet of black card in which numerous pin holes were lit from behind to produce a set of 'stars' moving towards and past the viewer. The film was then wound back a bit and re-exposed with a different set of holes in the card. By repeating the process a continuous sequence of moving through space was created. By stopping some passes early so the stars stayed in view, a shape could be built up out of points of light, such as the Doctor's face and the logo. Again, the sequence had to be redone when Peter Davison became the Doctor just a year later, and when Colin Baker took over in 1984 a third version was produced. This returned to more of a tunnel feel with rows of animated coloured flashes around the edges.

A new Doctor in 1987 required a new title sequence, and this time computer graphics were used — a relatively new field at the time. BBC graphic designer Oliver Elmes wanted to achieve a greater freedom of movement through space and around a galaxy to get a dizzying, 'rollercoaster' feel. He worked with Gareth Edwards at CAL Video to create the final sequence of the 'camera' passing through a galactic rim and around a bubble-encased TARDIS. Of course, since then computer-generated images have become ubiquitous, and all the later title sequences have been digitally created. Those for the TV Movie — by Canadian effects company Northwest Imaging & FX — and the revived series — devised by Dave Houghton and Chris Tucker at visual effects company The Mill — took similar approaches to adapting the feel of the Fourth Doctor sequence, but dropped the appearance of the Doctor's face. The latter had the logo tweaked from the Christmas 2006 special "The Runaway Bride", and was rendered in high-definition for the 2009 specials. For the arrival of the Eleventh Doctor, Christian Manz at digital effects company Framestore developed a sequence more in line with the fairytale feel the new production team was aiming for, maintaining the motion through a tunnel but one now made of clouds, lightning and fire.

The data

SEQUENCE	FIRST SEEN	LAST SEEN	No. OF EPISODES
1	An Unearthly Child 1	The Moonbase 4	152
2	The Macra Terror 1	The War Games 10	101
3	Spearhead from Space 1	The Green Death 6	102
4a	The Time Warrior 1	Planet of the Spiders 6	26
4b	Robot 1	The Horns of Nimon 4	144
5a	The Leisure Hive 1	Logopolis 4	28
5b	Castrovalva 1	The Caves of Androzani 4	69
5c	The Twin Dilemma 1	The Trial of a Time Lord 14	31
6	Time and the Rani 1	Survival 3	42
7	The TV Movie	The TV Movie	1
8	Rose	The End of Time 2	60
9	The Eleventh Hour	The Angels Take Manhattan	33

The title sequences on the TV screen opposite are sized proportionally to the number of episodes they appeared on. Although the Fourth Doctor sequence 4b was in use the longest — six years from 1974 to 1980 — the longer seasons of *Doctor Who*'s early years mean the original sequence actually appeared the most. Similarly sequences 2 and 3 fronted almost equal numbers of episodes despite the latter being used over more years.

The more frequently changing Doctors of the 1980s required fresh title sequences, although the various versions of sequence 5 together appeared almost as often as sequence 4b. Sequence 8 is the only one to cover the full tenures of two Doctors, fronting all Ninth and Tenth Doctor episodes, although it was tweaked during that time.

Ranking the techniques used, the original howl-around effect leads, used as the basis of titles for 45% of all episodes to date. Camera animation methods were seen on 37.8%, while 17.2% have had CG sequences.

CH
VOL
1
4b
3
2
9
5c
5b
6
5a
4a
7
8

FICTION

THE WORLD ACCORDING TO DOCTOR WHO

Locations of televised stories set on Earth

The Doctor has often stated that the Earth is quite his favourite planet, and it's by far his most frequent destination. Yet judging by his televised adventures, he has seen surprisingly little of it. He has barely visited a tenth of all the countries of the world, and the vast majority of his escapades have taken place in southern England (with a more recent increase in Welsh incidents).

The following three maps list stories with scenes set in London, the UK and worldwide. Some take place across multiple locations so are listed more than once. The events in "Amy's Choice" are not included as they were all a dream. Flashbacks are included if they feature new material, not just pre-seen clips. Stock-footage snapshots to show worldwide scale are ignored unless augmented with story-specific elements. Two-part New Series stories are listed by the episode title in which a location was first seen, but only once if a new location in the second part was in an already visited region.

Stories set in London

It's not surprising that a high proportion of *Doctor Who* stories are set in or visit London, as not only is it the country's capital but it's where the programme was produced for its first 26 years. Usually, unless featuring a major landmark like the Houses of Parliament or St Paul's Cathedral, the precise location in London is not specified on screen, but in the interests of placing as many stories as possible some can be reasonably estimated.

The distinctive obelisk nearby places Brendan School in Enfield (where "Mawdryn Undead" was filmed). Sarah's home in "The Five Doctors" may be in Croydon, as suggested in "The Hand of Fear", but here is taken to be in West London as that is where it was filmed (and where Sarah lived in her own series). Martha and her family's homes seen in "42", "The Sound of Drums" and "The Stolen Earth" could be anywhere in London. The script for "The Waters of Mars" puts Adelaide Brooke's house in London, while on-screen news reports give her a connection to Finchley, so it's assumed she still lives there. The National Museum in "The Big Bang" is probably in the museums district of South Kensington. The script for "The Doctor, the Widow and the Wardrobe" places the Arwell's pre-war home in Kew. The house the Doctor gives to Amy and Rory in "The God Complex" could have been in Leadworth but later events in "The Power of Three" suggest it's in London.

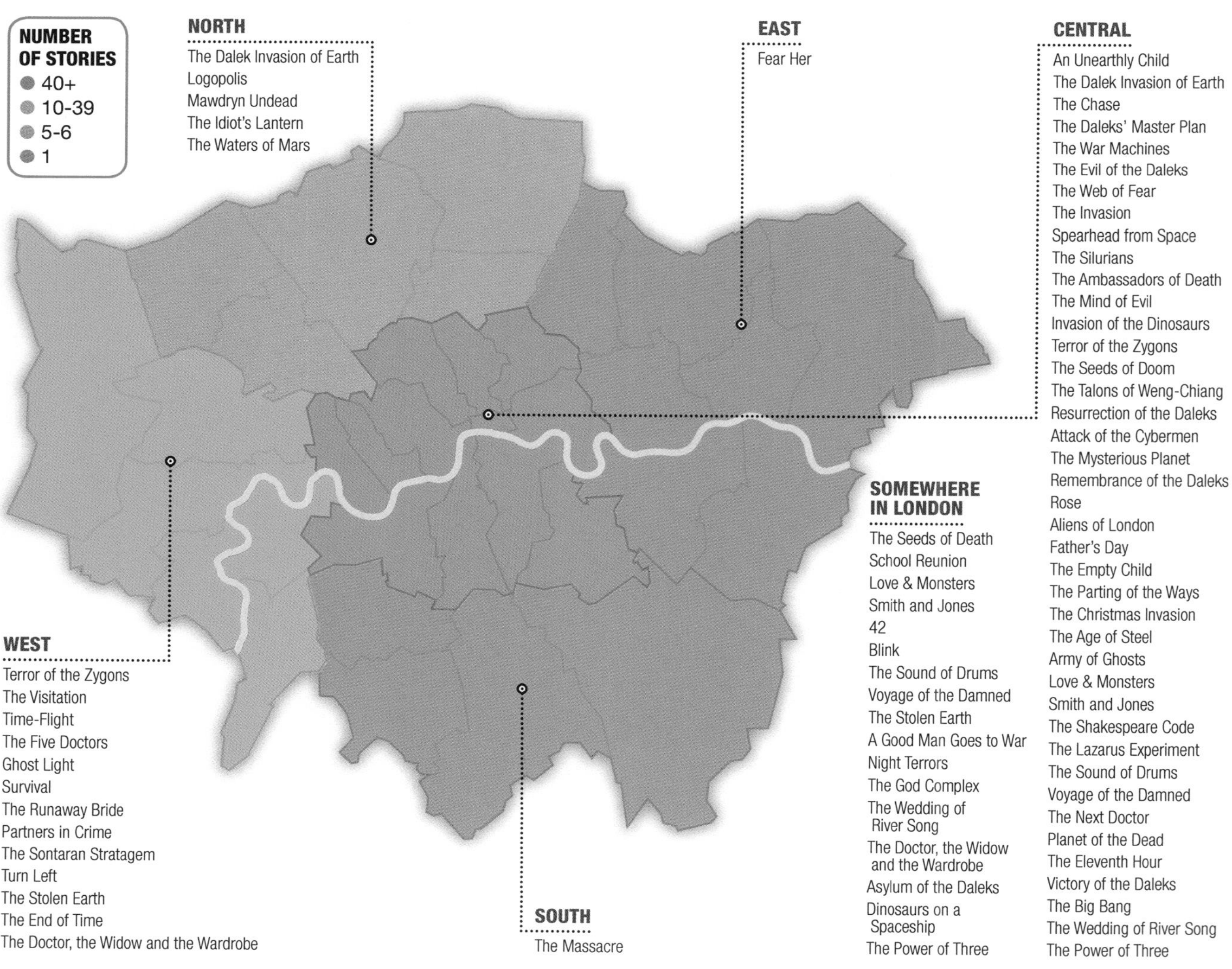

Stories set in the UK

Two-thirds of stories set on Earth take place in the UK (although none of them in Northern Ireland), and 60% of them in England. This is subject to revision, however — for example, we only discovered many years later that the closing scene of "The Hand of Fear" was in Aberdeen and not Croydon. Generic quaint English villages are assumed to be in the region where they were filmed, usually in South England (supported by the lack of Northern accents among the local yokels). Unless otherwise specified, the 1970s UNIT stories are assumed to happen in the Home Counties.

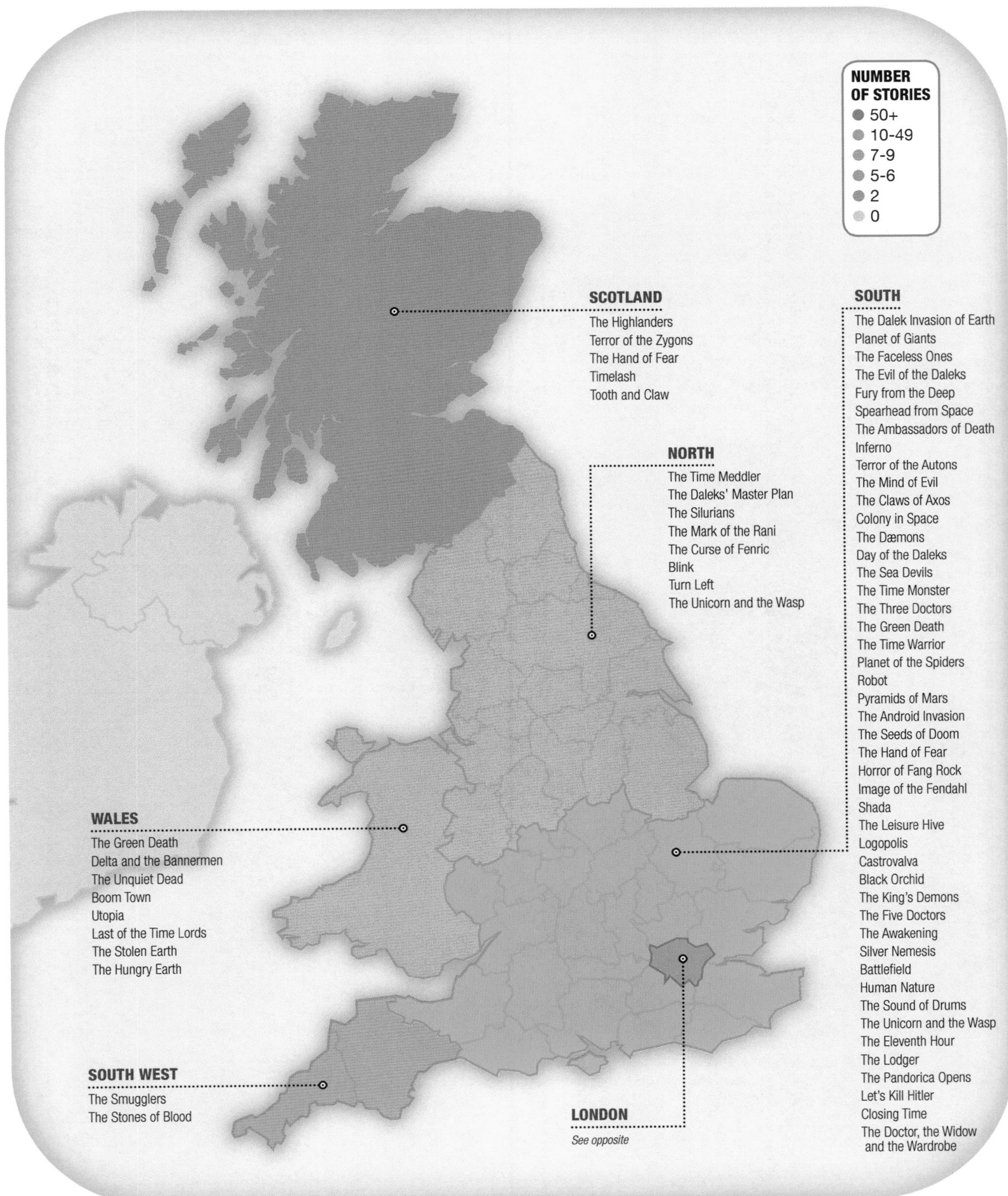

Number of stories set on Earth, by Doctor

In all, 148 different stories have been set or have included scenes on Earth. Somewhat surprisingly, the Doctor who has spent most time on Earth was not the Third, despite being exiled here, but the Tenth, followed by the Eleventh, whose total is only going to increase (see graph below).

However, when these figures are taken as a percentage of each Doctor's total number of stories, the balances change. The Third and Tenth Doctors are more even, with 76.3% and 75.0% respectively of their stories featuring Earth. Discounting the Eighth Doctor, whose one story was on Earth giving him a 100% hit rate, the Ninth Doctor is the one who couldn't get enough of our world, with 80% of his stories set here (and the remainder in nearby orbit). The Eleventh is again second, with 78.6% of his stories at least looking in on Earth events. Only the Fourth Doctor has fewer than half of his stories featuring Earth, at just 38.1%, although again one ("The Ark in Space") takes place in an orbiting space station.

- First Doctor
- Second Doctor
- Third Doctor
- Fourth Doctor
- Fifth Doctor
- Sixth Doctor
- Seventh Doctor
- Eighth Doctor
- Ninth Doctor
- Tenth Doctor
- Eleventh Doctor

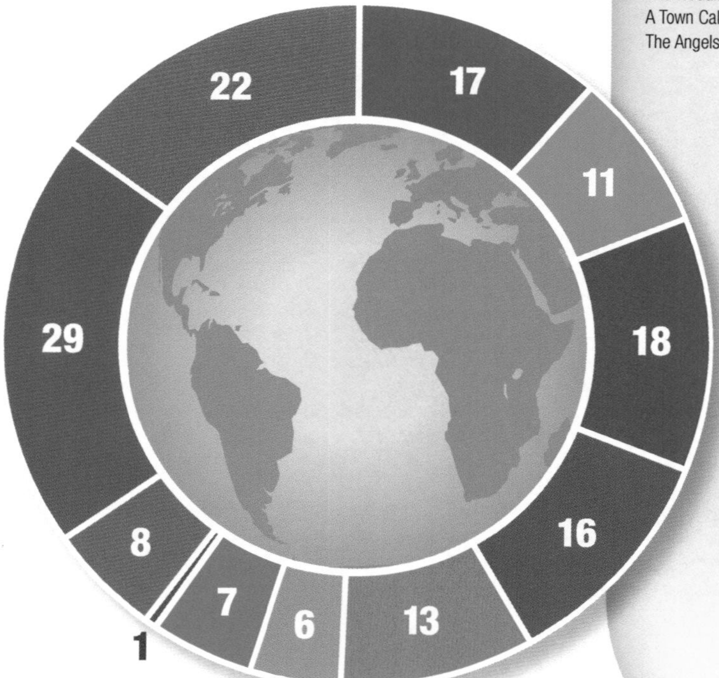

22
17
11
18
16
13
6
7
1
8
29

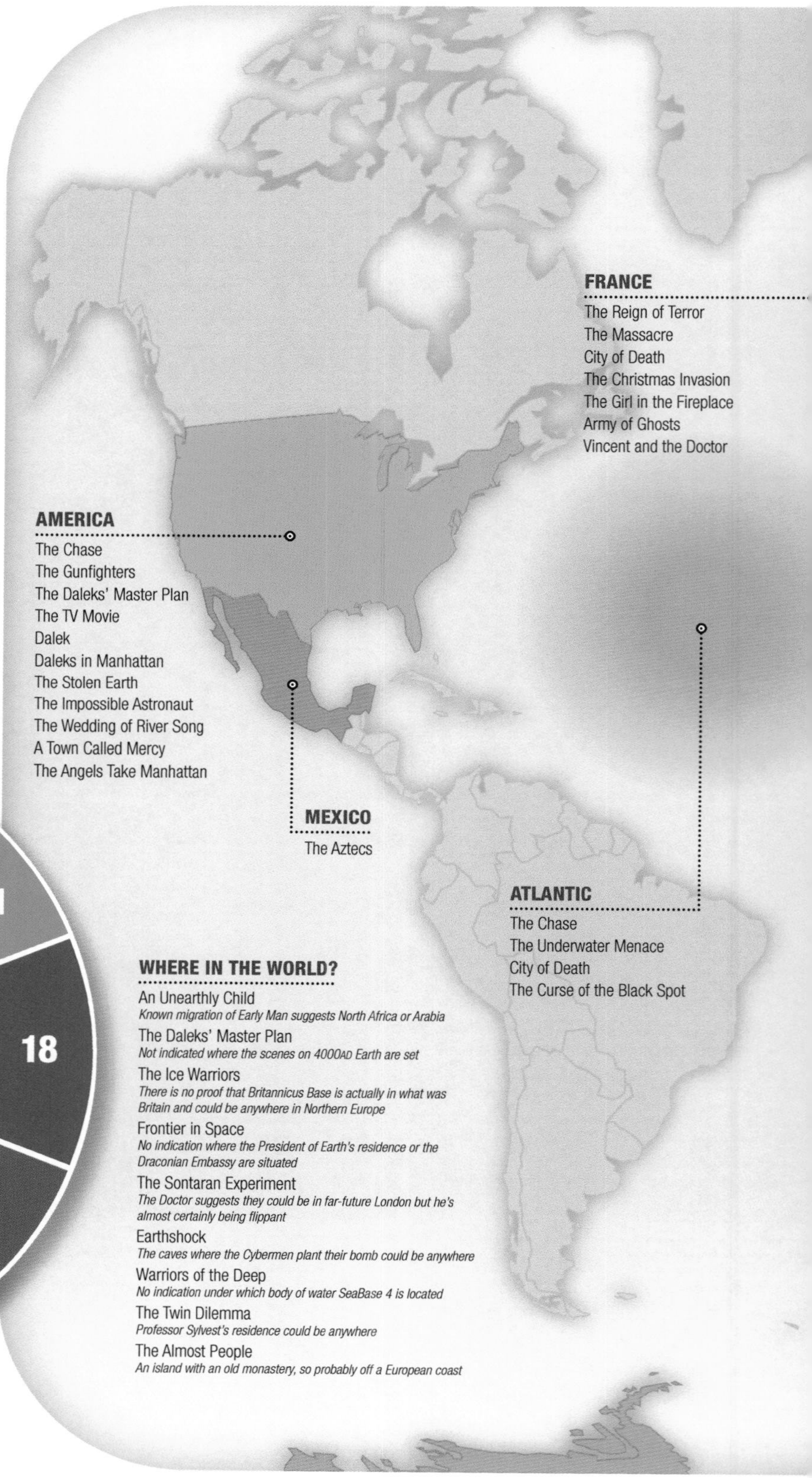

FRANCE
The Reign of Terror
The Massacre
City of Death
The Christmas Invasion
The Girl in the Fireplace
Army of Ghosts
Vincent and the Doctor

AMERICA
The Chase
The Gunfighters
The Daleks' Master Plan
The TV Movie
Dalek
Daleks in Manhattan
The Stolen Earth
The Impossible Astronaut
The Wedding of River Song
A Town Called Mercy
The Angels Take Manhattan

MEXICO
The Aztecs

ATLANTIC
The Chase
The Underwater Menace
City of Death
The Curse of the Black Spot

WHERE IN THE WORLD?

An Unearthly Child
Known migration of Early Man suggests North Africa or Arabia

The Daleks' Master Plan
Not indicated where the scenes on 4000AD Earth are set

The Ice Warriors
There is no proof that Britannicus Base is actually in what was Britain and could be anywhere in Northern Europe

Frontier in Space
No indication where the President of Earth's residence or the Draconian Embassy are situated

The Sontaran Experiment
The Doctor suggests they could be in far-future London but he's almost certainly being flippant

Earthshock
The caves where the Cybermen plant their bomb could be anywhere

Warriors of the Deep
No indication under which body of water SeaBase 4 is located

The Twin Dilemma
Professor Sylvest's residence could be anywhere

The Almost People
An island with an old monastery, so probably off a European coast

Stories set overseas

Only 22 countries other than the UK have featured in *Doctor Who* stories, and not all of them were actually visited by the Doctor himself. We see only the offices of global organisations in "The Tenth Planet" and "The Enemy of the World", where events are not witnessed by the Doctor. Similarly he is not physically present when he first says goodbye to Rose at Bad Wolf Bay (although he looks around as though he can see his projection's surroundings), or when people are seen to be hypnotised by the Sycorax in Paris and Rome, the Cybermen break through from their parallel world in Paris and India, or when the Daleks invade Germany.

Some countries are the location for fleeting stop-offs. The Doctor makes a whistlestop visit to the Empire State Building in "The Chase" (although he sees a lot more of it in "Daleks in Manhattan") and doesn't stay long at Ghana's strange festival. His second visit to Dårlig Ulf Stranden was unavoidably brief, and we only see him stop off in Kenya to seek Riddell's help in "Dinosaurs on a Spaceship". His trips to Egypt in the same story and Belgium in "The Unicorn and the Wasp" appear to have been more involved although we only see glimpses of his adventures there.

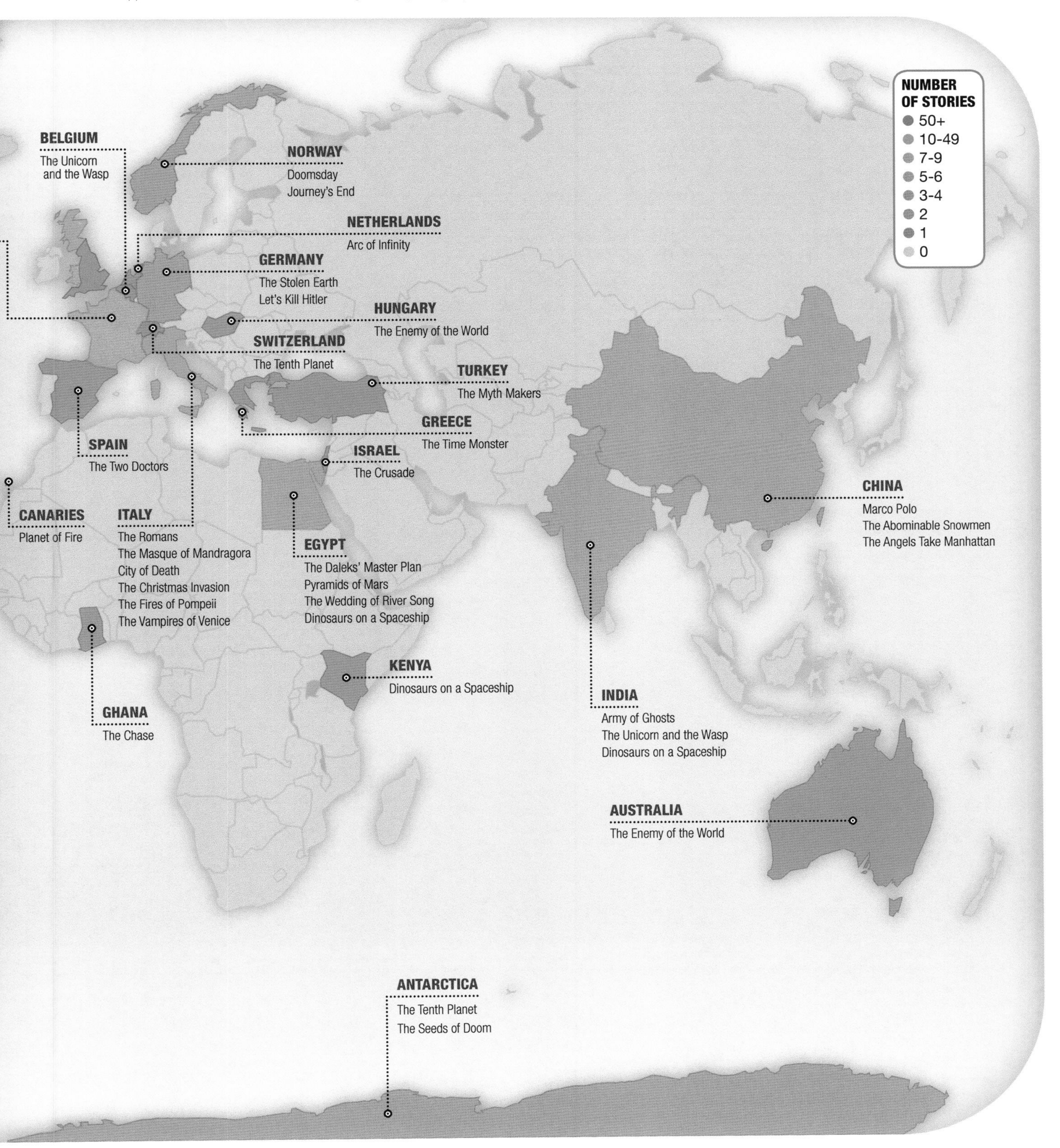

THE ROOF OF THE WORLD

Significant heights and depths experienced in *Doctor Who*

The Doctor's many visits to Earth have seen him not only venture around the globe but also far above and below its surface. Early on he was high in the Pamir Mountains, the highest peak of which reaches 7,495 metres, although the pass in which the travellers first met Marco Polo was probably nearer 4,200m — high enough for the elderly Doctor to succumb to altitude sickness. By comparison, the top of the Temple of Yetaxa was likely a mere 20m above the ground, offering grand vistas of the Aztec city but tiring to climb (and not a pleasant drop for Ixta). The TARDIS touched down briefly at the top of the Empire State Building in "The Chase". Although the tour guide claims they're on floor 102, it's clearly the observation deck on the 86th floor, at 320m (and as he exaggerates the height of the skyscraper, he's an unreliable guide). This puts the 457m down which the TARDIS crew had to lower themselves to escape the burning city on Mechanus in dizzying perspective. The First Doctor's last ascent was to the top of the GPO (now BT) Tower.

The Doctor's first venture into the depths of the planet came early in his second incarnation when he landed on an island near the Azores and was transported some 1,000m below sea level (based on the average sea depth in the area) to the remains of Atlantis. He would later descend an unknown distance into Euro Gas Refinery's impeller shaft to confront the Weed Creature, shortly after evading Yeti on London's Piccadilly Line just 20m below the surface. An earlier encounter with the robotic beasts had been his highest Earth adventure, around 4,600m above sea level in the Himalayas.

The Third Doctor was soon trying to make peace with cave-dwelling Silurians, some 250m down based on the depths of real Derbyshire cave systems, but nothing compared to the 32,187m (20 miles) Professor Stahlman's Inferno project had drilled into the Earth's crust. The Doctor himself didn't go that deep but the goo that came up the bore was not pleasant. A quick dive to some 27m, based on the depth of the eastern Solent, to meet the Sea Devils was a jaunt in comparison, although his venture down a Welsh coal mine — typically around 160m deep — at Llanfairfach was more harrowing.

The Fourth Doctor's encounter with the Zygons took him into the murky depths of Loch Ness, 227m at its deepest. Fang Rock lighthouse was probably around 30m, easy enough for a Rutan to climb, and nothing compared to the top level of Paris's Eiffel Tower at 273m, from which the Doctor and Romana flew (or did they take the lift?). If the Doctor wasn't scared of heights then, he soon had cause to be, falling to his fourth 'death' from the gangway of the Pharos Project radio telescope. Based on the similar Lovell telescope at Jodrell Bank, this would have been a plummet of some 40m.

The Doctor subsequently avoided high places (regenerative trauma presumably clouding his fear when he climbed up to the city of Castrovalva) but happily explored some caves where the Cybermen had planted a bomb (unknown depth but the troopers carry no climbing equipment) and visited SeaBase 4 at the bottom of an unknown body of water. The Sixth Doctor narrowly avoided a one-way trip down a mine shaft, although the one he landed the Rani's TARDIS in was likely not more than 30m deep as it was a drift mine with a ground-level entrance. The Seventh Doctor visited King Arthur's spaceship below the surface of Lake Vortigern — some 15m deep based on the reservoir where "Battlefield" was filmed.

The Tenth Doctor was understandably tentative when he had to climb Alexandra Palace's 67m transmitter (already atop a 24m-high building), being his first time that high since he visited the Pharos Project. He later learned 1 Canada Square in London's Canary Wharf was built to reach an anomaly 183m above sea level (so why they kept building to 235m is unclear). After swinging from the aerial of the Empire State Building 381m up, no wonder he kept to the lower chambers of Vesuvius given its pre-eruption peak was around 2,500m, reduced to 1,281m by the explosion the Doctor initiated.

The Eleventh Doctor took the TARDIS more then 21,000m below Cwmtaff in Wales to rescue Amy from the Silurian base there, but was later back above ground marrying River Song at the 139m apex of the Great Pyramid of Giza on a time-collapsing alternative Earth. From there the 46m-tall Weeping Angel Statue of Liberty wouldn't have seemed half as frightening as it did close up from the roof of a 16-storey New York apartment block.

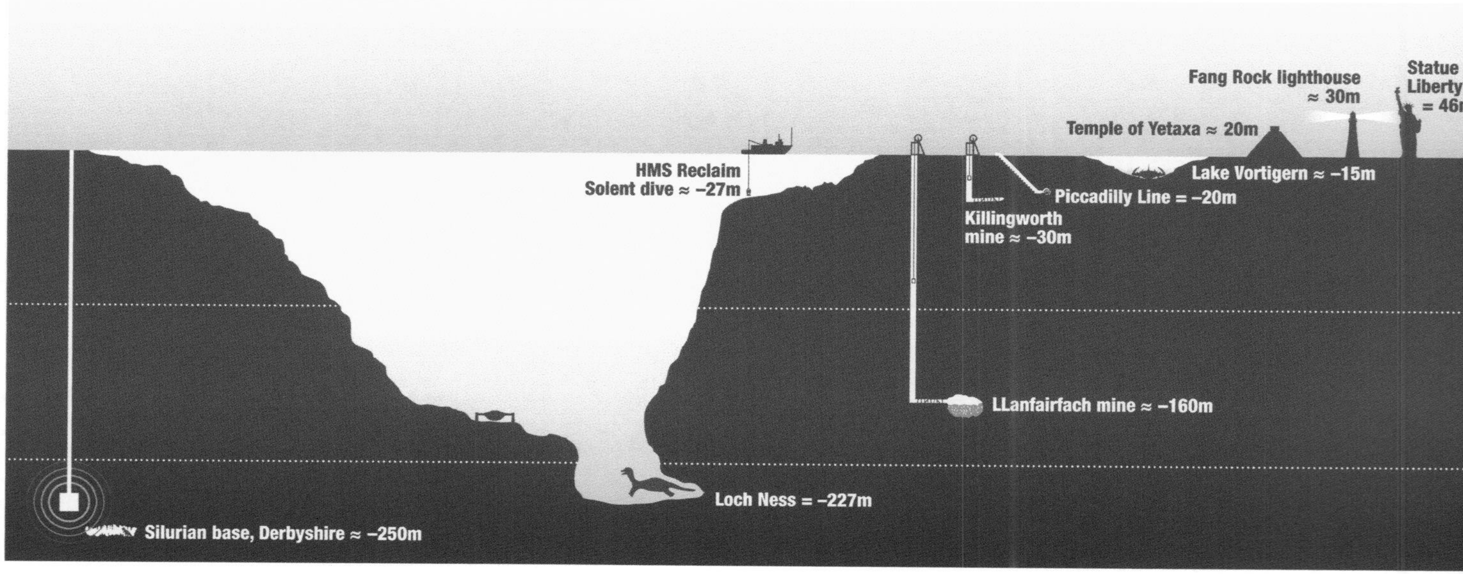

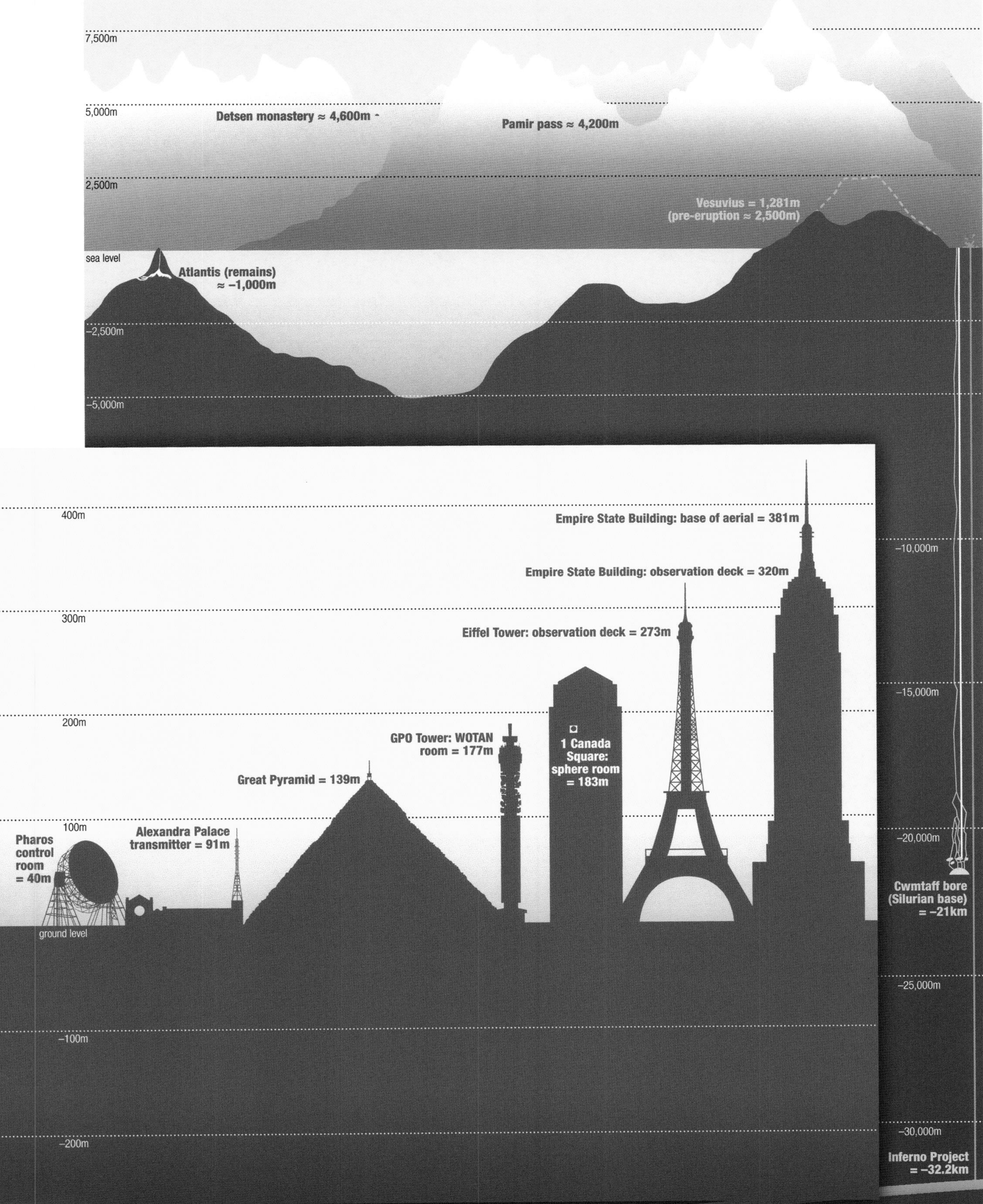

7,500m
5,000m
Detsen monastery ≈ 4,600m
Pamir pass ≈ 4,200m
2,500m
Vesuvius = 1,281m
(pre-eruption ≈ 2,500m)
sea level
Atlantis (remains)
≈ –1,000m
–2,500m
–5,000m
400m
Empire State Building: base of aerial = 381m
–10,000m
Empire State Building: observation deck = 320m
300m
Eiffel Tower: observation deck = 273m
–15,000m
200m
GPO Tower: WOTAN
room = 177m
1 Canada
Square:
sphere room
= 183m
Great Pyramid = 139m
100m
–20,000m
Pharos
control
room
= 40m
Alexandra Palace
transmitter = 91m
Cwmtaff bore
(Silurian base)
= –21km
ground level
–25,000m
–100m
–30,000m
–200m
Inferno Project
= –32.2km

THE SWOLLEN EARTH

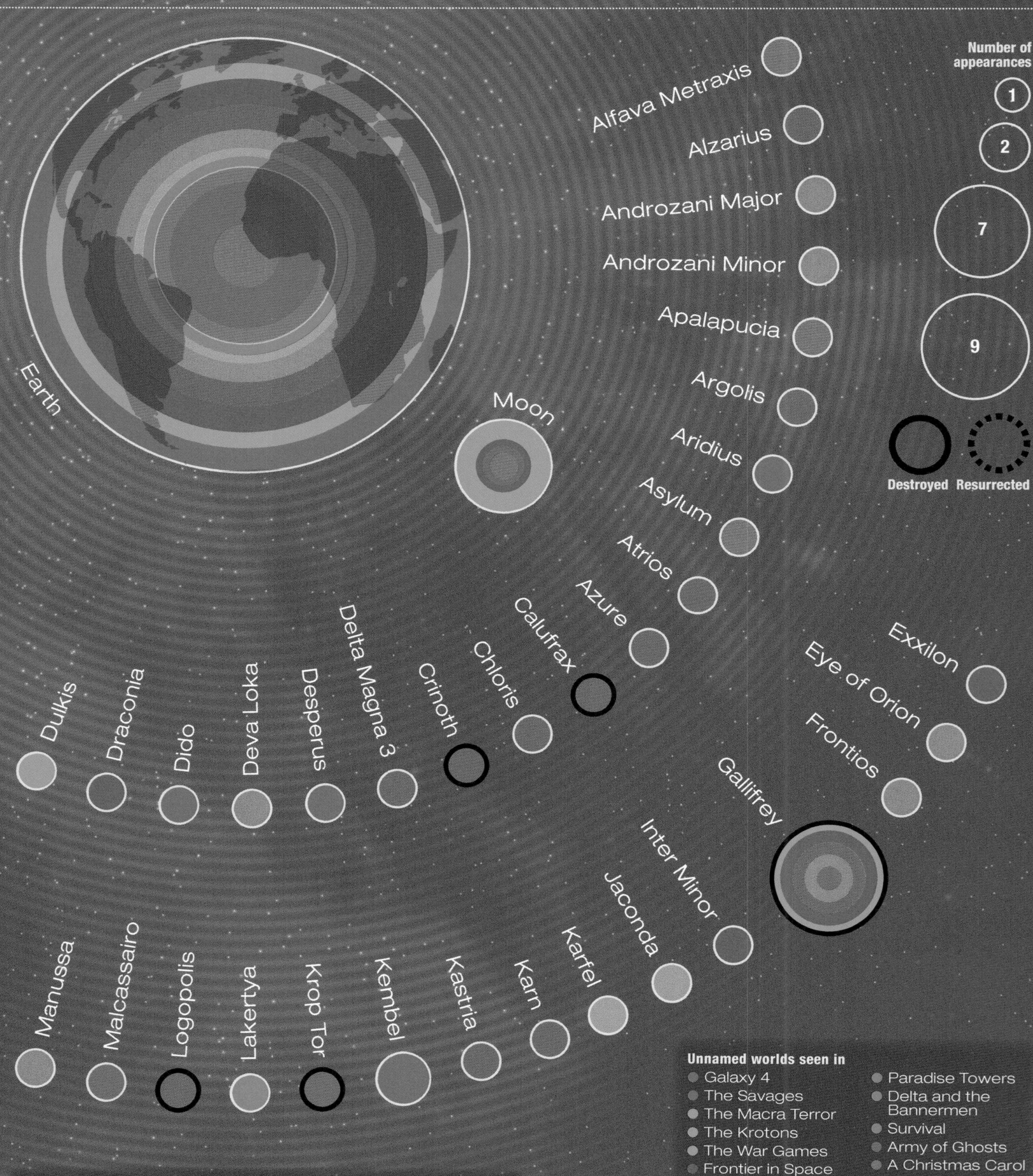

Seen in stories featuring

- First Doctor
- Second Doctor
- Third Doctor
- Fourth Doctor
- Fifth Doctor
- Sixth Doctor
- Seventh Doctor
- Eighth Doctor
- Ninth Doctor
- Tenth Doctor
- Eleventh Doctor

Unnamed worlds seen in

- Galaxy 4
- The Savages
- The Macra Terror
- The Krotons
- The War Games
- Frontier in Space
- The Face of Evil
- The Robots of Death
- State of Decay
- Castrovalva
- Paradise Towers
- Delta and the Bannermen
- Survival
- Army of Ghosts
- A Christmas Carol
- A Good Man Goes to War
- The Doctor, the Widow and the Wardrobe

Planets visited or seen from close orbit, sized relative to number of appearances

Whereas the vast majority of planets featured in *Doctor Who* (85.9%) are only ever seen once, the Earth has been visited or seen from orbit in 151 stories — nearly twice as often as all other planets put together. That Gallifrey and Skaro are the most frequently seen other worlds is not surprising given they're home to the Time Lords and Daleks respectively, and the Moon (popular with the Second Doctor) gains exposure from its proximity to Earth.

Only the Eighth and Ninth Doctors were never seen to visit another world, spending all their televised time on or orbiting Earth (although we do see Skaro at the start of the TV Movie), whereas the Fourth Doctor spent the most time elsewhere, visiting other planets almost twice as often as he did ours.

THE HUNGRY EARTH

Stories' cumulative shift between Earth and elsewhere over Doctor's timeline

We've seen how much of a tendency the Doctor has for visiting Earth relative to other planets in the universe, and which incarnations have been here most. So what are the trends over his own timeline in his movements between Earth and elsewhere? When has the series felt most tied to our planet?

For this chart, each story was assigned a score of +1 if it predominantly took place on Earth and –1 if it took place somewhere else. As much as possible only a story's primary setting was included, so this isn't a strict list of consecutive TARDIS landing sites, and returns to a previously seen setting within a story aren't counted again. A few stories have more than one score, however, if they switched between significant locations (such as "Attack of the Cybermen", which starts out on Earth [+1] but then moves the main action to Telos [–1]) or took a tour of multiples places (for example, "Frontier in Space" takes us from various contemporaneous future Earth settings (spaceships, Earth itself and the Moon) to the planet Draconia then the planet of the Ogrons, so that scores +1,–1,–1). Stories that took place in some 'nowhere' realm were scored 0 (namely "The Celestial Toymaker", "The Mind Robber" and "Warriors' Gate"). "The Edge of Destruction" and "The Doctor's Wife" were also scored 0 as they take place in the TARDIS (or outside the universe), so too "The War Games" as although strictly speaking it all takes place on an alien world, some areas of which we see, much of the action is in simulations of past Earth environments. (Other unusual locations that were scored 0 were the haunted house in "The Chase" (revealed to be on Earth but mainly presented as somewhere 'other'); Omega's domain inside a black hole in "The Three Doctors"; the space race in "Enlightenment"; the scenes in the Matrix at the end of "The Trial of a Time Lord"; and the Minotaur's touring prison in "The God Complex".) Stories set solely on the Moon were scored +1, but those in nearby space stations depended on their connection to Earth: so "The End of the World" was scored +1 as we see Earth and its presence is a major element of the story, whereas "The Ark in Space" was scored –1 as the planet is only briefly seen/mentioned and most of the action is unrelated to the Ark's proximity to Earth. These scores were then accumulated in sequence and plotted to produce a trend line in which movement to the left indicates a focus on Earth and movement to the right reflects a venture beyond our world.

The line is coloured to indicate whether Earth-bound stories are set in the past, present or future, while off-world destinations are split between those set among an alien society on their world, and those focusing on future humans who have ventured beyond Earth. Some subjective decisions had to me made here: for example, the people on Marinus appear human and could be a future colony, but they're presented as being an alien society; conversely, while the alien nature of the Solonians is examined in "The Mutants", this is presented through the eyes of the human colonists.

The switches between alien futures and historical Earth of the early series creates a zig-zagging line around the vertical. A slight run of Earth-based stories around the end of Season 1 and start of Season 2 pulls the line to the left, but this is quickly rectified during the rest of Season 2. Towards the end of the First Doctor's time the series embarks on a significant drift Earthwards for the next two years, not venturing back out into the unknown frequently until Season 6. The Third Doctor's loss of TARDIS travel is represented by a single extended 'Contemporary Earth' data point so as not to suggest continued returns to present-day (or near-future if you prefer) Earth by choice, followed by his first off-world story, "Colony in Space". For the incarnation who was supposedly stuck on Earth, the rest of his time actually sees tighter zig-zagging than the Second Doctor's.

The arrival of the Fourth Doctor shifts the balance slightly to the right in his first two seasons, then in his third a swing back Earthwards is followed by a larger one away again. After "Image of the Fendahl" in the middle of Season 15, the series takes a determined move away from Earth, with only three stories set here over the next four years, all in contemporary times: "The Stones of Blood", "City of Death" and "Logopolis" (the brief sojourn in Brighton in "The Leisure Hive" is not included). The second half of Season 19, the Fifth Doctor's first, features a run of Earthly tales, which hold their own through Season 20 but then the trend edges back towards alien adventures until Season 24's "Paradise Towers". With the Seventh Doctor now at the TARDIS controls, the planet hopping slows and then, from Season 26, sharply reverses. Coupled with the revived series' early devotion to Earth, the line jumps hard to the left, not really slowing until Series 4. Another, smaller leap Earthwards during the Eleventh Doctor's first year consolidates the trend, and although after that it slows a little, the overall drift is still towards Earth-based tales.

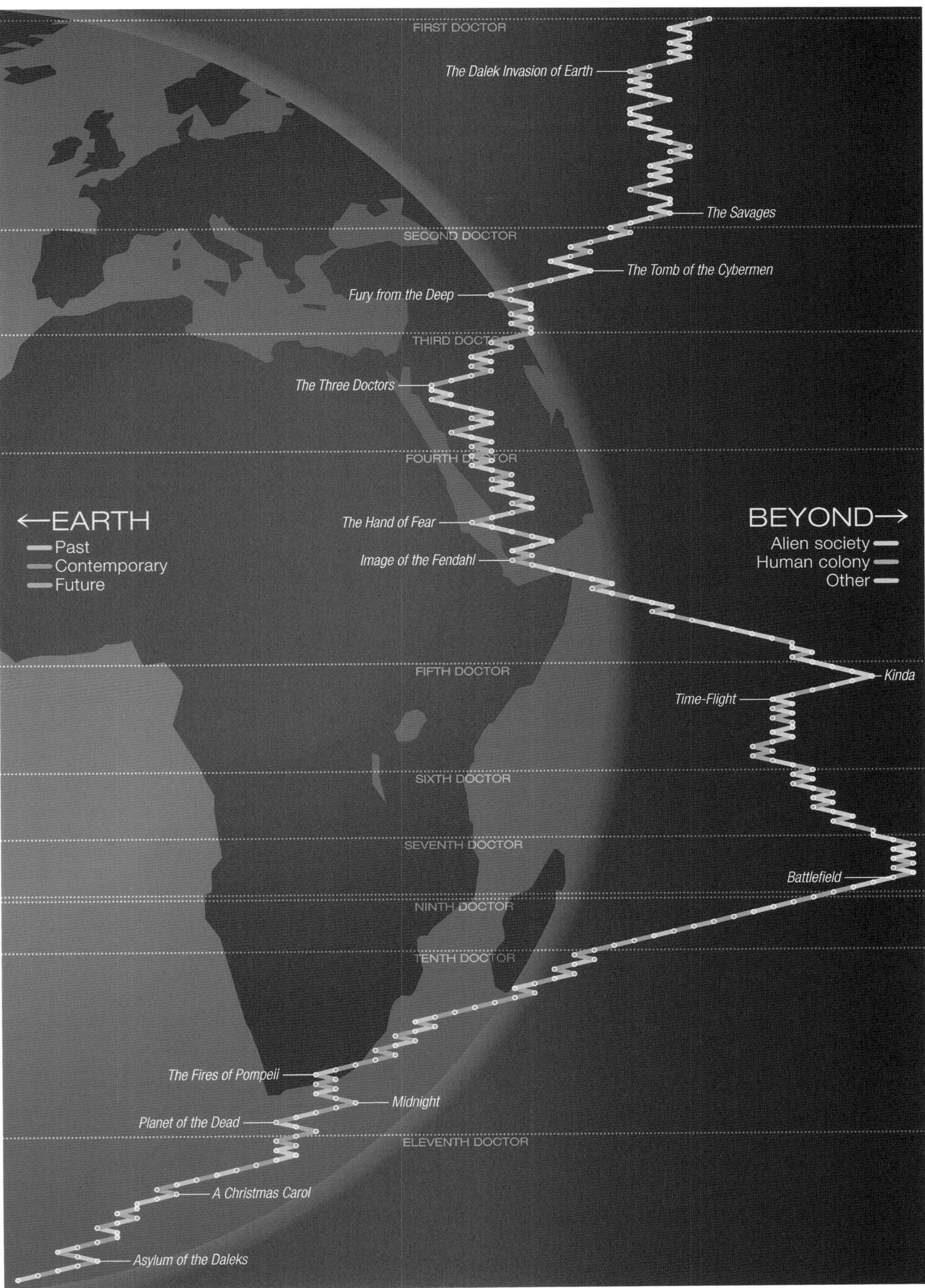
FIRST DOCTOR
The Dalek Invasion of Earth
The Savages
SECOND DOCTOR
The Tomb of the Cybermen
Fury from the Deep
THIRD DOCTOR
The Three Doctors
FOURTH DOCTOR
←EARTH
Past
Contemporary
Future
The Hand of Fear
Image of the Fendahl
BEYOND→
Alien society
Human colony
Other
FIFTH DOCTOR
Kinda
Time-Flight
SIXTH DOCTOR
SEVENTH DOCTOR
Battlefield
NINTH DOCTOR
TENTH DOCTOR
The Fires of Pompeii
Midnight
Planet of the Dead
ELEVENTH DOCTOR
A Christmas Carol
Asylum of the Daleks

STRANGERS IN SPACE

What we learn about the lives of the Doctor's travelling companions relative to their origins

Do we discover more about a companion's family, home life and career if they're from contemporary Earth as opposed to a historical period or an alien planet? By grouping travelling companions according to their birthplace and time, and linking to several life factors that might help the viewer know and understand them better, if there were any correlation then each colour group would lead to similar end points.

Most major companions are humans from contemporary Earth, with only five being from the past or future, and five from another world. (Leela is unique in that she is human but born on another world in the future among a relatively primitive society.) While those we observe most about are Tegan (all but two factors) and Rose (all but three), for some humans we learn very little of their lives outside the TARDIS, such as Harry or Ben & Polly. We discover as much background about Adric, from the planet Alzarius, as we do about Martha, from modern Earth. Companions from Earth's future fare particularly badly, with little revealed about Vicki's or Zoe's lives, and nothing at all about Steven's, while Romana and Mel remain mysteries also. These last three, along with Dodo, of whom we briefly hear of an aunt, have consequently been omitted from the chart. Liz and the members of UNIT are not included as they didn't travel with the Doctor and their characters were almost exclusively conveyed in terms of their roles within UNIT.

The chart confirms the lack of any correlation between a companion's birthplace and our knowledge about them, with origin group colours distributed across the range of life factors. With three-fifths of characters charted being from contemporary Earth (blue), they unsurprisingly feature in all life factor categories. However, there are some notable biases. Meeting other members of a companion's family after their introductory story has happened only once for someone born on another planet (Turlough's brother in "Planet of Fire"). Until the new series, none of those who couldn't be returned to their home when leaving the TARDIS were from contemporary Earth (the recent stranding of the Ponds on Earth but not in their time mirrors Rose being stuck in the right time but on a parallel Earth). Indeed, while 64% of companions charted are modern-day humans, they account for 78.6% of those who returned home after their travels with the Doctor. So if you want to get home again, it's best to be from Earth.

The data

	SPECIES	HOME LIFE		FAMILY				HOMESICKNESS			LIFE STAGES	
		See them at their home	See them doing job	Hear about their family	Meet family in first story	Meet family in later story	Family death leads to travels	Asks to go home during travels	Returns home	Can't return home	Seen as a child	Seen as older
Susan	alien				●					●		●
Barbara & Ian	contemporary human		●					●	●			
Vicki	future human			●			●					
Steven	future human											
Dodo	contemporary human			●					●			
Ben & Polly	contemporary human		●						●			
Jamie	historical human	●							●			
Victoria	historical human	●		●	●		●					
Zoe	future human		●						●			
Liz	contemporary human		●						●			
Jo	contemporary human		●	●					●			●
Sarah	contemporary human		●	●					●			●
Harry	contemporary human		●						●			
Leela	future/historical human	●	●		●		●					
Romana	alien											
Adric	alien	●			●		●	●		●		
Nyssa	alien	●	●	●	●		●			●	●	●
Tegan	contemporary human		●	●	●	●	●	●	●		●	●
Turlough	alien			●		●		●	●			
Peri	contemporary human			●	●							
Mel	contemporary human											
Ace	contemporary human		●	●		●						
Rose	contemporary human	●	●	●	●	●	●			●	●	
Mickey	contemporary human	●	●	●		●			●		●	
Martha	contemporary human	●	●		●				●			
Donna	contemporary human	●	●		●	●	●		●			
Amy & Rory	contemporary human	●	●	●		●				●	●	●

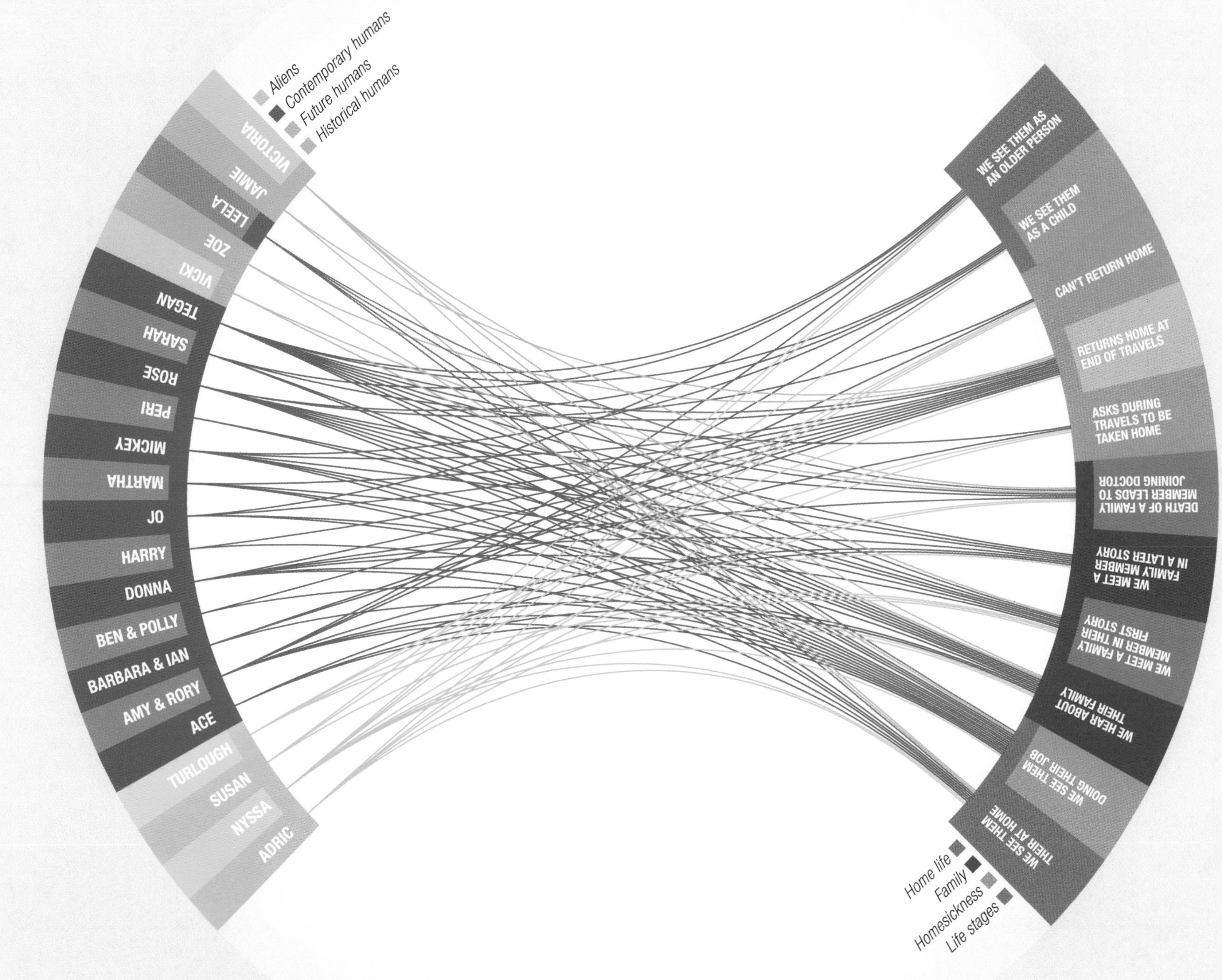

Aliens
Contemporary humans
Future humans
Historical humans
VICTORIA
JAMIE
LEELA
ZOE
VICKI
TEGAN
SARAH
ROSE
PERI
MICKEY
MARTHA
JO
HARRY
DONNA
BEN & POLLY
BARBARA & IAN
AMY & RORY
ACE
TURLOUGH
SUSAN
NYSSA
ADRIC
WE SEE THEM AS AN OLDER PERSON
WE SEE THEM AS A CHILD
CAN'T RETURN HOME
RETURNS HOME AT END OF TRAVELS
ASKS DURING TRAVELS TO BE TAKEN HOME
DEATH OF A FAMILY MEMBER LEADS TO JOINING DOCTOR
WE MEET A FAMILY MEMBER IN A LATER STORY
WE MEET A FAMILY MEMBER IN THEIR FIRST STORY
WE HEAR ABOUT THEIR FAMILY
WE SEE THEM DOING THEIR JOB
WE SEE THEM THEIR AT HOME
Home life
Family
Homesickness
Life stages

JOURNEY INTO TERROR

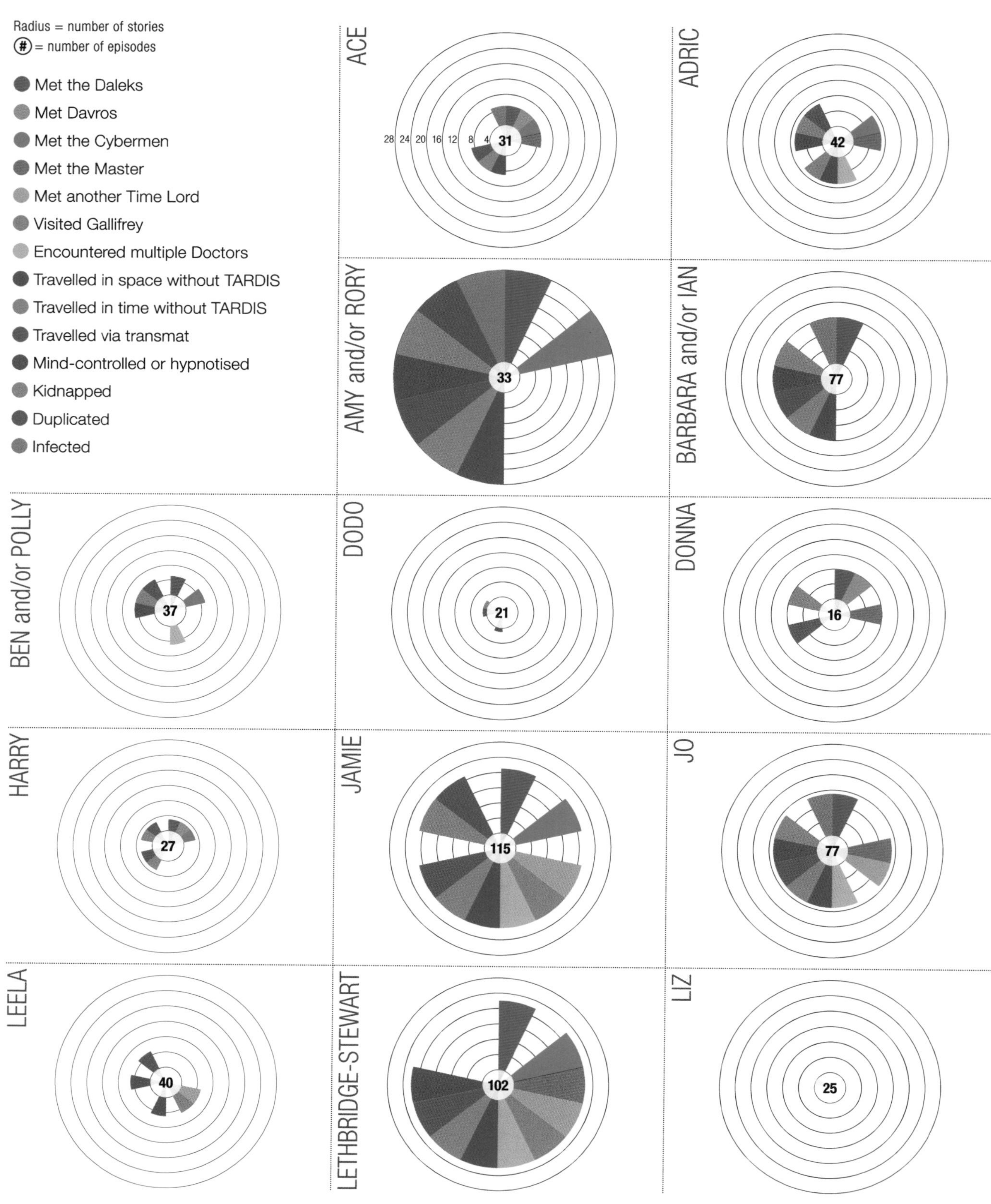

Radius = number of stories
(#) = number of episodes
Met the Daleks
Met Davros
Met the Cybermen
Met the Master
Met another Time Lord
Visited Gallifrey
Encountered multiple Doctors
Travelled in space without TARDIS
Travelled in time without TARDIS
Travelled via transmat
Mind-controlled or hypnotised
Kidnapped
Duplicated
Infected
ACE
28 24 20 16 12 8 4
31
ADRIC
42
AMY and/or RORY
33
BARBARA and/or IAN
77
BEN and/or POLLY
37
DODO
21
DONNA
16
HARRY
27
JAMIE
115
JO
77
LEELA
40
LETHBRIDGE-STEWART
102
LIZ
25

Range of experiences gained by the Doctor's closest companions

There is a range of events the Doctor's companions can expect to encounter, from meeting his archest enemies to being flung bodily through time and space, and undergoing various forms of attack. One might presume the more adventures they have, the more of these experiences they'll gain, so the radius of the slices indicates the number of stories each companion appeared in, while the centre number is their number of episodes. It's no surprise, then, that Dodo or Liz gained less from their time with the Doctor, and yet Mel and Harry undergo more in a similar number of episodes. While Amy and Rory were in the highest number of stories, their knowledge of the Doctor and his people is notably lacking. Sarah is the only companion to face the full range of common terrors that travelling with the Doctor involves (Tegan just missing out by not actually meeting Davros in "Resurrection of the Daleks").

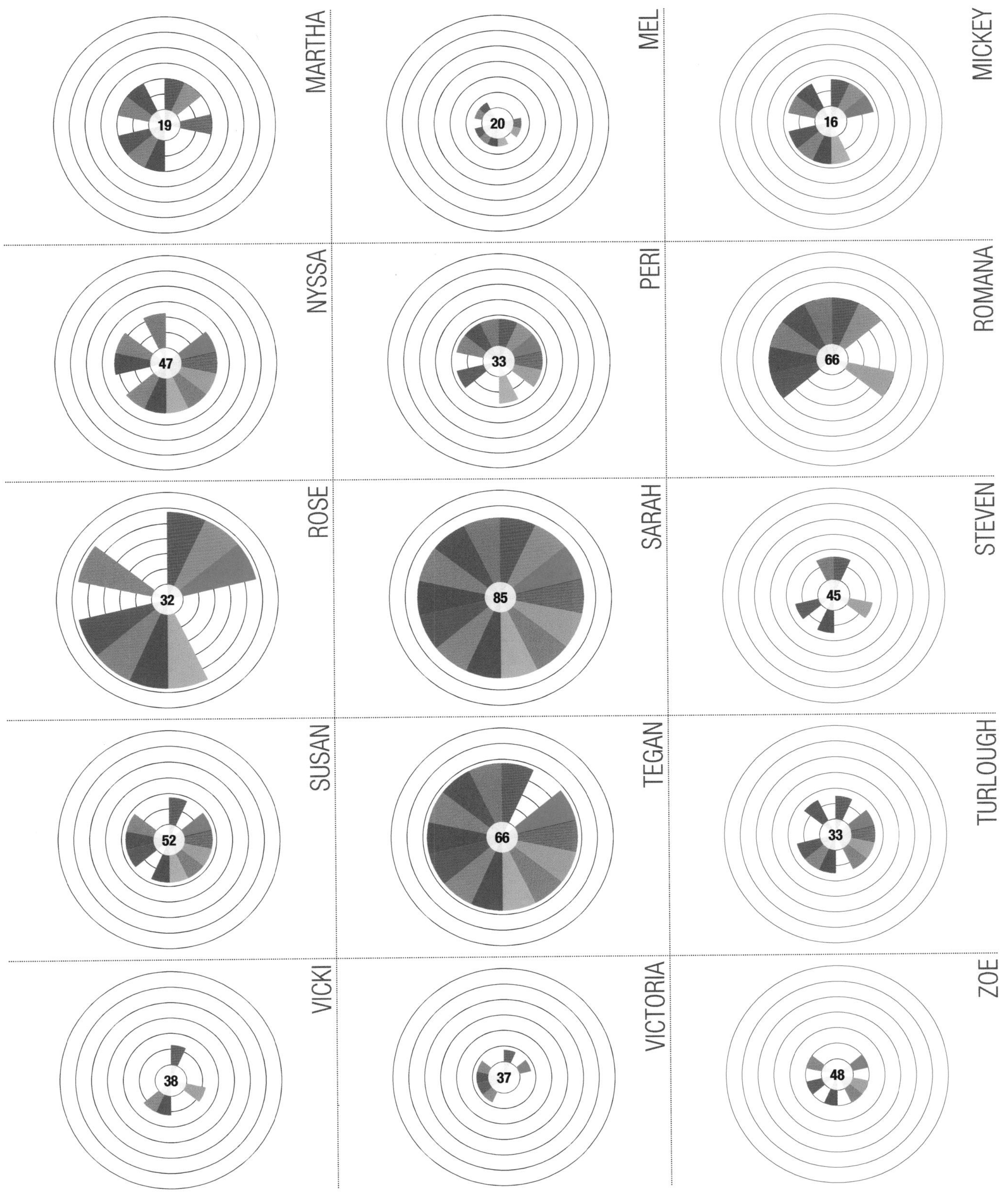

JOURNEYS END

Circumstances in which the Doctor's humanoid travelling companions joined and left the TARDIS

On all but a handful of occasions, the Doctor has had at least one companion journeying with him in the TARDIS. Indeed, it's a common refrain of the current series that he can get carried away when he travels alone and that having someone with him, particularly a human, is a calming influence. But as recently seen in "The Angels Take Manhattan", the Doctor doesn't like to deal with his friends leaving him, yet leave him they do, although not always of their own accord. For as the Doctor goes on ageing and regenerating, his shorter-lived companions must eventually go their own way.

Curiously, for most of the original series, the Doctor never voluntarily invited anyone to come with him — they either were carried off in the TARDIS by accident, asked to go with him or were forced upon him by circumstances or higher powers. Only towards the end of the Classic series was he seen to specifically ask Ace to travel with him (although prompted by Mel), whereas in the revived series it's his most common way of finding a new companion. Perhaps the loss of the Time Lords has made him more open to needing company.

Happily, the most common reason for a companion to leave the TARDIS is they have come back home and so choose to move on with their lives. While Mickey initially elected to stay on a parallel Earth, he eventually made it back to our universe. Of those who have not made it home, often they have chosen to settle somewhere new because they've fallen in love, although some have been less lucky. While Steven was slightly pressganged by the Doctor into taking on the leadership of an alien society, he went along with it willingly, whereas Rory was unwittingly sent back in time by a Weeping Angel. While the same fate befell Amy, this was her choice in order to be with her husband. Peri is not counted as having left to be with a partner for, although she reportedly ended up marrying King Yrcanos, this wasn't her reason for leaving and she seems to have been making the best of a bad situation after the Time Lords stranded her on Thoros Beta.

Only three main companions have been seen to die as a result of their travelling with the Doctor, and none in the revived series (despite the prospect often being hinted at when a regular is due to leave the show). While Rose was reported as dead in our universe, she actually survived on a parallel world, so not quite a return home but not really ending up somewhere else either. Donna's mind-wipe was presented as a form of death, but in effect she just ended up back where she started. And despite both Amy's and Rory's many reversed demises, they eventually ended up living together in 1930s New York (as far as we know).

Not included here are Liz and the various members of UNIT as, although they assisted the Doctor while he was exiled to Earth, they didn't travel with him and carried on their regular lives during and after their association. Liz could have been listed as having been imposed on the Doctor (by the Brigadier) and then 'returned home' to her academic life in Cambridge. Also missing are the Doctor's two robotic companions, K9 and Kamelion. Two versions of K9 travelled in the TARDIS: the first the Doctor gave to Leela when she elected to remain on Gallifrey, while the second he left with Romana in E-Space. Kamelion only appeared in his joining and leaving stories so wasn't a full-time companion; he was arguably rescued by the Doctor from the Master's control but ended up being destroyed at the Doctor's own hand.

Other potential inclusions are Adam Mitchell, who was invited aboard (more by Rose than the Doctor) but dumped back home (with a futuristic USB port in his forehead); Captain Jack Harkness, who was rescued from being exploded by a World War Two bomb, then exterminated by a Dalek before being resurrected by Rose but left by the Doctor on a space station orbiting Earth in the distant future. He briefly returned, imposing himself on the Doctor, but ultimately elected to return to his duties at Torchwood in 21st Century Cardiff (not his native time). And the criss-crossing paths of the Doctor and River Song are so complicated that it's hard to say how or even if she ever joined or left the TARDIS!

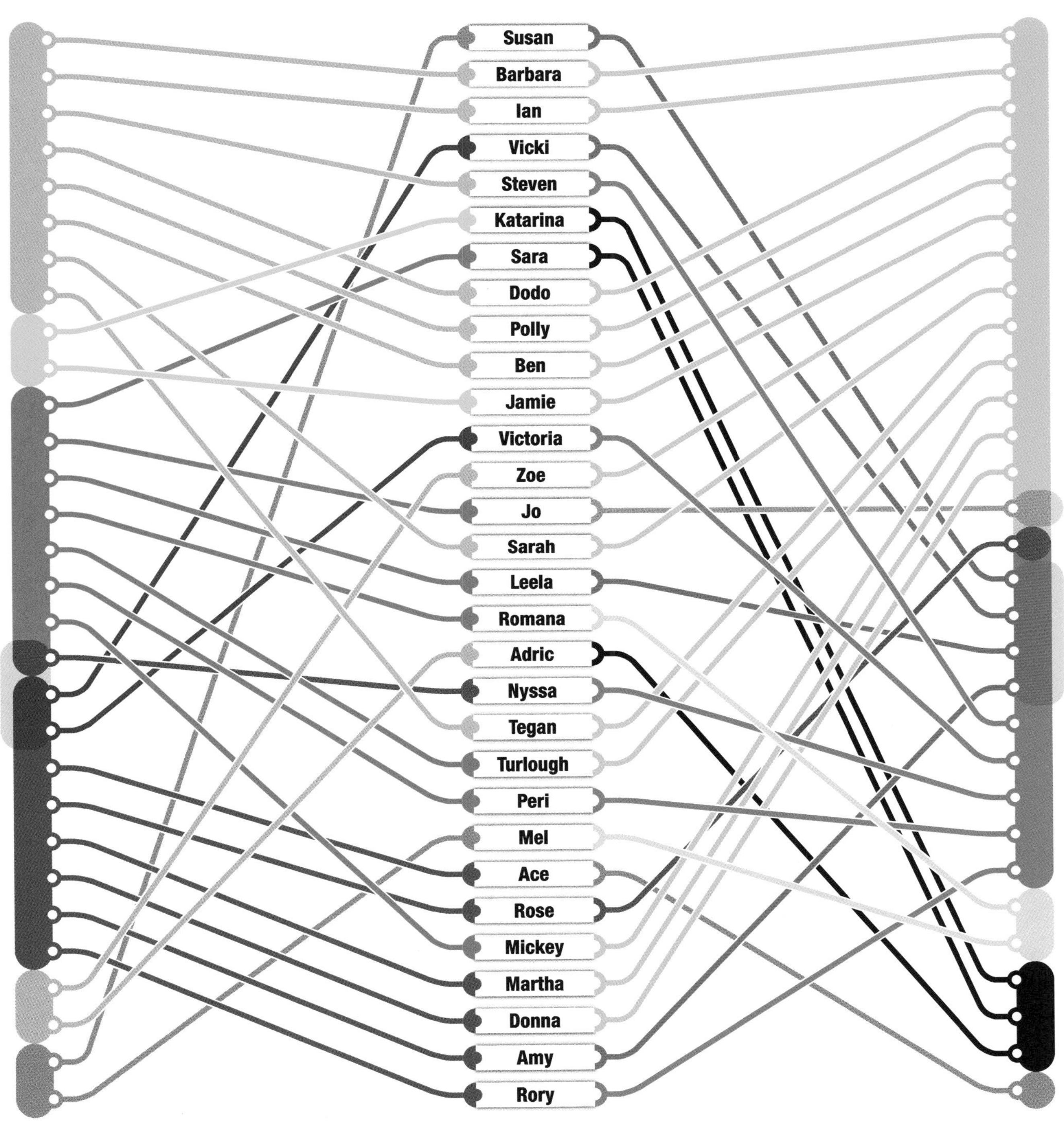

ARRIVALS

- **ACCIDENTAL** – unaware what they were getting themselves into
- **RESCUED** – brought aboard to save them
- **IMPOSED** – forced on the Doctor or requested to join him
- **ORPHAN** – lack of parents reason for joining Doctor
- **INVITED** – directly asked by the Doctor to accompany him
- **STOWAWAY** – hid aboard the TARDIS
- **UNKNOWN** – circumstances of joining the Doctor not seen on TV

DEPARTURES

- **RETURNED HOME** – ended up back in their original location and time period
- **WITH PARTNER** – left the Doctor to be with a loved one
- **DIDN'T RETURN HOME** – left on non-homeworld or in a different time period
- **CONTINUED OWN TRAVELS** – left the Doctor but didn't settle down
- **DIED** – killed during their travels with the Doctor
- **UNKNOWN** – reason for leaving not seen on TV

SMITH AND JONES

Number of appearances in stories by characters named Smith and Jones

It should come as no surprise that the Doctor has had companions named both Smith and Jones, given they're two of the most common surnames in the English-speaking parts of the world. Yet of all the characters encountered in nearly 50 years of TV adventures, we've seen only eight Smiths and ten Joneses. Perhaps writers thought such common names would be uninteresting in a fantasy adventure show like *Doctor Who*, given it was more than ten years before the Doctor ever met a Smith. Ironically she became his companion, his previous one having left to marry a man called Jones.

Then, within the first series of the show's revival, we were introduced to characters called both Smith and Jones who would go on to make further appearances, before getting our first Jones companion, along with her sizeable family. She even united the two names by ultimately marrying a Smith. Since we've had a Doctor played by a genuine Smith, there have been no further Smiths (nor Joneses) in the programme.

The Doctor's occasional use of the pseudonym 'Dr John Smith' isn't included, until that alter ego becomes a separate character in his own right in "Human Nature". Martha Jones's brother Leo had an infant daughter, Keisha, who was barely seen and obviously had no lines so is not counted here.

The data

STORIES	SMITHS	JONESES
Fury from the Deep		Megan Jones
The Dæmons		Mr Jones
The Green Death		Clifford Jones
The Time Warrior	Sarah Jane Smith	
Invasion of the Dinosaurs	↳ Sarah Jane Smith	
Death to the Daleks	↳ Sarah Jane Smith	
The Monster of Peladon	↳ Sarah Jane Smith	
Planet of the Spiders	↳ Sarah Jane Smith	
Robot	↳ Sarah Jane Smith	
The Ark in Space	↳ Sarah Jane Smith	
The Sontaran Experiment	↳ Sarah Jane Smith	
Genesis of the Daleks	↳ Sarah Jane Smith	
Revenge of the Cybermen	↳ Sarah Jane Smith	
Terror of the Zygons	↳ Sarah Jane Smith	
Planet of Evil	↳ Sarah Jane Smith	
Pyramids of Mars	↳ Sarah Jane Smith	
The Android Invasion	↳ Sarah Jane Smith	
The Brain of Morbius	↳ Sarah Jane Smith	
The Seeds of Doom	↳ Sarah Jane Smith	
The Masque of Mandragora	↳ Sarah Jane Smith	
The Hand of Fear	↳ Sarah Jane Smith	
The Five Doctors	↳ Sarah Jane Smith	
Remembrance of the Daleks	Mike Smith	
	Mrs Smith	
Ghost Light	Josiah Samuel Smith	
Rose	Mickey Smith	
Aliens of London/World War Three	↳ Mickey Smith	Harriet Jones
Father's Day	↳ Mickey Smith	
Boom Town	↳ Mickey Smith	
Bad Wolf/The Parting of the Ways	↳ Mickey Smith	
The Christmas Invasion	↳ Mickey Smith	↳ Harriet Jones
School Reunion	↳ Mickey Smith	
	↳ Sarah Jane Smith	
The Girl in the Fireplace	↳ Mickey Smith	
Rise of the Cybermen/The Age of Steel	↳ Mickey Smith	
	Ricky Smith	
Army of Ghosts/Doomsday	↳ Mickey Smith	
Smith and Jones		Martha Jones
		Francine Jones
		Letitia Jones
		Clive Jones
		Leo Jones
The Shakespeare Code		↳ Martha Jones
Gridlock		↳ Martha Jones
Daleks in Manhattan/Evolution of the Daleks		↳ Martha Jones
The Lazarus Experiment		↳ Martha Jones
		↳ Francine Jones
		↳ Letitia Jones
		↳ Leo Jones
42		↳ Martha Jones
		↳ Francine Jones
Human Nature/The Family of Blood	John Smith	↳ Martha Jones
Blink		↳ Martha Jones
Utopia		↳ Martha Jones
The Sound of Drums/Last of the Time Lords		↳ Martha Jones
		↳ Francine Jones
		↳ Clive Jones
		↳ Letitia Jones
		↳ Leo Jones
The Sontaran Stratagem/The Poison Sky		↳ Martha Jones
The Doctor's Daughter		↳ Martha Jones
The Stolen Earth/Journey's End	↳ Sarah Jane Smith	↳ Martha Jones
	Luke Smith	Ianto Jones
	↳ Mickey Smith	↳ Francine Jones
		↳ Harriet Jones
The End of Time	↳ Mickey Smith	↳ Martha Jones
	↳ Sarah Jane Smith	
	↳ Luke Smith	

45
Number of stories
40
Smiths
Joneses
35
30
25
20
15
Number of characters
10
5

THE WEB OF FEAR

Stories featuring more than one returning foe

Given the Doctor's propensity for making enemies, he has faced relatively few more than twice. This is perhaps not surprising for someone who can travel anywhere in the whole history of the entire universe (so the chances of bumping into someone again should be low), but the demands of making an adventure television series mean return matches with popular adversaries are inevitable. It surely follows that more than one showing up in a story would be even more popular, and if they were actually working together against the Doctor, well, he'd have no chance, would he?

This chart shows the story links between major returning foes. Adversaries are included if they have appeared in three or more stories. The outer ring is proportional to each race's number of appearances, clockwise in the order in which they first appeared (see below). Stories are counted if they include newly recorded material, not just past clips or photographs. 'Time Lords' counts any story in which a Gallifreyan other than the Doctor, Romana or the Master appeared. Not all races were villainous in every story but they are counted anyway.

The coloured links indicate appearances by more than one of these monsters in the same story. These may be in unconnected scenes or as a unified force. The story with the most recurring enemies is, not surprisingly, "The Pandorica Opens", in which the Daleks, Cybermen, Autons, Silurians, Sontarans and Judoon join many other one-off races in an alliance against the Doctor to prevent him, they believe, from destroying the universe. "The Five Doctors" features five recurring adversaries, each transported to the Gallifreyan Death Zone to battle the Doctor on his birthday, as does "The War Games" thanks to the Doctor's defence plea that all the nasty creatures in the universe need to be put in their place. There are four major monster appearances in "A Good Man Goes to War", although the Cybermen were not involved with the others, who were actually fighting on the Doctor's side for once. The Weeping Angels are the only enemy to have appeared more than twice but never in a story with any other.

The data

DALEKS The Daleks, The Dalek Invasion of Earth, The Space Museum, The Chase, Mission to the Unknown, The Daleks' Master Plan, The Power of the Daleks, The Evil of the Daleks, The War Games, Day of the Daleks, Frontier in Space, Planet of the Daleks, Death to the Daleks, Genesis of the Daleks, Destiny of the Daleks, The Five Doctors, Resurrection of the Daleks, Revelation of the Daleks, Remembrance of the Daleks, Dalek, Bad Wolf/The Parting of the Ways, Army of Ghosts/Doomsday, Daleks in Manhattan/Evolution of the Daleks, The Stolen Earth/Journey's End, The Waters of Mars, Victory of the Daleks, The Pandorica Opens/The Big Bang, The Wedding of River Song, Asylum of the Daleks

TIME LORDS The Time Meddler, The War Games, Terror of the Autons, Colony in Space, The Three Doctors, Planet of the Spiders, Genesis of the Daleks, The Brain of Morbius, The Deadly Assassin, The Invasion of Time, The Armageddon Factor, Arc of Infinity, The Five Doctors, The Twin Dilemma, The Mark of the Rani, The Trial of a Time Lord, Time and the Rani, The End of Time

CYBERMEN The Tenth Planet, The Moonbase, The Tomb of the Cybermen, The Wheel in Space, The Invasion, The War Games, Carnival of Monsters, Revenge of the Cybermen, Earthshock, The Five Doctors, Attack of the Cybermen, Silver Nemesis, Rise of the Cybermen/The Age of Steel, Army of Ghosts/Doomsday, The Next Doctor, The Pandorica Opens/The Big Bang, A Good Man Goes to War, Closing Time

YETI The Abominable Snowmen, The Web of Fear, The War Games, The Five Doctors

ICE WARRIORS The Ice Warriors, The Seeds of Death, The War Games, The Curse of Peladon, The Monster of Peladon

AUTONS Spearhead from Space, Terror of the Autons, Rose, Love & Monsters, The Pandorica Opens/The Big Bang

HOMO REPTILIA The Silurians, The Sea Devils, Warriors of the Deep, The Hungry Earth/Cold Blood, The Pandorica Opens/The Big Bang, A Good Man Goes to War, The Wedding of River Song, Dinosaurs on a Spaceship

THE MASTER Terror of the Autons, The Mind of Evil, The Claws of Axos, Colony in Space, The Dæmons, The Sea Devils, The Time Monster, Frontier in Space, The Deadly Assassin, The Keeper of Traken, Logopolis, Castrovalva, Time-Flight, The King's Demons, The Five Doctors, Planet of Fire, The Caves of Androzani, The Mark of the Rani, The Trial of a Time Lord, Survival, The TV Movie, Utopia, The Sound of Drums/Last of the Time Lords, The End of Time

SONTARANS The Time Warrior, The Sontaran Experiment, The Invasion of Time, The Two Doctors, The Sontaran Stratagem/The Poison Sky, The Pandorica Opens/The Big Bang, A Good Man Goes to War

DAVROS Genesis of the Daleks, Destiny of the Daleks, Resurrection of the Daleks, Revelation of the Daleks, Remembrance of the Daleks, The Stolen Earth/Journey's End

OOD The Impossible Planet/The Satan Pit, Planet of the Ood, The Waters of Mars, The End of Time, The Doctor's Wife

JUDOON Smith and Jones, The Stolen Earth/Journey's End, The Pandorica Opens/The Big Bang, A Good Man Goes to War

WEEPING ANGELS Blink, Time of Angels/Flesh and Stone, The God Complex, The Angels Take Manhattan

SILENTS The Impossible Astronaut/Day of the Moon, Closing Time, The Wedding of River Song

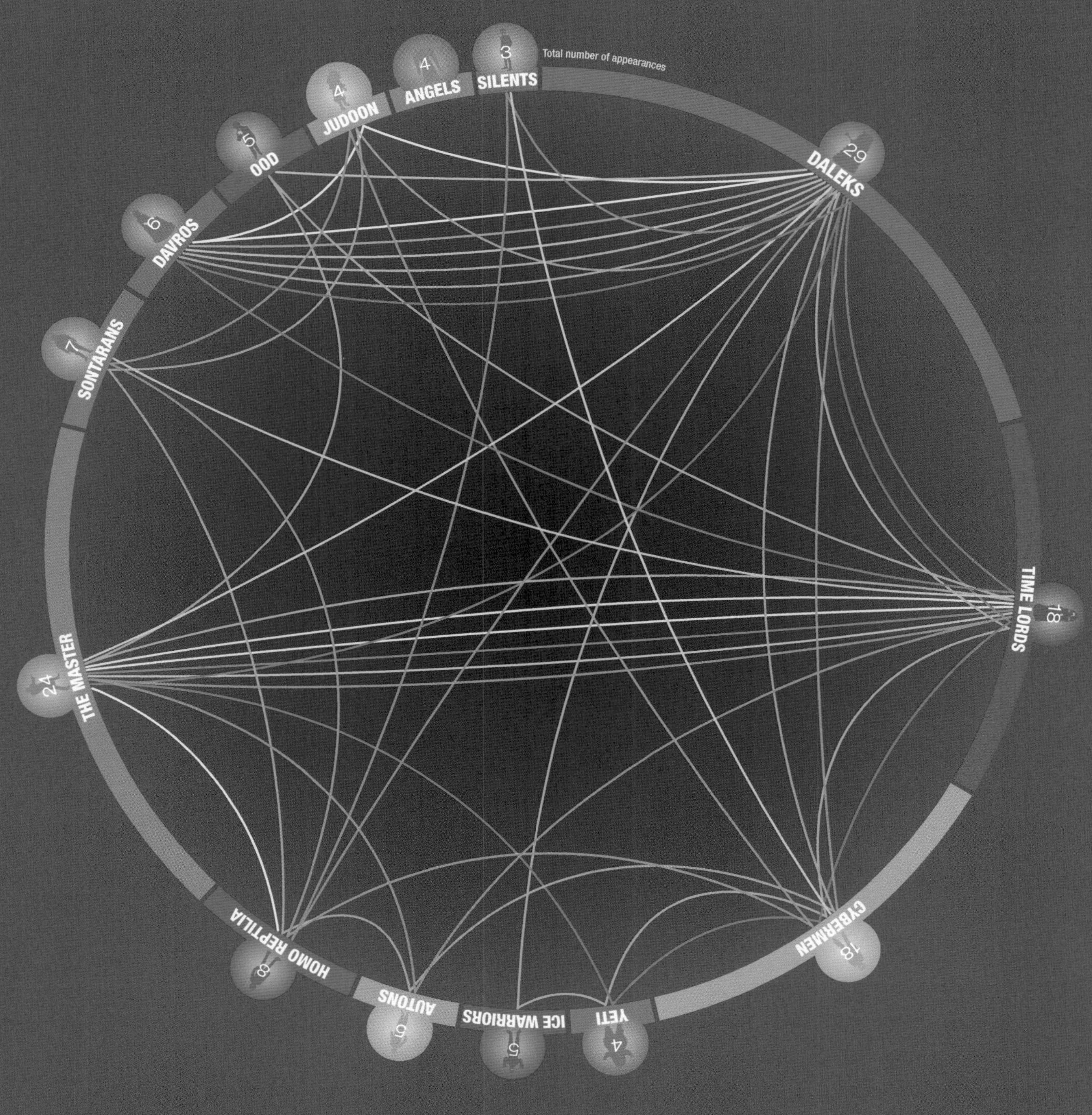

- The War Games
- Terror of the Autons
- Colony in Space
- The Sea Devils
- Frontier in Space
- Genesis of the Daleks
- The Deadly Assassin
- The Invasion of Time
- Destiny of the Daleks
- The Five Doctors
- Resurrection of the Daleks
- The Mark of the Rani
- Revelation of the Daleks
- The Trial of a Time Lord
- Remembrance of the Daleks
- Army of Ghosts/Doomsday
- The Stolen Earth/Journey's End
- The Waters of Mars
- The End of Time
- The Pandorica Opens/The Big Bang
- A Good Man Goes to War
- Closing Time
- The Wedding of River Song

THE POWER OF THE DALEKS

Minimum sizes of Dalek taskforces as seen on screen

Given the immediate impact of the Daleks' first appearance in *Doctor Who*, it was inevitable they would make a comeback despite having apparently all been killed. So a throwaway line in their first sequel, "The Dalek Invasion of Earth", allowed for the planet's occupation by Daleks, and throughout the original series it was taken as read that Dalek forces existed in the universe and that whenever the Doctor defeated one lot, there were more plotting away elsewhere. The revived series made things tricky for itself in this regard as all Daleks were said to have been wiped out in the Time War, so writers had to devise excuses for new empires of Daleks, only to have them eradicated once more. The creation of a new species of pure Dalek in "Victory of the Daleks" was an attempt to return to the assumptions of old that there were always Daleks out there, somewhere.

In real life, however, the programme's budget has always limited how many Daleks can be shown on screen at any one time. For their first story, just four props could afford to be built. Over the years these were repaired and supplemented with new casings, but also became damaged beyond use such that there were never more than six working Dalek props in any one story (plus occasional static 'dummy' casings) — except for their final appearance in the original series, "Remembrance of the Daleks", when a new design of Dalek was introduced. Despite this, the top half of one of the original props from "The Daleks" survived right through the original series, having been used in all but two Dalek stories.

Of course, a certain number of casings didn't mean only that number of Daleks could be portrayed. The same props were used to represent different Daleks in difference scenes, benefitting from the fact that Daleks look more or less the same (at least within any one story) or being repainted to represent a different rank. This chart tallies the minimum number of Daleks required to represent all those seen on screen in each story, allowing for time, location and those that are destroyed during the story. For example, although "Day of the Daleks" used only three props, within the story there are three Daleks (including the gold leader) in their control room at all times, two seen chasing the Doctor in the tunnels, one is destroyed by rebels and then at least five return to the 20th Century to attack Auderley House. The two grey Daleks in the control room cannot be the same as those in the tunnels, as the latter's failure to capture the Doctor is reported to them, but the one gold and four grey Daleks that emerge from the tunnels in episode four could be those we've already seen, so the minimum number of Daleks is six (those five plus the one destroyed earlier). Of course, within the fiction of the story there are probably many more Daleks occupying the Earth, but from the on-screen evidence, there can be no fewer than six.

Only those Dalek stories that exist in full are included, as it's impossible to know how many Daleks were on screen in the missing episodes. Over the years, different effects have been used to show more Daleks than there were props, from photographic blowups in the background to computer-generated Dalek hordes. It's impractical to try to count the Daleks seen streaming across space in "The Parting of the Ways", for example, so instances where such large numbers are seen acting in unison are not counted. But where they appear individually, even if augmented by green-screen multiplication, such as those seen invading the Game Station, they are counted. Minor differences in the condition or colouring of the props are not taken as indication of a different character if otherwise two Daleks could be the same one within the story, but in-story differences are, such as the standard and ballistic weapons in "Death to the Daleks". Further story-specific decisions are given below.

THE DALEKS Tally includes nine full-size photographic Daleks seen in the control room as these are clearly intended to be real Daleks (however unconvincingly to modern viewers). The point-of-view shot of the Dalek in 'section three' infected by the Thal drugs shows six other Daleks in the same room (three photographic). These must be different to those in the control room as the latter receive a report on section three's incapacitation.

THE DALEK INVASION OF EARTH Tally includes three photographic Daleks in the area around the saucer. Those patrolling London after the main saucer has taken off must be different, but could be the same ones as in the saucer that later attacks Barbara and Jenny, so the latter are not counted again.

THE CHASE Tally includes one photographic Dalek seen descending in the time machine's lift, and three dummy props hired from the makers of the "Dr Who and the Daleks" movie.

PLANET OF THE DALEKS The models of the frozen Dalek army are not included, nor are the full-size equivalents seen as the Doctor is setting the bomb.

GENESIS OF THE DALEKS Although it doesn't affect the final tally, it's assumed the test Dalek at the end of episode one is the same as the one that recognises the Doctor's alienness in episode two.

RESURRECTION OF THE DALEKS Four Daleks are seen arriving in the warehouse to eradicate Davros's two Daleks (although only three could be seen in the transmat cubicle), one of each faction being promptly destroyed. The Doctor then blows up two more, but at least three are seen succumbing to the Movellan virus, so more must have arrived while the Doctor was in the TARDIS.

REVELATION OF THE DALEKS Tally includes the glass Dalek that solidifies to kill Natasha and Grigory, but not that containing Stengos.

THE PARTING OF THE WAYS Tally includes the Daleks around the captured Rose and the Emperor, but not his black-domed guards nor the CGI swarms. Those that invade the Game Station make up the rest of the total.

DOOMSDAY Only the Cult of Skaro are counted, not the (CGI) "millions" released from the Genesis Ark.

THE STOLEN EARTH/JOURNEY'S END Daleks seen in London, New York, Cardiff and Germany are counted separately as the same ones could not have travelled in the time seen. One shot of the Reality Bomb test group has the humans surrounded by a mix of CGI and physical Daleks – only the two seen escorting the victims in the previous scene are counted.

ASYLUM OF THE DALEKS Of the Parliament, only the two Dalek escorts, Supreme and Prime Minister are counted. Those in the Asylum first encountered by Rory are counted separately to those later seen by the Doctor and Amy. The tally includes Oswin-Dalek.

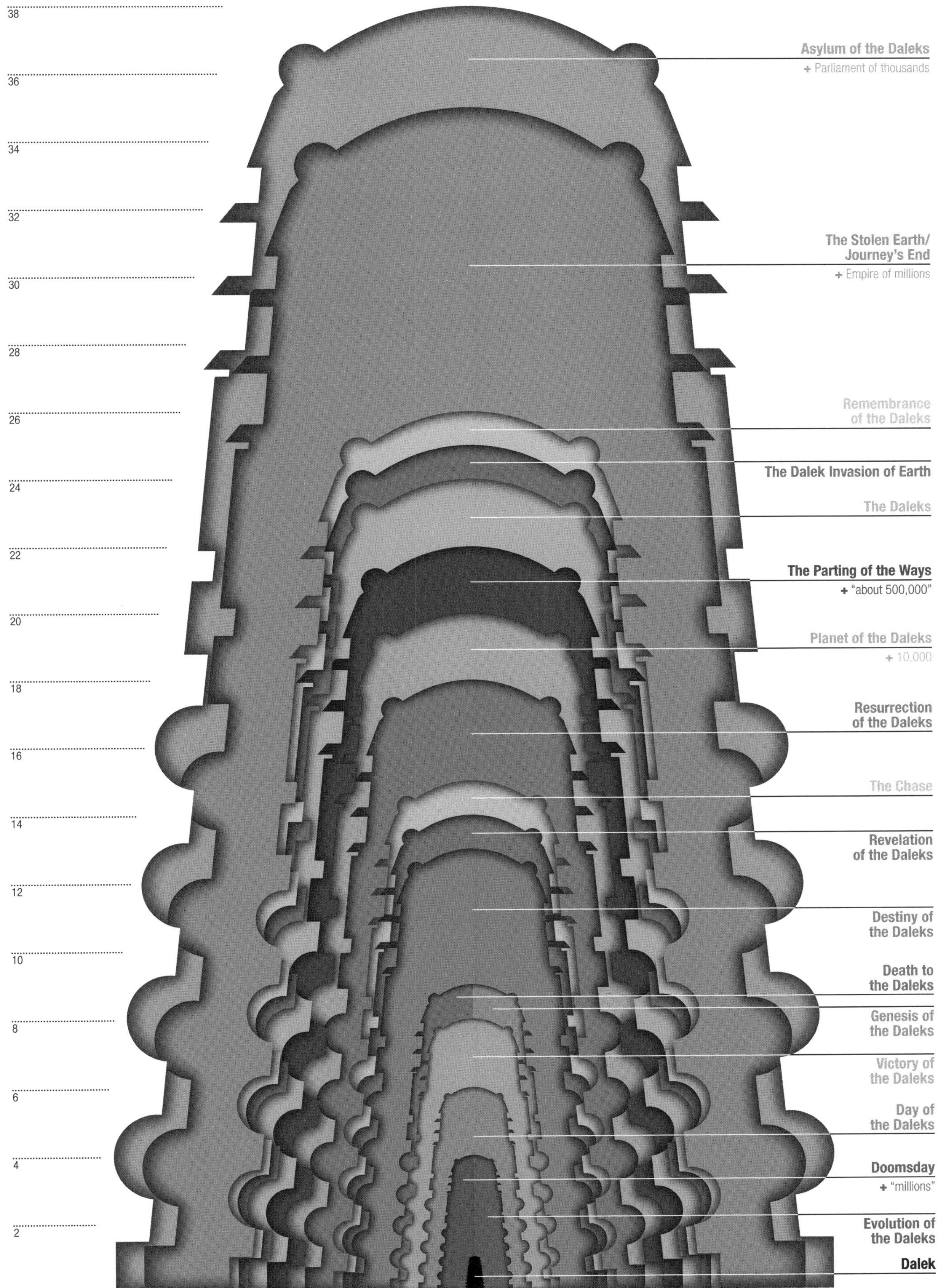

38
36
34
32
30
28
26
24
22
20
18
16
14
12
10
8
6
4
2
Asylum of the Daleks
+ Parliament of thousands
The Stolen Earth/ Journey's End
+ Empire of millions
Remembrance of the Daleks
The Dalek Invasion of Earth
The Daleks
The Parting of the Ways
+ "about 500,000"
Planet of the Daleks
+ 10,000
Resurrection of the Daleks
The Chase
Revelation of the Daleks
Destiny of the Daleks
Death to the Daleks
Genesis of the Daleks
Victory of the Daleks
Day of the Daleks
Doomsday
+ "millions"
Evolution of the Daleks
Dalek

BAD WOLVES

Changes in the gender balance of major villains in *Doctor Who* across four decades

The Doctor has had many more female than male companions and, despite the stereotype, they have rarely been screaming girls who need constantly rescuing by a man. But what about the villains the Doctor has come up against over the years? It could be argued that a sign of true sexual equality in drama is the willingness to present women to be just as scheming, self-serving and vicious as men can be. If producers and audiences shy away from female malefactors as unbelievable or merely uncomfortable, then surely they're not treating the genders equally.

This chart shows the number and proportion of male versus female villains during the four decades *Doctor Who* has been televised, each ring sized relative to the overall number of villains appearing in each decade. The full list of counted villains is given below. Such a selection is bound to be slightly subjective but specifically excludes gender-indeterminate monsters (what sex is a Dalek, or even Styggron for that matter?) except where they adopt a human form for much of their appearance or are clearly presented as male or female (clearest when it's the latter, a notable point in itself). Most, therefore, are human/humanoid where it's clear what sex they are. The aim has been to highlight that writers choose whether to make the evildoers in their stories men or women. Even in historical stories featuring characters based on real people, it was the writer's choice to focus on those characters.

What defines a villain is also subjective. The list here focuses on the main adversaries who get enough character development and screen time that it's clear their morals are suspect, so no thuggish henchmen unless they're significant enough to get a name and clearly support their bosses' goals and relish their role in forcing others to comply (such as Packer in "The Invasion"). A character is counted if they can be described as closed-minded to all but their own ambitions, regardless of any impact on others, whether the aim itself is malicious (usually) or not. If someone who has acted despicably comes to realise their error or relents on learning the consequences of their actions, then they are considered to be not inherently evil and aren't included (such as the Controller in "Day of the Daleks"). It's those who choose their behaviour, know it has a harmful effect on others but continue anyway and will not be deterred whom we can call demonstrably evil.

It's perhaps unsurprising that the balance of male to female villains has become more even between the 1960s and today, as societal attitudes to women have grown fairer. It's nevertheless notable that in its very first year, *Doctor Who* featured a female murderer who clearly felt no remorse for her actions. And while 1965's "Galaxy 4" is generally seen as a hackneyed example of the 'good isn't always beautiful' cliché, it did have the nerve to present a strong, clear-minded woman in a position of command (she just happened to be a nasty, self-important harridan).

The 1970s showed little improvement, despite a greater number of villainous characters overall, with barely a 1% shift in the balance. Indeed, there were no female villains at all during the Pertwee era, and few during Tom Baker's time until Graham Williams became producer, with Season 16 featuring three stories in a row that had immoral women, two the prime adversaries. The 1980s took the ratio almost to 1:3 female to male villains. It's up for debate whether this was in part due to the presence of Margaret Thatcher leading the country — Helen A and her female-run police force in "The Happiness Patrol" notwithstanding — but clearly there was greater consideration given to making the bad guys into bad girls more often.

The revived series has struck a more even balance, although men are still more evil than women by a factor of 3:2. This is also across a lower number of villains overall, despite there being more individual stories than in each of the preceding decades. Perhaps human villainy is seen as less of a novelty for a family adventure series these days, but at least it's not always the men who are up to no good.

The data

1960s **MALE** Kal, Tegana, Vasor, Eyesen, Yartek, Tlotoxl, Léon Colbert, Robespierre, Forester, Bennett, Sevcheria, Nero, El Akir, Lobos, The Monk, Mavic Chen, Zephon, Kirksen, Karlton, The Abbot of Amboise, Marshal Tavannes, The Toymaker, Cyril, Ike Clanton, Phineas Clanton, Billy Clanton, Seth Harper, Johnny Ringo, Edal, Captain Pike, Cherub, Bragen, Solicitor Gray, Captain Trask, Professor Zaroff, Ola, The Director, Kennedy, Theodore Maxtible, Eric Klieg, Salamander, Benik, Giles Kent, Rago, Toba, Tobias Vaughn, Packer, Eelek, Caven, General Smythe, Major Von Weich, The War Chief, The Security Chief, The War Lord
FEMALE Kala, Locusta, Maaga, Cassandra, Catherine de Medici, Kaftan

1970s **MALE** Channing, Major Baker, General Carrington, Reegan, Professor Stahlman, Brigade Leader, The Master, Harry Mailer, Captain Dent, Morgan, Bert, Hepesh, The Marshal, Professor Jaeger, Omega, Kalik, Cross, Hinks, Irongron, Sir Charles Grover, Butler, General Finch, Eckersley, Ettis, Lupton, Jellicoe, Vural, Davros, Nyder, Kellman, The Duke of Forgill/Broton, The Caber, Professor Sorenson, Salamar, Sutekh, Mehendri Solon, Morbius, Harrison Chase, Scorby, Count Federico, Hieronymous, Captain Rossini, Eldrad, Chancellor Goth, Taren Capel, Magnus Greel, Li H'sen Chang, Lord Palmerdale, James Skinsale, Gatherer Hade, The Collector, Castellan Kelner, Graff Vynda-K, Pirate Captain, Count Grendel, Thawn, Rohm-Dutt, Ranquin, The Marshal, The Shadow, Scaroth, Tryst, Dymond, Soldeed, Skagra
FEMALE Hilda Winters, Sister Lamont/Odda, Eldrad, Queen Xanxia, Vivien Fay/Cessair, Madame Lamia, Countess Scarlioni, Lady Adrasta

1980s **MALE** Pangol, Meglos, General Grugger, Dexeter, Aukon, Zargo, Rorvik, The Master, Proctor Neman, Monarch, Persuasion, Hindle, Ringway, The Castellan, Commander Maxil, Lon, Mawdryn, Captain Striker, Marriner, President Borusa, Nilson, Sir George Hutchinson, Joseph Willow, Lytton, Timanov, Sharaz Jek, Morgus, Stotz, Chief Officer, Quillam, Shockeye, The Borad, Tekker, Jobel, The Valeyard, Glitz, Dibber, Crozier, Doland, Chief Caretaker/Kroagnon, Gavrok, Kane, Ratcliffe, De Flores, Captain Cook, Chief Clown, Josiah Samuel Smith, Commander Millington
FEMALE Lexa, Camilla, Kassia, Enlightenment, Captain Wrack, Solow, The Rani, Chessene, Kara, Belazs, Helen A, Daisy K, Priscilla P, Lady Peinforte, Mrs Pritchard

2000s **MALE** Sneed, Joseph Green, General Asquith, Henry van Statten, The Editor, Father Angelo, Finch, John Lumic, Magpie, Toby Zed/Beast, Victor Kennedy, Lance Bennett, Diagoras, Professor Lazarus, Jeremy Baines/Son of Mine, The Master, Rickston Slade, Max Capricorn, Lucius Petrus Dextrus, Klineman Halpen, Luke Rattigan, General Cobb, Rassilon, Francesco Calvierri, The Dream Lord, Kazran Sardick, Colonel Manton, Solomon, The Shakri
FEMALE Cassandra, Margaret Blaine, Matron Casp, Sister Jatt, The Wire, Yvonne Hartman, Empress of the Racnoss, Florence Finnegan, Lilith, Jenny/Mother of Mine, Lucy Saxon, Matron Cofelia, Sky Silvestry/Entity, Mercy Hartigan, Rosanna Calvierri, Alaya, Restac, Jennifer Lucas ganger, Madame Kovarian

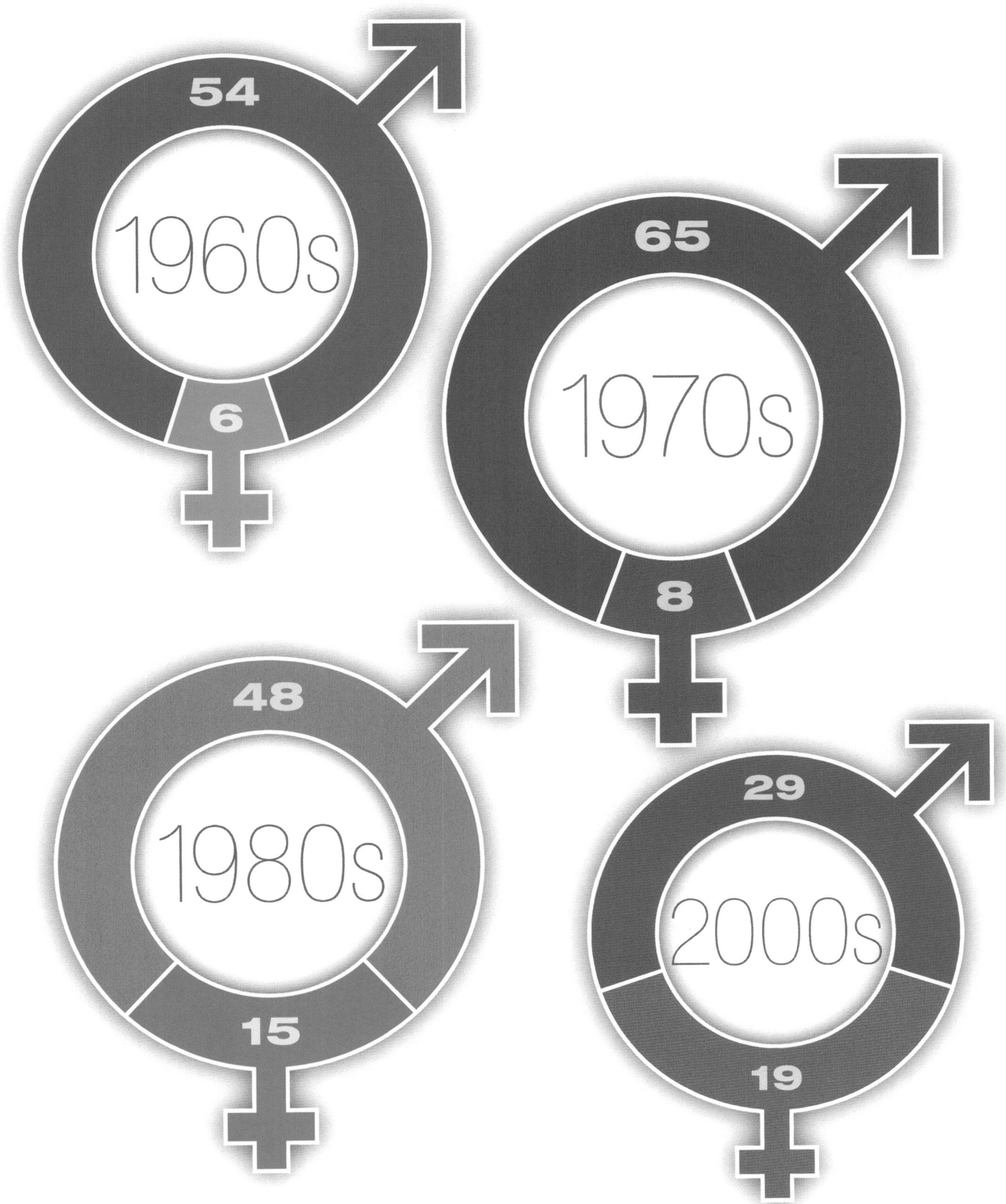
54
1960s
6
65
1970s
8
48
1980s
15
29
2000s
19

THE FINAL PHASE

Categorisation of episode cliffhangers

From the outset, *Doctor Who* was devised as a serial adventure made up of multi-part stories with each episode ending on a dramatic moment intended to lure the audience back the following week to see how it was resolved. This is a technique that dates back to the serialisation of novels in 19th Century newspapers, but is most associated with the film serials of the early 20th Century, such as *The Perils of Pauline* and *Flash Gordon*. *Doctor Who* stuck with the model throughout its original run, but the revived series moved to mainly single-episode stories.

This chart tallies the types of cliffhanger script writers have adopted over the years, to see which are most common. Only the episode endings within a particular story are counted, not those leading from one story to the next, as was common in the early years of *Doctor Who*. The latter tend to be simply a tacked-on surprise rather than arising from the preceding drama, often added by the story editor rather than the serial's writer. Some episodes end with multiple cliffhangers for different characters in different situations. In these cases, only the very final scene of the episode is counted. For example, at the end of "Aliens of London", the Doctor, Rose and Jackie Tyler are separately menaced by Slitheen, but the final scene is of the Doctor being electrocuted, so this is counted under 'Doctor in Peril'.

Categories for the cliffhangers were created as needed, but grouped as much as possible to keep the number of options to a minimum.

DOCTOR or **COMPANION IN PERIL** Instances where a regular is in direct and imminent danger of death or appears already dead. If both are in the same predicament, this is counted as Doctor in Peril only, as he's the prime protagonist.

DOCTOR or **COMPANION IN DISTRESS** Instances where a regular is scared, threatened or otherwise put in clear danger but not at immediate risk of dying. If both are in the same predicament, this is counted as Doctor in Distress only, as he's the prime protagonist.

MONSTER REVEAL Instances where the episode ends with our first sight of the monster in full. Often this is as they threaten a regular, but are categorised separately as the key impact of the cliffhanger is based on the appearance of the monster.

IT'S BEHIND YOU Instances where a threat is apparent to the audience but not the characters in the scene.

VILLAIN IN CONTROL A moment of apparent triumph for the antagonist, when everything seems to be going their way and their defeat seems impossible.

TRAPPED OR CAPTURED One or more regulars are imprisoned or fall into a trap but are not otherwise in immediate danger of death.

SOMEONE IS KILLED The episode ends with the death of a character. Sometimes this implies the same fate is imminent for a regular but the focus of the cliffhanger is on the person's death.

SURPRISE REVELATION Something that hasn't been anticipated is announced or revealed — those classic 'shock' endings.

WORRYING DISCOVERY A regular learns or finds something that increases the danger of the general situation but doesn't put them in immediate danger.

DANGEROUS DEVELOPMENT A more general event that the audience can see spells trouble, generally not involving a regular.

BETRAYED Someone is revealed as a traitor, putting other characters in danger.

DISAPPEARED Someone has apparently vanished without trace or is seen to disappear without explanation.

WHO'S THAT? Instances where someone is only partially seen, or shown fully but the audience knows they can't be the person they appear.

WHAT'S GOING ON? Those instances where the episode ending is just so weird the audience has no idea what's going to come next.

OTHER Inevitably some cliffhangers don't fit into a category, either because they're unique or are a development the impact of which is not apparent.

In "The Trial of a Time Lord", the Valeyard prosecuting the Doctor claimed his companions have been put in danger twice as often as he has. While this line probably wasn't based on comprehensive research of the series to date, going by cliffhangers alone it's clearly not true as by far the most common episode climax is to have the Doctor the one in danger. One in five cliffhangers have him threatened, put at risk, ordered killed or generally not having a fun time, while a further 11.8% have him about to be or apparently already eliminated. His companions, meanwhile, are only in peril or distress in 9.1% of cliffhangers, although this doesn't include when they're side by side with the Doctor facing danger.

Perhaps surprisingly, the reveal of a monster accounts for less than one in 12 cliffhangers, and a fifth of those are the appearance of a Dalek, often in stories with the word 'Daleks' in the title. Other examples included in this category are the first sight of a Sensorite at the end of "The Sensorites" part 1, the true face of Magnus Greel in "The Talons of Weng-Chiang" part 5, and the Cybermen in "Earthshock" part 1, which could also class as a Surprise Revelation but as it's the return of an old enemy the cliffhanger is seen not as 'Ooh, someone is watching!' but as 'Ooh, it's the Cybermen!'.

Dangerous Developments include instances like the Daleks' time machine closing in on the TARDIS ("The Chase" parts 2, 3 and 4), WOTAN ordering the requisition of "Doctor Who" ("The War Machines" part 1), the Master unable to control Azal ("The Dæmons" part 3, a rare instance of a cliffhanger being the villain in danger), Davros ready to launch the Daleks on the universe ("Genesis of the Daleks" part 1), the Valeyard escalating the stakes in the Doctor's trial ("The Trial of a Time Lord" part 1) and the mysterious pit on Krop Tor opening ("The Impossible Planet").

Just under one in five episode endings see the villain apparently undefeatable. The classic example of this is "The Underwater Menace" part 3 (all together now, "Nothing in the world can stop me now!"), but also parts 3, 4 and 5 of "The Power of the Daleks" see the Daleks confident of victory, "Kinda" part 1 has the unhinged Hindle in charge, and "The Sound of Drums" has the Master victorious at last. While these could be considered shock endings themselves, Surprise Revelations here include the Monk's possessing a TARDIS ("The Time Meddler" part 3), the true boss of Global Chemicals being a computer ("The Green Death" part 4) and the Doctor's apparent regeneration in "The Stolen Earth".

Deaths and captures account for just under 3% each of cliffhangers. The first cliffhanger death was in "The Daleks" part 5 (although not at the hands of the Daleks themselves), the last the hapless Edwardes in "The Trial of a Time Lord" part 9. The regulars were being taken prisoner from the word go, twice in the first story ("An Unearthly Child" parts 2 and 3). Of the five betrayal cliffhangers, three have been the Doctor's apparent treachery, in "The Reign of Terror" part 5, "The War Games" part 8 and "The Invasion of Time" part 2.

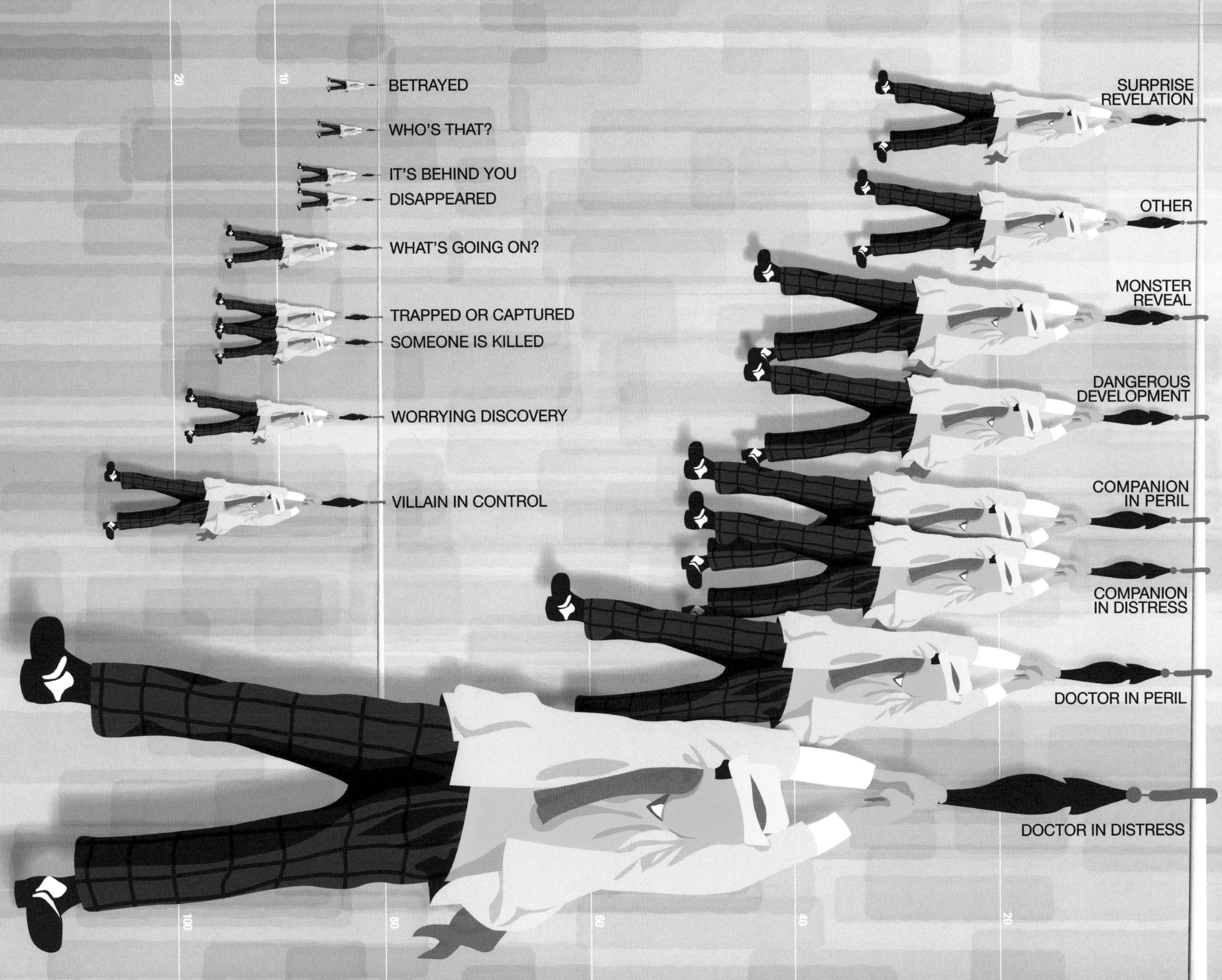

SURPRISE REVELATION
OTHER
MONSTER REVEAL
DANGEROUS DEVELOPMENT
COMPANION IN PERIL
COMPANION IN DISTRESS
DOCTOR IN PERIL
DOCTOR IN DISTRESS
20
40
60
80
100
BETRAYED
WHO'S THAT?
IT'S BEHIND YOU
DISAPPEARED
WHAT'S GOING ON?
TRAPPED OR CAPTURED
SOMEONE IS KILLED
WORRYING DISCOVERY
VILLAIN IN CONTROL
10
20

How the main antagonists got their comeuppance at the conclusion of New Series stories

It's said there are only seven different types of story at heart, but judging by the revived series of *Doctor Who* there are many more potential endings, at least when it comes to giving the bad guys their just desserts. The villains and monsters have faced a range of retributions once the Doctor has foiled their plans, from that trusty standby of being blown up to more unusual punishments like being trapped on an old Betamax videotape.

While the details of each adversary's comeuppance may vary, they can be broadly categorised. For example, whether it's a Dalek deciding it has become too tainted by humanity or the Master turning on his Time Lord tormentors, they involve the threat being ended through an act of self-sacrifice. While no attempt was made to limit the number of categories — if an outcome had not been shown before it was assigned a new set — endings were grouped if they held a broad similarity. Sometimes a story has two entries if it had separate antagonists or one who was soundly trounced.

The colour-coded traces reveal any repetition of similar denouements and whether a writer displays a bias towards any outcomes. For example, the three most recent of Toby Whithouse's four scripts have the antagonists willingly going to their deaths, be it Rosanna accepting her race's fate, the Minotaur tiring of its existence or Kahler Jax selecting his own punishment for his crimes. Similarly, Steven Moffat is the only writer to have redeemed any of his villains, both Kazran Sardick and Melody Pond seeing the error of their ways and performing a selfless act.

Blowing up the bad guys (arguably an easy way out) is joined as the most common outcome by the threat being resolved through the clarification of a misunderstanding, each accounting for an eighth of endings. Steven Moffat was the first to use this latter technique, with the nanogenes in "The Empty Child/The Doctor Dances" learning how to heal humans properly, returning to it for "The Beast Below" and 2011's Christmas special. Close on their heels is the villain's self-sacrifice, followed by the problem being negated through some temporal effect. This 'pressing reset' method is *Doctor Who*'s timey-wimey equivalent of the 'it was all a dream' cliché and risks invalidating the audience's investment in the drama. That the series' two showrunners have been responsible for six of its eight uses is either worrying or a sign they know it should only be used by experienced writers.

Only three resolutions can be classed as genuinely unique: the Wire's being recorded onto video in Mark Gatiss's "The Idiot's Lantern", the Vespiform's death by drowning in Gareth Roberts' "The Unicorn and the Wasp", and the routing of the Headless Monks by the Doctor's army of recruits. The Monks are not merely scared away by the threat of the Doctor's wrath, as the Sycorax, Vashta Nerada and Atraxi are, but their defeated withdrawal doesn't really count as escaping to fight another day; the link to that from "A Good Man Goes to War" is for Madame Kovarian.

The abbreviations of writers' names are: **CC** Chris Chibnall; **GR** Gareth Roberts; **DF** Russell T Davies and Phil Ford; **DR** Russell T Davies and Gareth Roberts; **HR** Helen Raynor; **JM** James Moran; **KT** Keith Temple; **MG** Mark Gatiss; **Mg** Matthew Graham; **MJ** Matt Jones; **NG** Neil Gaiman; **PC** Paul Cornell; **RC** Richard Curtis; **RD** Russell T Davies; **RS** Robert Shearman; **SG** Stephen Greenhorn; **SM** Steven Moffat; **SN** Simon Nye; **ST** Steve Thompson; **TM** Tom MacRae; **TW** Toby Whithouse

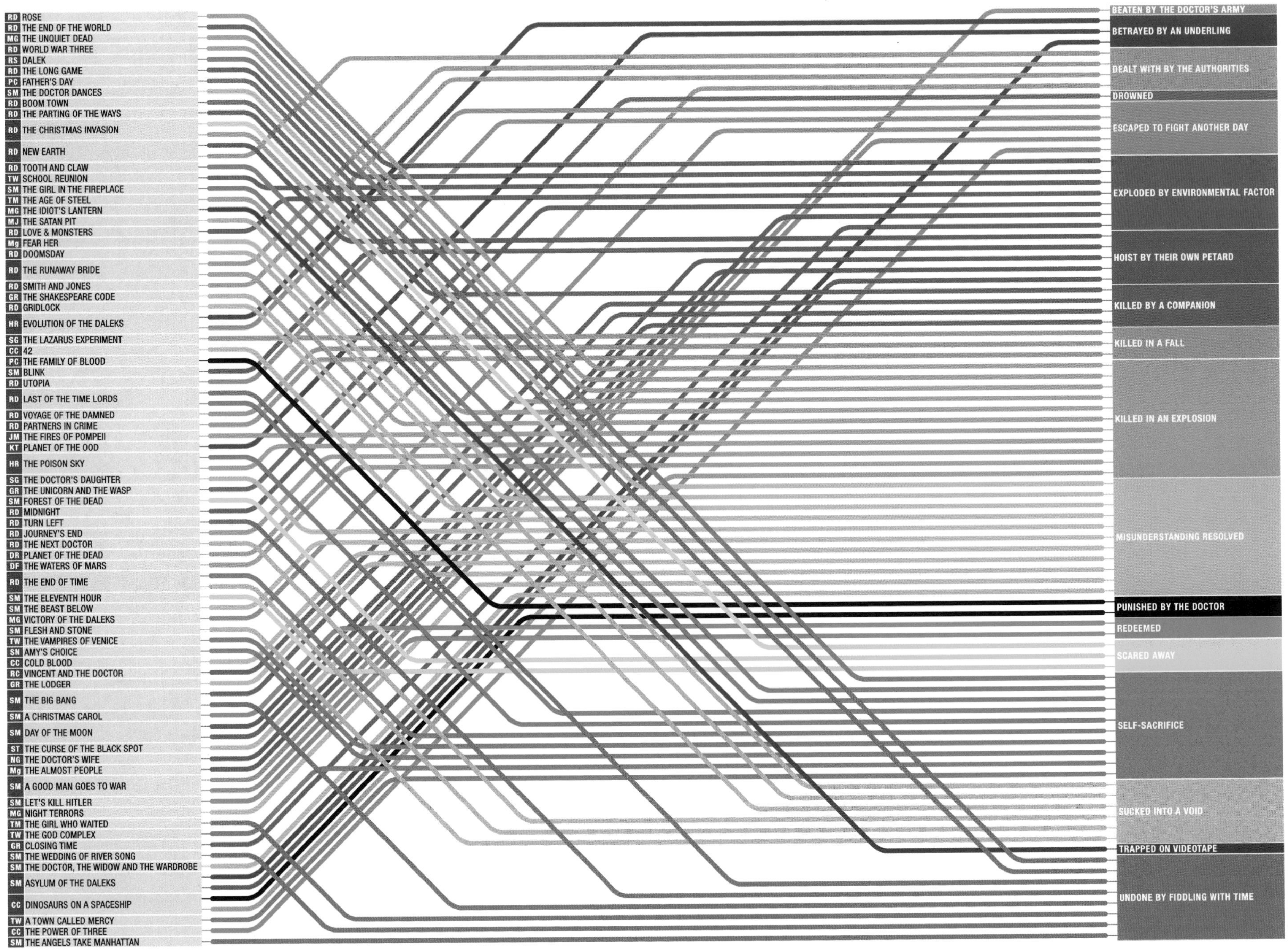

RD ROSE
RD THE END OF THE WORLD
MG THE UNQUIET DEAD
RD WORLD WAR THREE
RS DALEK
RD THE LONG GAME
PC FATHER'S DAY
SM THE DOCTOR DANCES
RD BOOM TOWN
RD THE PARTING OF THE WAYS
RD THE CHRISTMAS INVASION
RD NEW EARTH
RD TOOTH AND CLAW
TW SCHOOL REUNION
SM THE GIRL IN THE FIREPLACE
TM THE AGE OF STEEL
MG THE IDIOT'S LANTERN
MJ THE SATAN PIT
RD LOVE & MONSTERS
Mg FEAR HER
RD DOOMSDAY
RD THE RUNAWAY BRIDE
RD SMITH AND JONES
GR THE SHAKESPEARE CODE
RD GRIDLOCK
HR EVOLUTION OF THE DALEKS
SG THE LAZARUS EXPERIMENT
CC 42
PC THE FAMILY OF BLOOD
SM BLINK
RD UTOPIA
RD LAST OF THE TIME LORDS
RD VOYAGE OF THE DAMNED
RD PARTNERS IN CRIME
JM THE FIRES OF POMPEII
KT PLANET OF THE OOD
HR THE POISON SKY
SG THE DOCTOR'S DAUGHTER
GR THE UNICORN AND THE WASP
SM FOREST OF THE DEAD
RD MIDNIGHT
RD TURN LEFT
RD JOURNEY'S END
RD THE NEXT DOCTOR
DR PLANET OF THE DEAD
DF THE WATERS OF MARS
RD THE END OF TIME
SM THE ELEVENTH HOUR
SM THE BEAST BELOW
MG VICTORY OF THE DALEKS
SM FLESH AND STONE
TW THE VAMPIRES OF VENICE
SN AMY'S CHOICE
CC COLD BLOOD
RC VINCENT AND THE DOCTOR
GR THE LODGER
SM THE BIG BANG
SM A CHRISTMAS CAROL
SM DAY OF THE MOON
ST THE CURSE OF THE BLACK SPOT
NG THE DOCTOR'S WIFE
Mg THE ALMOST PEOPLE
SM A GOOD MAN GOES TO WAR
SM LET'S KILL HITLER
MG NIGHT TERRORS
TM THE GIRL WHO WAITED
TW THE GOD COMPLEX
GR CLOSING TIME
SM THE WEDDING OF RIVER SONG
SM THE DOCTOR, THE WIDOW AND THE WARDROBE
SM ASYLUM OF THE DALEKS
CC DINOSAURS ON A SPACESHIP
TW A TOWN CALLED MERCY
CC THE POWER OF THREE
SM THE ANGELS TAKE MANHATTAN

BEATEN BY THE DOCTOR'S ARMY
BETRAYED BY AN UNDERLING
DEALT WITH BY THE AUTHORITIES
DROWNED
ESCAPED TO FIGHT ANOTHER DAY
EXPLODED BY ENVIRONMENTAL FACTOR
HOIST BY THEIR OWN PETARD
KILLED BY A COMPANION
KILLED IN A FALL
KILLED IN AN EXPLOSION
MISUNDERSTANDING RESOLVED
PUNISHED BY THE DOCTOR
REDEEMED
SCARED AWAY
SELF-SACRIFICE
SUCKED INTO A VOID
TRAPPED ON VIDEOTAPE
UNDONE BY FIDDLING WITH TIME

TRANSMISSION

DAYS OF RECKONING

Variations in the transmission times of *Doctor Who*

Doctor Who has been shuffled around the TV schedules several times over its long life. Initially episodes were made one a week and the programme was shown almost all year round, with just a month or two's break at the end of the summer. This was a punishing process, especially for the regular cast and crew, as they were working almost solidly year after year. This is why occasional episodes didn't feature either the Doctor or one of his companions, so that the actor could take a much-needed holiday.

By the time the show moved to colour in the 1970s, television production techniques were changing as videotape editing became easier, allowing programmes to be recorded in a different scene order to that shown in the final episodes. *Doctor Who* also moved to shorter seasons broadcast over 26 weeks or so, initially from January to June, then later from September to March. Further shortening came in 1982 when the programme was shown twice a week over 13 weeks. Then in 1985 the length of each episode was changed from 25 minutes to 45 minutes, still over 13 weeks, but when the programme returned in 1986 it was back to 25-minute episodes running for 14 weeks.

The return of *Doctor Who* in 2005 saw it adopt the same structure as 1985's season: 45-minute episodes broadcast over 13 weeks. 2009 saw the show take some time out, with just three hour-long specials (with part 2 of the last on New Year's Day 2010), before briefly returning to form in 2010, since when it was experimented with shorter 'half-seasons' of five to seven episodes twice a year.

Transmission pattern through each year from 1963-1989 and 2005-2012 *(opposite)*

This charts the transmission of *Doctor Who* during each year in blocks indicating the weeks in which a new episode was shown, with paler colours marking repeats of past episodes on BBC1 or 2. It highlights the near-all-year broadcast during the first two Doctor's eras (1968 had only four weeks when no *Doctor Who* was shown), dropping to half-yearly seasons for the Third and Fourth Doctors, and three-month runs for the rest.

Once the programme moves to shorter seasons, the changes in its starting time become clearer: initially New Year, drifting back to pre-Christmas before shifting to early autumn for most of the Fourth Doctor's era. Even then, it often took a mid-season break over Christmas before returning in January (often billed as a 'new series'). It returned to a New Year start for the early 1980s, shifting back to autumn after the 1985 suspension.

July and August are clearly the months with the fewest showings of new episodes, no doubt avoided as this is the most common time for family holidays so a poor time to schedule a family show like *Doctor Who* — although during the show's high popularity in the late-1970s summer repeats became common. But from the mid-1970s the second quarter also becomes barren until the return of the series in 2005. (The TV movie starring the Eighth Doctor, not included here, was shown in the last week of May 1996.) This post-hiatus period also highlights the prevalence of the Christmas special in the final week of each year.

Number of episodes first broadcast on each day of the week *(overleaf)*

Saturday is the traditional day for *Doctor Who*, with 84.2% of episodes being first broadcast on this day. Indeed, for the show's first 18 years it was only ever shown on early Saturday evening (excluding repeats), as have each of the revived series' regular episodes. But in the 1980s the BBC's schedulers were trying out new models, and *Doctor Who* was moved to twice-weekly broadcasts in 1982 – seen by many as a test run for the launch of *EastEnders* in 1984. Before returning to Saturdays in 1985, it was shown on each weekday at some time, although Wednesday gets a boost to 5.2% of all episodes thanks to the last two years of the original series being shown on that day.

It wasn't until the series returned that it saw an episode broadcast on a Sunday, thanks to Christmas specials showing on Christmas Day.

(Note: to keep the count to a square number, this chart only includes episodes up to "The Doctor, the Widow and the Wardrobe". The five episodes of the 2012 series were each first broadcast on a Saturday.)

Number of episodes first broadcast on each day of the year *(overleaf)*

Although most episodes have been shown on a Saturday, the actual days of the month these fall on shifts, so this chart highlights which dates have had the most *Doctor Who* showings (excluding repeats). The summer dip is again most noticeable, and hotspots naturally fall into seven-day patterns, particularly at the start of the year, highlighting the predominance of a January start for seasons. Thanks to the New Series' regular Christmas specials, Christmas Day has become the most common day of the year on which to see a new episode. Only two achieve the double-whammy of being on both a Saturday and Christmas Day, however: 1965's "The Daleks' Master Plan" part 7 and 2010's "A Christmas Carol".

Transmission pattern through each year from 1963-1989 and 2005-2012

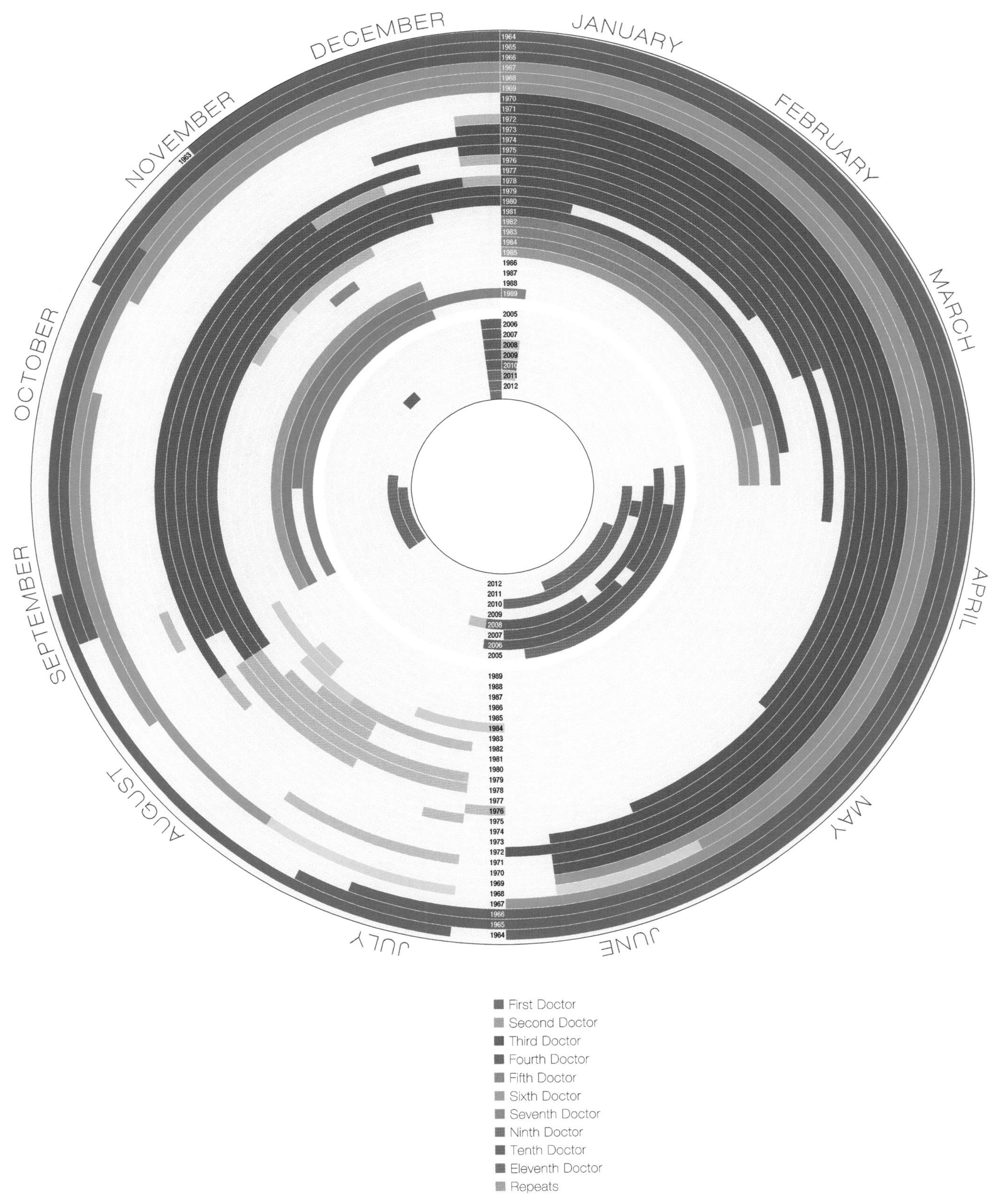

Number of episodes first broadcast on each day of the week

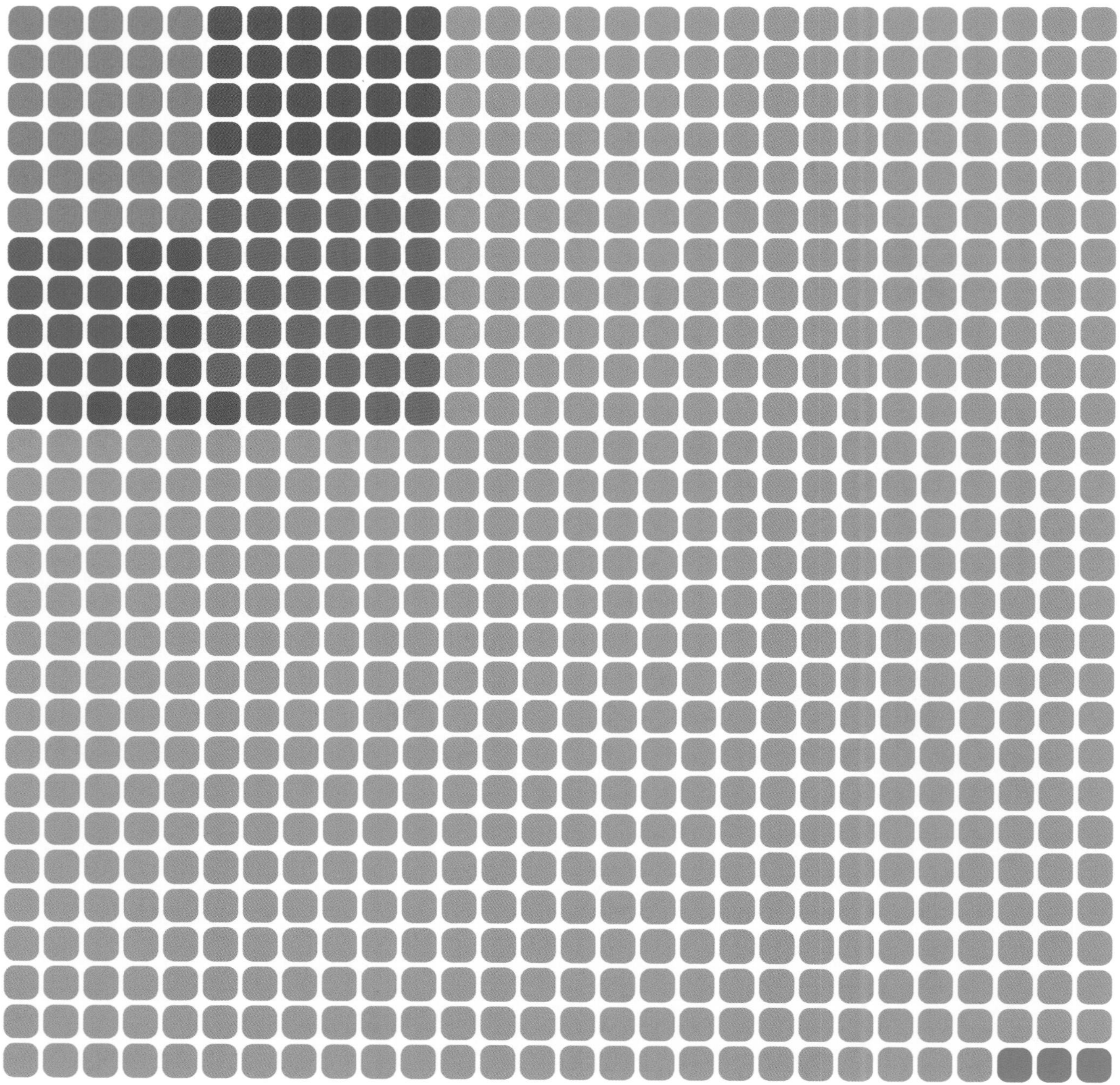

= one episode

- Mondays
- Tuesdays
- Wednesdays
- Thursdays
- Fridays
- Saturdays
- Sundays

Number of episodes first broadcast on each day of the year

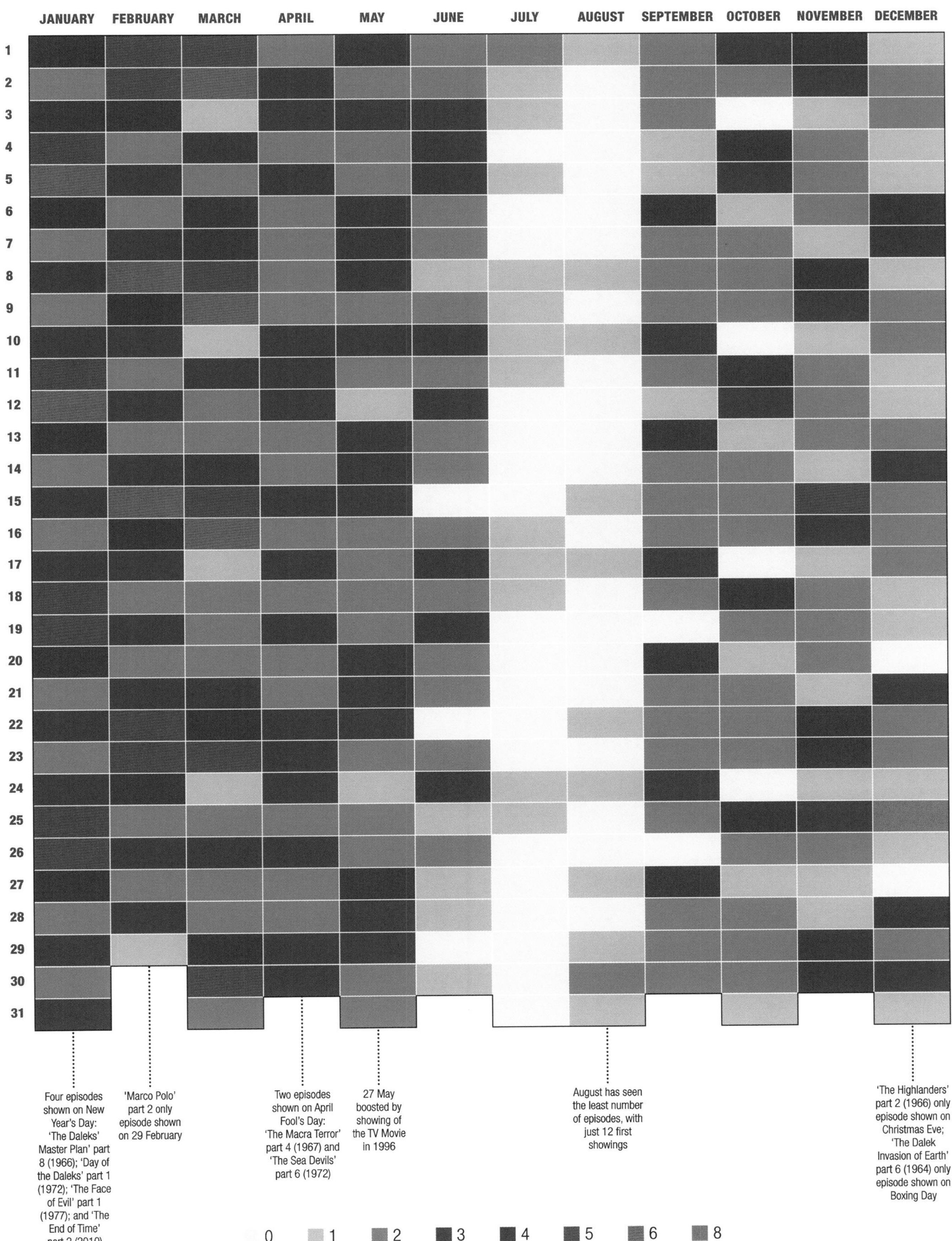
JANUARY
FEBRUARY
MARCH
APRIL
MAY
JUNE
JULY
AUGUST
SEPTEMBER
OCTOBER
NOVEMBER
DECEMBER
1
2
3
4
5
6
7
8
9
10
11
12
13
14
15
16
17
18
19
20
21
22
23
24
25
26
27
28
29
30
31
Four episodes shown on New Year's Day: 'The Daleks' Master Plan' part 8 (1966); 'Day of the Daleks' part 1 (1972); 'The Face of Evil' part 1 (1977); and 'The End of Time' part 2 (2010)
'Marco Polo' part 2 only episode shown on 29 February
Two episodes shown on April Fool's Day: 'The Macra Terror' part 4 (1967) and 'The Sea Devils' part 6 (1972)
27 May boosted by showing of the TV Movie in 1996
August has seen the least number of episodes, with just 12 first showings
'The Highlanders' part 2 (1966) only episode shown on Christmas Eve; 'The Dalek Invasion of Earth' part 6 (1964) only episode shown on Boxing Day
0
1
2
3
4
5
6
8

THE DIMENSIONS OF TIME

Most common time slots for first broadcast of *Doctor Who* episodes

Many fans would say the best time to watch *Doctor Who* was well into the evening hours of a dark autumn night, just like when they were children. But as we've seen from the yearly transmission pattern, there are only three periods when the programme was broadcast in the latter months of the year: the first six years (when it was on nearly all year anyway), the Fourth Doctor's era and the Seventh Doctor's. Similarly, it has predominantly been shown in the early evening, between five and six o'clock, with 58.5% of episodes starting broadcast within this hour. Only 12.7% have started after seven o'clock. Those beginning after 7.30pm are almost exclusively the Seventh Doctor stories, when the programme was shown on Wednesday evenings opposite *Coronation Street* — but those fans harking back to the thrill of watching on an autumn evening are not usually proponents of this era.

Excluding the TV Movie, which had an unusually late showing at 8.29pm on a May Day Bank Holiday Monday, the latest an episode has begun broadcast is 7.40pm, "The Greatest Show in the Galaxy" part 3 and "Gridlock" going out at this time. The earliest is 5.09pm, for the first three parts of "The Keeper of Traken" and episodes one, two and four of the following story "Logopolis". The most common time for an episode to start is 5.15pm, with 80 (10.2%) doing so, while a further 48 began within three minutes either side (taking the share to 16.2%).

The chart shows the hours of five to eight o'clock divided into ten-minute segments, with the radius of each span indicating the number of episodes starting within that slot. The hour hand indicates the earliest time an episode has been shown, the minute hand the latest, while the second hand marks the average across all episodes — specifically, 3 minutes and 6.6 seconds after six o'clock. The median falls at 5.51pm, a time at which 47 episodes have begun broadcast.

After the dominance of the 5.10-5.19pm slot, with 135 episodes starting then, the next most common is 5.50-5.59pm, with 128 episodes. 89 began between 5.40 and 5.49pm, while 56 started in the ten minutes after 5.30. All other time slots have fewer than 50 episodes beginning during those ten minutes. The least common time, with just four episodes starting in this slot, is 7.20-7.29pm, one of which was "The Five Doctors", broadcast on a Friday evening as part of 1983's Children In Need telethon. After the six earliest episodes mentioned above, which began just a little ahead of their 5.10pm scheduled starting time, the next least common time to show an episode is 7.10-7.19pm, with 14 episodes beginning then, all Tenth and Eleventh Doctor stories. The last segment with fewer than 25 episodes showing is 6.30-6.39pm, these 18 episodes including all six parts of "The Talons of Weng-Chiang".

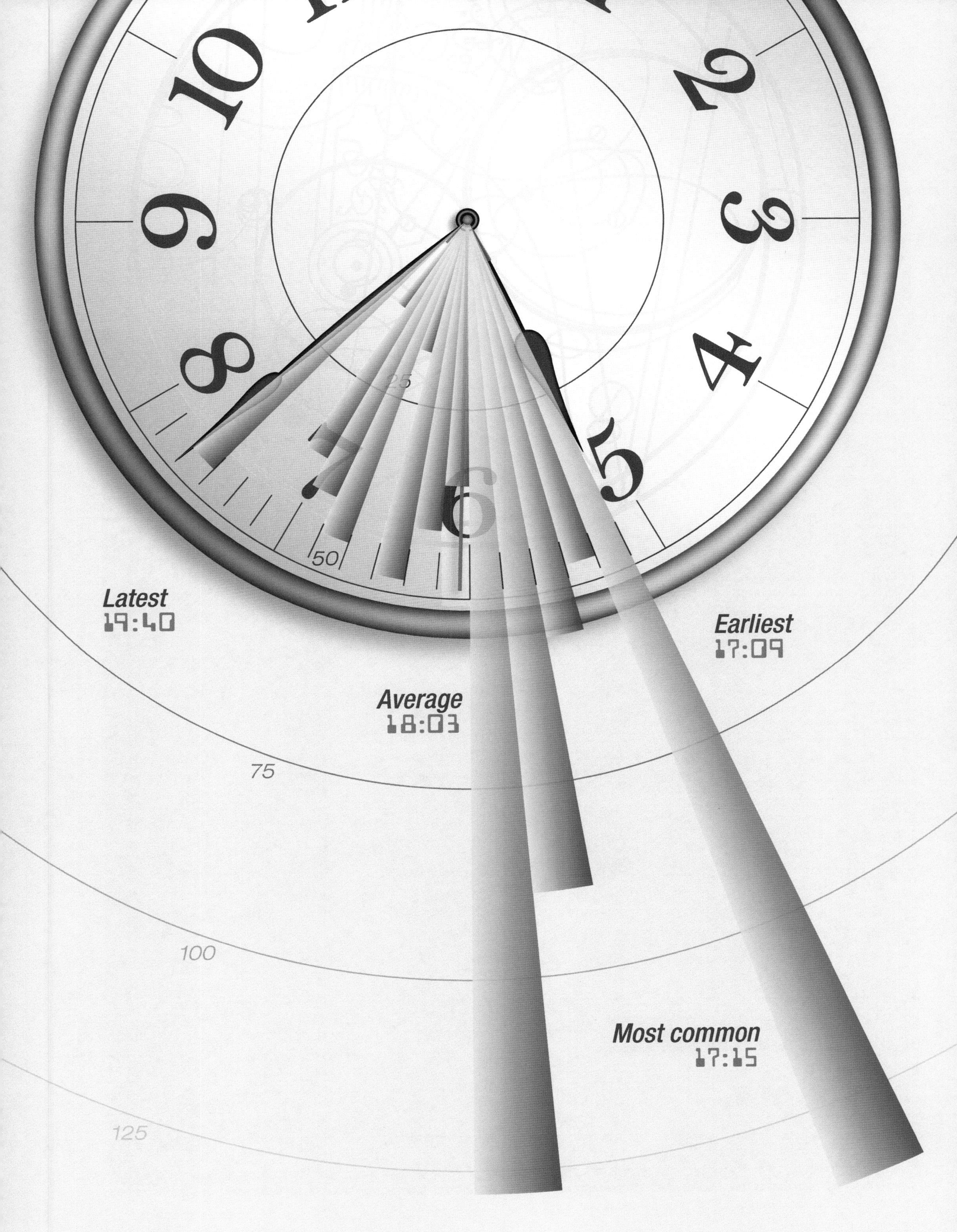

Latest
19:40
Earliest
17:09
Average
18:03
Most common
17:15
25
50
75
100
125

CLOSING TIMES

Total number of '25-minute' episodes: **679**

39.6% within 30 seconds of 25m

Average duration: **24m 14s**

Most common duration: **24m 30s**

Base: All episodes from 'An Unearthly Child' 1 to 'Survival' 3 excluding 'The Five Doctors', 'Resurrection of the Daleks' and Season 22

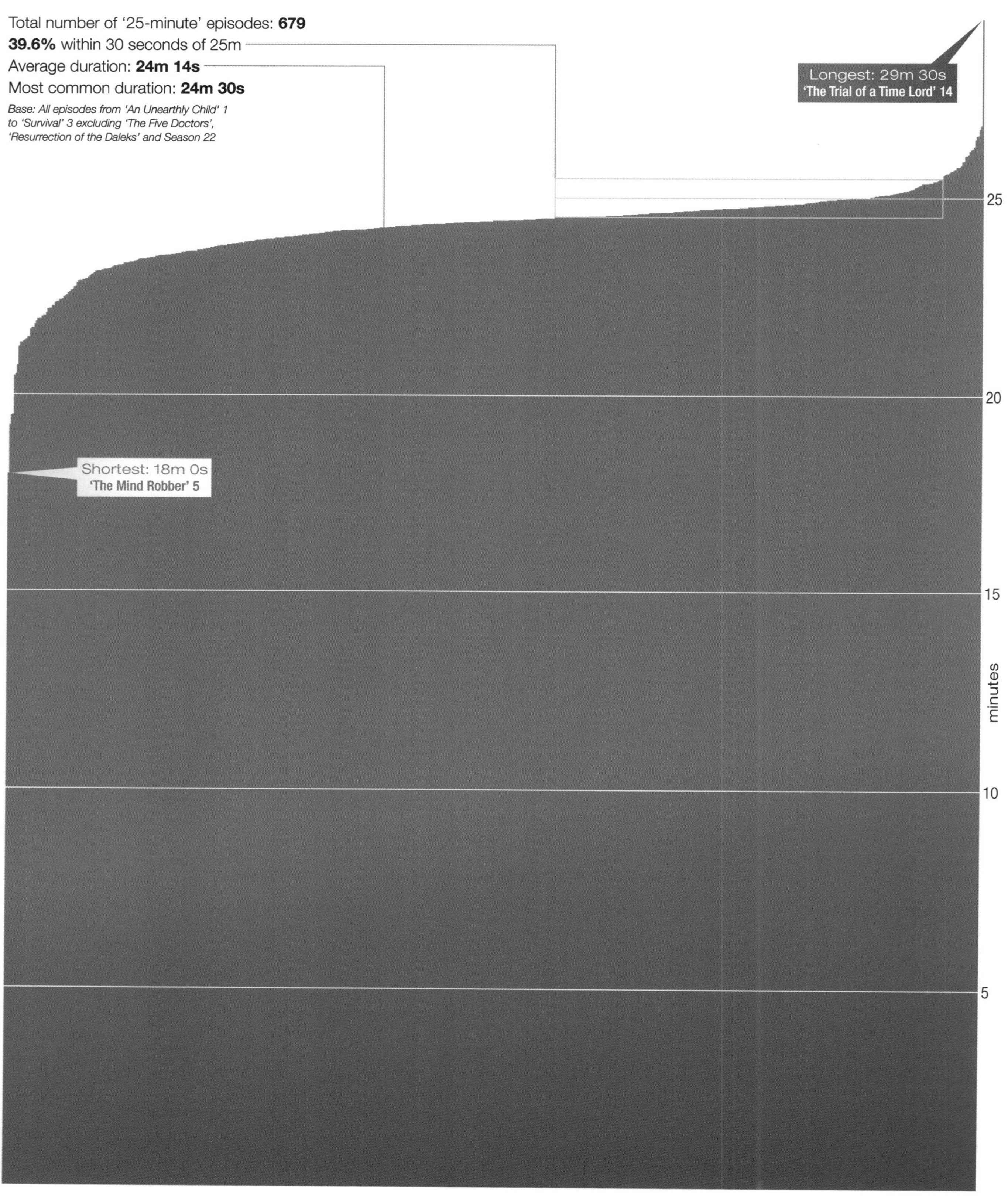

Spread of durations for *Doctor Who*'s two standard episode lengths

For the majority of the original series, *Doctor Who* followed a format of multi-part stories show in approximately 25-minute episodes. Since its return it has adopted the structure more common to today's television series of one- or two-part stories of 45 minutes each, which the original series only dabbled with once for Season 22. The only episodes outside these standards are season finales and specials (and one season opener, "The Eleventh Hour"). These are included with the 45-minute episodes in the chart below, except the 90-minute "The Five Doctors" and the 85-minute TV movie. The original series was better at hitting its target, with a higher percentage of episodes within 30 seconds of the standard duration. Indeed, if one takes this to actually be 24½ minutes, which was the true target for the 25-minute slot, then an impressive 60% of episodes were within 30 seconds of this length.

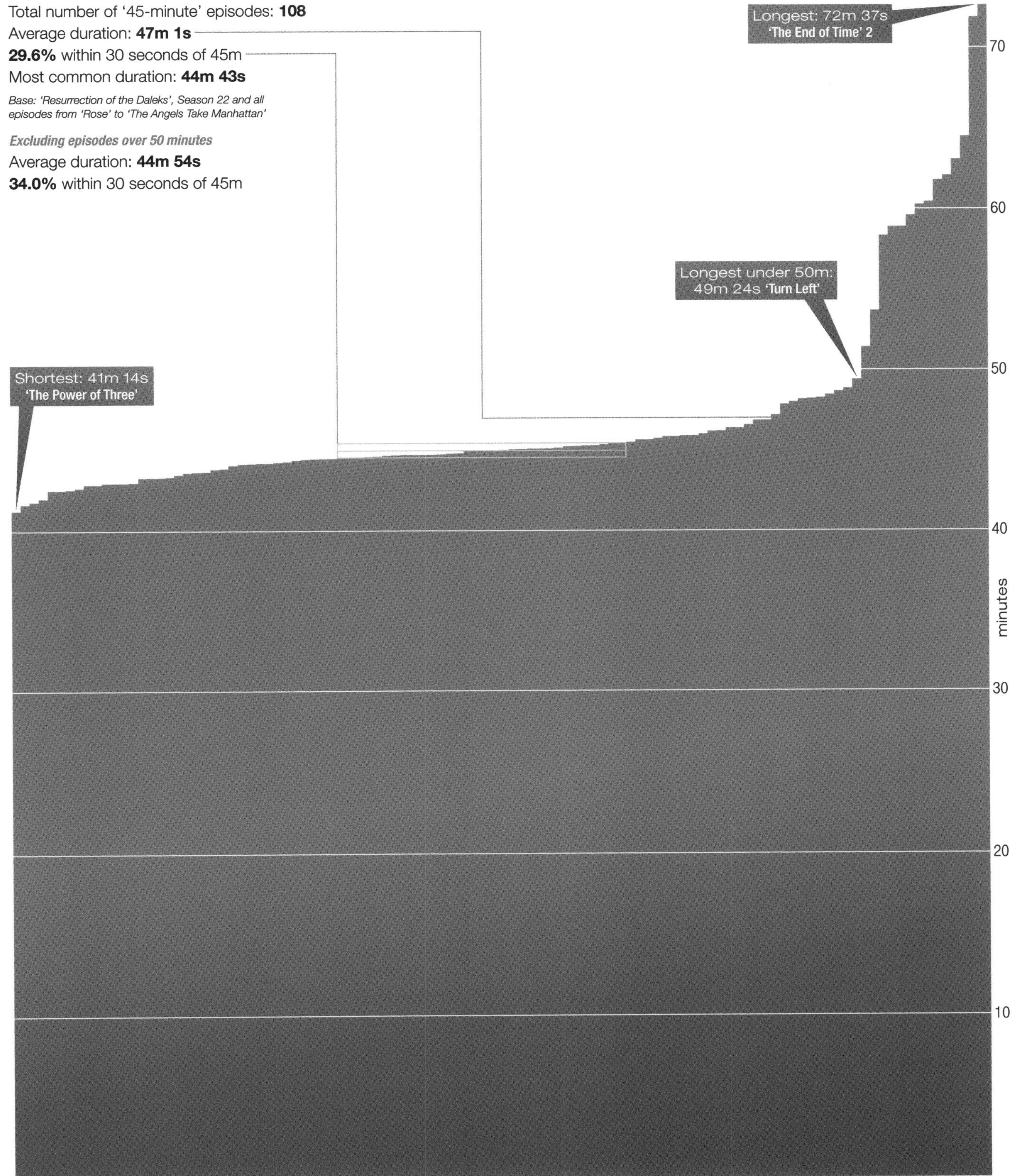

THE POWER OF FOUR

The dominance of the four-part story in Classic *Doctor Who*

When *Doctor Who* was first produced, each episode had its own on-screen title and viewers generally didn't know how many weeks a particular story would last. Without knowing when the current storyline would finish, therefore, the end-of-episode cliffhangers carried more weight as one could never be certain if this was the true climax. For the writers, stories could be whatever length they needed to best convey the plot — in theory. In practice, the series surprisingly quickly fell into regular story lengths of four or six parts.

The reasons were practical as much as narrative. Longer stories were cheaper to make, on average, as sets, costumes and props could be reused for a greater number of weeks. However, they ran the risk of deterring viewers who had missed the first parts from joining the story midway. Thus four episodes — which at around 25 minutes each added up to a typical feature film length of 80-90 minutes — came to be seen as the ideal runtime, with occasional six-parters thrown in for 'event' stories such as the return of the Daleks.

By the end of the First Doctor's era, just three years into the programme, nearly all stories were four episodes long, and at this time individual episode titles were dropped in favour of overall story titles with part numbers, making it clearer how far into a story the viewer was. Rising costs then pushed the producers towards longer stories, and six-parters became the norm for most of the Second Doctor's era, with additional script problems towards the end leading to eight- and even ten-episode stories.

With the shorter seasons of the 1970s, more thought had to be given to structuring each year's run of stories and, after a brief flirtation with seven-part serials, a mix of two four-parters and three six-parters — making up the 26-episode seasons — was settled on. A change of producer in 1975 led to a rethink and an extra story was added by switching to five four-parters and a six-part season finale. With further changes to the scheduling in the 1980s, seasons were extended again to seven stories by dropping six-parters in favour of another four-episode story and one just two episodes long. After the 1985 suspension, however, the cut to 14-episode seasons led to a mix of four- and three-part stories.

Throughout all these changes, the four-parter held its regard as the best length in which to tell a *Doctor Who* story. Plotting the total number of stories of each episode count starkly highlights the prominence of the four-parter, with more stories being that length than any other combined. By happy coincidence, the Fourth Doctor had the most four-parters in his era, more even than all six-parters from all eras combined.

The count includes all Classic stories from "An Unearthly Child" to "Survival". For parity, the 90-minute 20th anniversary special "The Five Doctors" is counted as a four-parter, being of equivalent length and shown in that format abroad. Similarly, the 45-minute episodes of Season 22 are each counted as equivalent to two parts, so the stories are tallied as though they were four-parters and "The Two Doctors" as a six-parter.

The data

	Number of stories	Number of episodes	Average episodes per story	Longest story (episodes)	Shortest story (episodes)	Most common episode count
FIRST DOCTOR	29	134	4.62	12	1	4
SECOND DOCTOR	21	119	5.67	10	4	6
THIRD DOCTOR	24	128	5.33	7	4	6
FOURTH DOCTOR	41	172	4.20	6	2	4
FIFTH DOCTOR	20	74*	3.70	4	2	4
SIXTH DOCTOR	8	44†	5.50	14	4	4
SEVENTH DOCTOR	12	42	3.50	4	3	3/4
TOTALS	**155**	**713**	**4.60**			

* 'The Five Doctors' counted as four parts † Season 22 counted as five four-parters and one six-parter

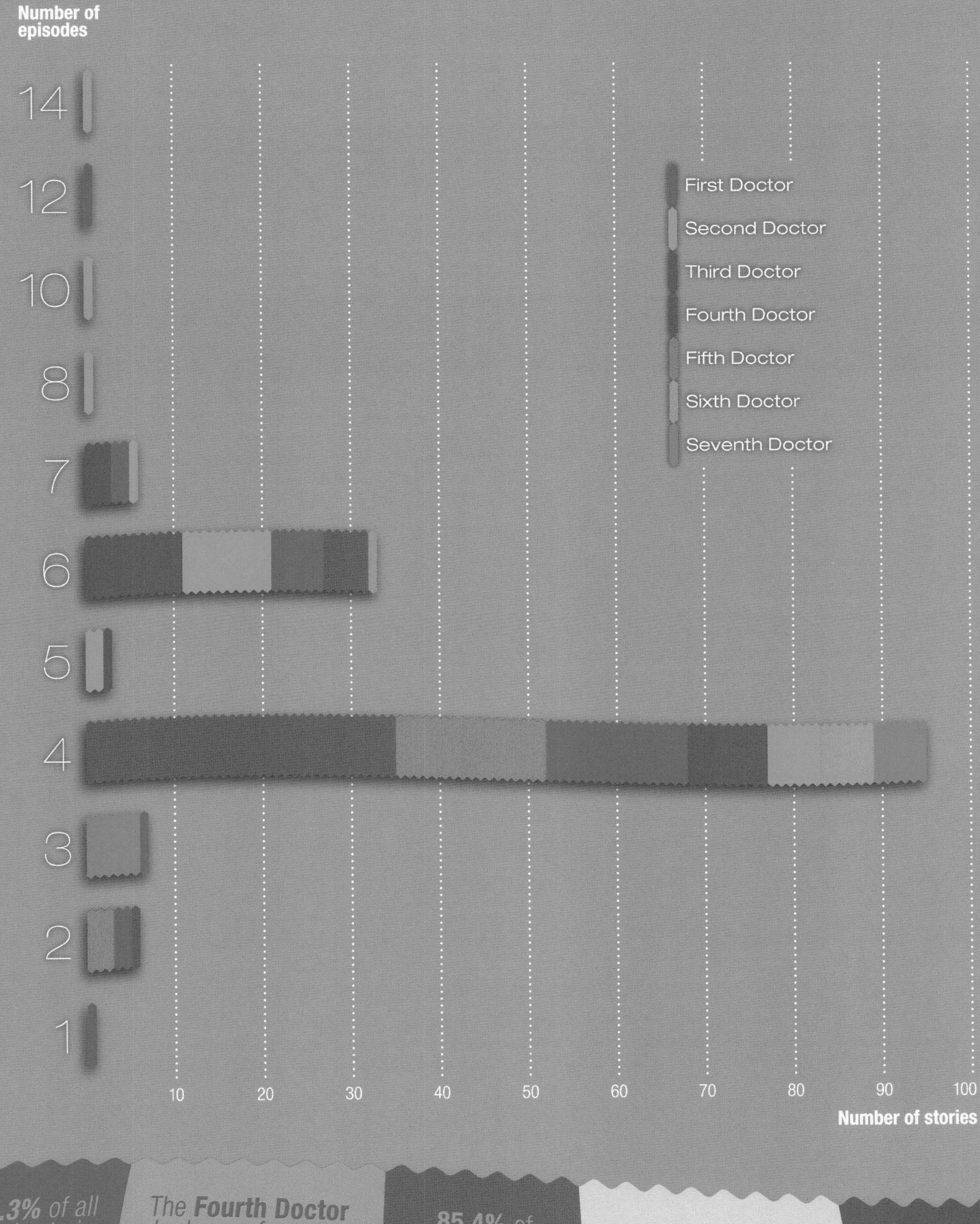

***61.3%** of all Classic stories are **four episodes** long*

*The **Fourth Doctor** had more four-part stories than the total number of **six-parters***

85.4% of Fourth Doctor stories are **four parts**

Four episodes is the **most common** story length for four of the **first seven** Doctors

Four parts is the only story length **every Doctor** had

THE TIME MONSTER

Total time required to watch all of *Doctor Who* to date

Up to "The Angels Take Manhattan", there have been 231 *Doctor Who* stories (not including "Shada", counting "The Trial of a Time Lord" as one story, and "Utopia" as a separate story from "The Sound of Drums/Last of the Time Lords") made up of 789 individual episodes. These have been broadcast over a span of 48 years, 10 months and 6 days. But how long would it take if you were to sit down and watch all the episodes in one consecutive run?

The answer is surprisingly short. For a show approaching its 50th anniversary (even taking into account that it was off the air for 15 years), all those episodes run end to end would take up just 15.08 days. Still, that would be quite a marathon and doesn't account for tea or toilet breaks. Perhaps watching (or, in the case of the missing episodes, listening to) one story a day is more realistic. While the single episode "Mission to the Unknown" would be easy to fit in, it would take you nearly six hours to watch all of the 14-episode "The Trial of a Time Lord" in one sitting, and close to eight months to get through the whole series — still doesn't sound long, perhaps, for such a long-lived programme.

Most people should be able to find time to watch an episode a day, surely, even if they're 45 minutes long in some cases. Then it would take you more than two years to get through the lot, by which time there would be a couple more seasons to add on. If you have a particularly busy life and can only manage time at the weekend to watch one story, then you'd need to keep going for nearly four and a half years, by which time we'll almost certainly be watching the Twelfth Doctor in action. And at just one episode a week — mirroring the original broadcast but without all those annoying gaps between seasons — then you should just be finished in time for *Doctor Who*'s 65th anniversary. If you're a long-time fan who's old enough to remember watching the first episode on broadcast, then this might not be a wise option to undertake...

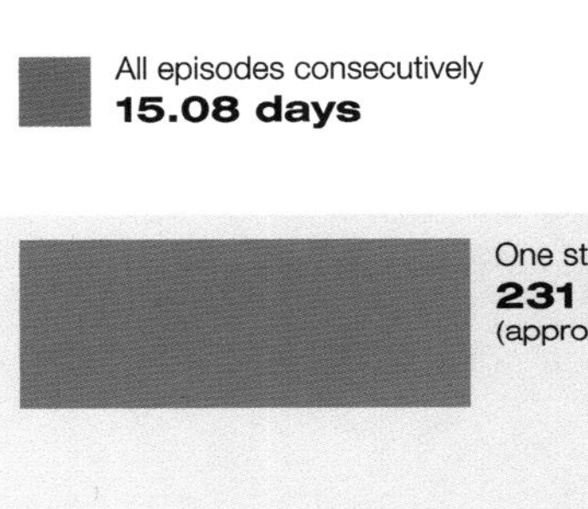

All episodes consecutively
15.08 days

All existing episodes consecutively
13.26 days

One story per day
231 days
(approx 7.6 months)

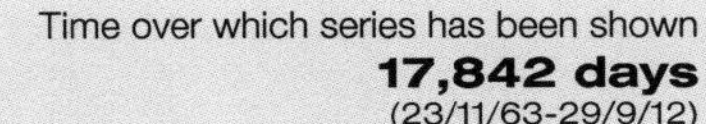

Time over which series has been shown
17,842 days
(23/11/63-29/9/12)

One episode per day
789 days
(approx 25.9 months/2.16 years)

One story per week
1,611 days
(approx 53 months/4.4 years)

One episode per week
5,517 days
(approx 181.4 months/15.1 years)

THE WATCHERS

Audience sizes for *Doctor Who* episodes based on recorded number of viewers

Nobody knows exactly how many people in the UK watch *Doctor Who*. Short of asking everyone in the country, all anyone can do is estimate the size of the audience for any television programme by recording what a representative sample of the population watches and extrapolating this to all households with a TV. This is what the Broadcasters' Audience Research Board (BARB) has been doing since 1981, before which the BBC and ITV recorded their own audience figures. As the television landscape expands in terms of the number of channels, and technological developments add more ways for viewers to watch at their convenience, the figures for the first showing of a programme may seem less relevant. Yet arguably they give a more accurate measure of a show's popularity than ever. In the days of only two main channels and no remote controls, as when *Doctor Who* began, families would often pick the BBC or ITV for their Saturday evening's viewing and watch whatever was shown. These days, with so many alternatives available, the fact that some eight million choose to put on *Doctor Who* rather than watch or do something more appealing is significant.

Nevertheless, variations are inevitable, caused by anything from the weather to what the preceding programme happened to be. The next few charts group in various ways the viewing figures for each episode of *Doctor Who* shown on the BBC's main two channels to see how audiences have waxed and waned at different times. Repeat showings have been included in this analysis as, while these typically get a much lower number of viewers than first showings, they still speak to people's desire to watch the programme and perhaps give a truer representation of its genuinely dedicated audience.

Average, minimum and maximum number of viewers for each episode, including repeats, by month of broadcast *(opposite)*

Grouping viewer numbers by the month in which each episode was broadcast illustrates any seasonal variances in people's viewing habits. This chart shows the average figure for all episodes shown each month (iris), the lowest rated episode in that month (pupil) and the highest rated (sclera). The segments run clockwise from January to December, with the radius of each segment proportional to the number of viewers. As we've seen, *Doctor Who* has been more commonly shown in the early months, and even on average these gain higher audiences than other times, slowly descending as summer approaches. July and August fare worst, partly from the relative lack of episodes shown then and also that many are repeats which generally get a smaller number of viewers. September's average gets a boost from many season openers being broadcast that month, although October improves on this. The higher minima for June, September and October reflect the lack of repeats in those months, so these are the lower end of first showings. November's is also relatively high in spite of it containing the "Five Faces of Doctor Who" repeat season. The peak of 16.1m viewers in October is thanks to an ITV strike in 1979 that left the BBC the only broadcaster for several weeks, greatly benefitting the start of Season 17. But even without this, the month would score an impressive high of 12m viewers for episode four of "The Hand of Fear" in 1976. The winter and spring months are more even before the fall-off towards summer. June's apparent low peak audience is still a healthy 9.5m for the final part of "The Chase" in 1965, and July only beats it thanks to the final episode of Series 4 slipping into that month and benefitting from a watercooler cliffhanger the week before.

Average, minimum and maximum number of viewers for each episode, including repeats, by year of broadcast *(overleaf)*

This chart shows the viewer numbers grouped for each year of broadcast, rather than the more common Season/Series grouping, and includes repeat showings to indicate which years people were most inclined to watch some *Doctor Who*. The bars are coloured by Doctor, although a year doesn't always fall entirely within one Doctor's reign. For example, the regeneration from the First to Second Doctor occurred mid-1966, but most of that year showed First Doctor episodes so it has been coloured blue rather than green. From this it's clear the First, Fourth and Third Doctors' eras had the greatest audiences, backed up by their years also including many of the most highly viewed individual episodes of all. The Ninth and Tenth Doctors' years follow closely behind, again with some high maximum audiences for the Tenth Doctor Christmas specials. (Note that the 2012 figure doesn't include that year's Christmas special so its maximum figure is lower than for the preceding few years.) It's notable that while 1982 was a good first year for the Fifth Doctor, averaging 8.49m viewers, there's then a drop for the 20th anniversary year — although still ahead of the last two years of the Fourth Doctor's era. After the attempted cancellation in 1985 and long gap between Seasons 22 and 23, *Doctor Who* never regained its previous audience levels as the show dropped in the public's awareness (and was more harshly placed in the television schedules), although it wasn't so far behind the lower reaches of previous years as some would claim. 1992 and 1993 each featured three-month blocks of repeats on BBC2 which, while never likely to reach the viewer numbers of first-run episodes on BBC1, achieved a creditable average of 2.64m and 2.42m viewers respectively. The 4m maximum in 1993 is for an episode of the "Planet of the Daleks" repeat on BBC1, beating the lowest ratings for some late-1980s episodes, suggesting that if even old *Doctor Who* could gain a good audience when scheduled well, new episodes would do even better. Indeed, the TV Movie alone made 1996 the fifth highest year for the show in average viewer numbers, beating all the revived series' averages.

Episodes with the highest and lowest numbers of viewers on first broadcast *(overleaf)*

A rundown of the most and least widely seen episodes of all. The top five, all from the start of Season 17 in 1979, benefit from that ITV strike giving Saturday night viewers less choice of what to watch. Even so, the last is only just ahead of Season 12's "The Ark in Space" episode 2, followed by Season 2's "The Web Planet" episode 1, with further instalments of that story within the top 20. The revived series comes in with the Kylie Minogue-starring Christmas special as eighth most seen episode, with the Tenth Doctor's expected swan song (although it turned out not to be) just 40,000 viewers behind. Over half of the bottom end of the table is comprised of Seventh Doctor stories, when the series was scheduled against top soap opera *Coronation Street*. These include three-quarters of Season 26, giving support to the BBC's decision to end the series.

Average, minimum and maximum number of viewers for each episode, including repeats, by month of broadcast

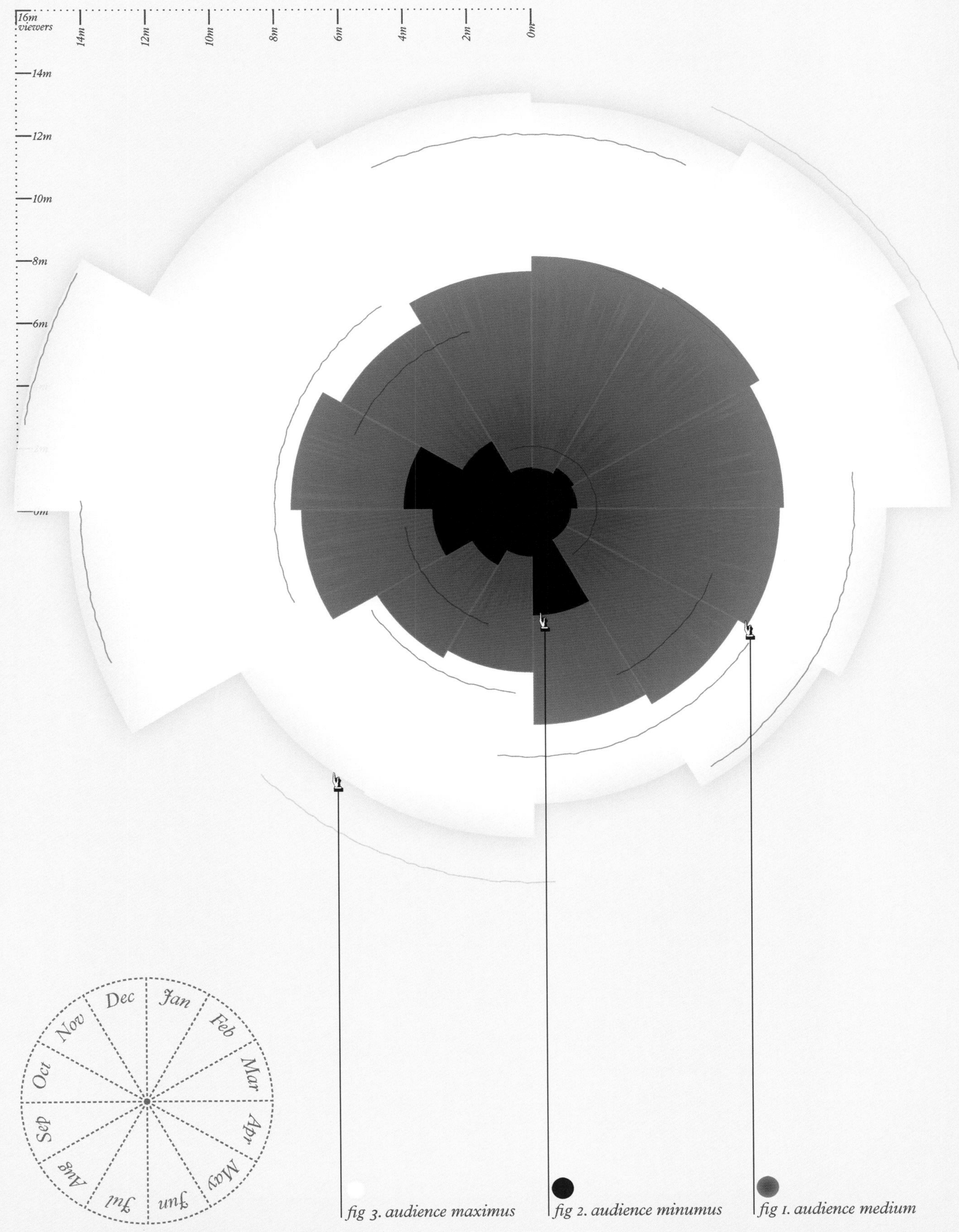

Average, minimum and maximum number of viewers for each episode, including repeats, by year of broadcast

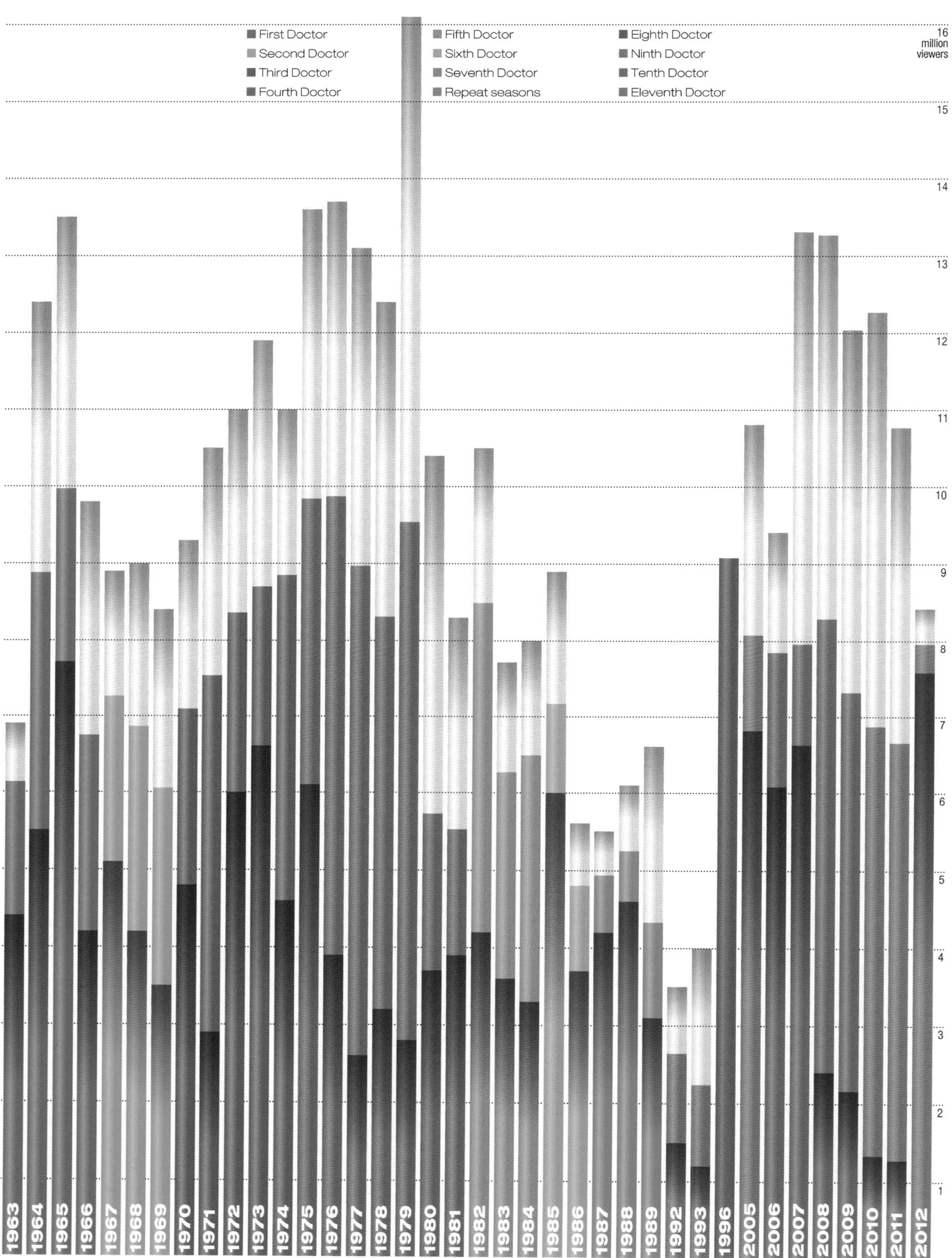

Episodes with the highest and lowest numbers of viewers on first broadcast

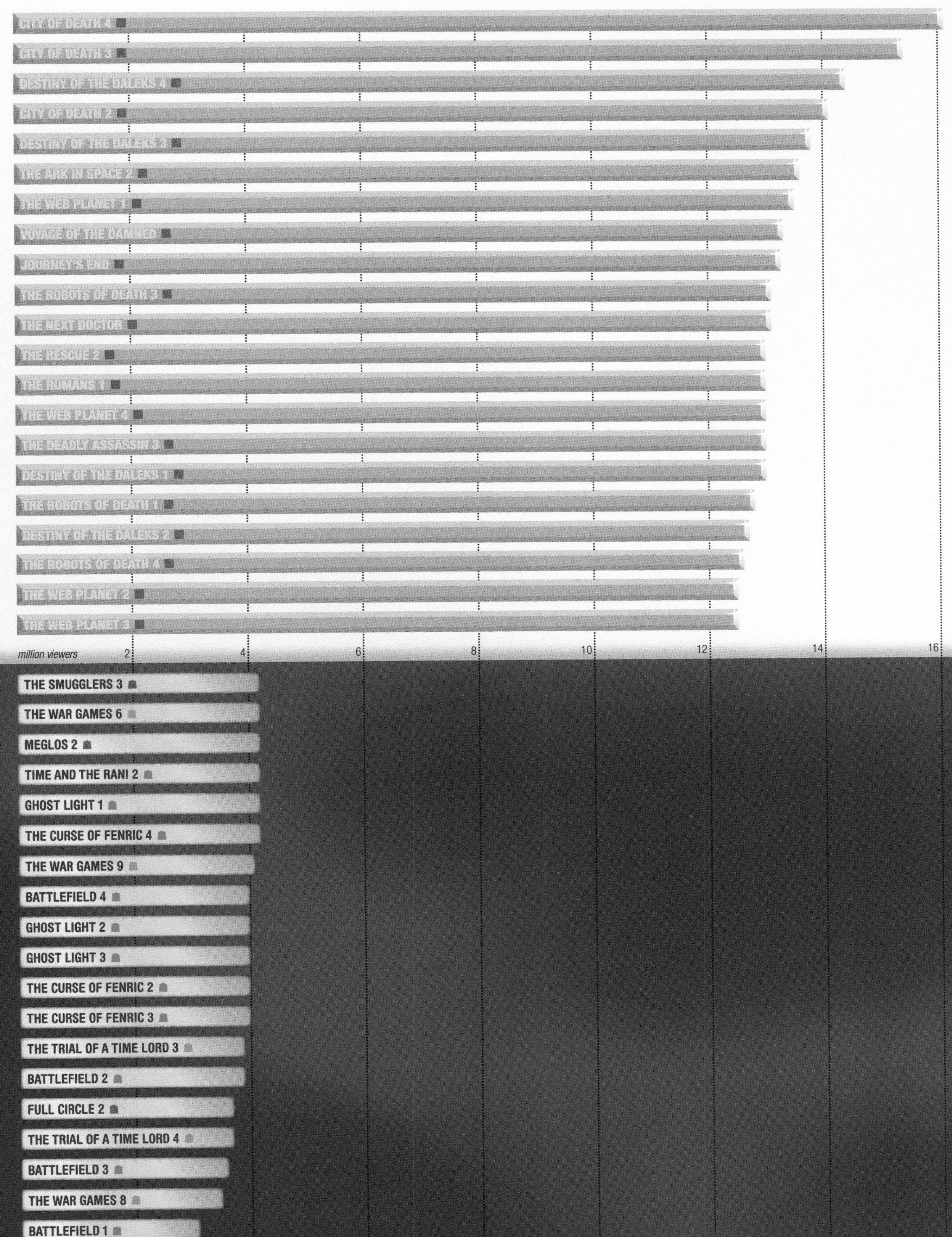
CITY OF DEATH 4
CITY OF DEATH 3
DESTINY OF THE DALEKS 4
CITY OF DEATH 2
DESTINY OF THE DALEKS 3
THE ARK IN SPACE 2
THE WEB PLANET 1
VOYAGE OF THE DAMNED
JOURNEY'S END
THE ROBOTS OF DEATH 3
THE NEXT DOCTOR
THE RESCUE 2
THE ROMANS 1
THE WEB PLANET 4
THE DEADLY ASSASSIN 3
DESTINY OF THE DALEKS 1
THE ROBOTS OF DEATH 1
DESTINY OF THE DALEKS 2
THE ROBOTS OF DEATH 4
THE WEB PLANET 2
THE WEB PLANET 3
million viewers
2
4
6
8
10
12
14
16
THE SMUGGLERS 3
THE WAR GAMES 6
MEGLOS 2
TIME AND THE RANI 2
GHOST LIGHT 1
THE CURSE OF FENRIC 4
THE WAR GAMES 9
BATTLEFIELD 4
GHOST LIGHT 2
GHOST LIGHT 3
THE CURSE OF FENRIC 2
THE CURSE OF FENRIC 3
THE TRIAL OF A TIME LORD 3
BATTLEFIELD 2
FULL CIRCLE 2
THE TRIAL OF A TIME LORD 4
BATTLEFIELD 3
THE WAR GAMES 8
BATTLEFIELD 1

Cumulative changes in weekly audience numbers

We've seen from the average audience sizes for each year how *Doctor Who* has fared over time, but how many viewers come and go over the course of a season? To compare the weekly shifts in viewer numbers, and to see which seasons held on to their starting audiences, which won more viewers and which saw people drift away, the following charts normalise each year's debut episodes to zero and plot the subsequent rises and falls in audience size each week. The revived series are shown opposite, while the original series are presented in groups over the next four pages.

These charts use the official viewing figures for the first broadcast of each episode on BBC1, which for recent years include people who have watched a recording within a week of broadcast, but not BBC iPlayer users. For Series 5 onwards they include viewers watching on BBC HD channels when showing episodes simultaneously to BBC1. Influences on the size of such initial audiences are numerous and hard to catalogue. Not only is the perceived quality of the ongoing series a factor but also things like how well received the previous episode was, what publicity and anticipation has been generated for an episode, how popular the programme scheduled before or after is, the time of day the episode is shown, whether it was delayed by preceding programmes, what was on other channels, whether an episode falls on a bank holiday, and even what the weather is like. Individual rises and falls may be hard to explain without this full context, therefore, but the trend for each season overall can be discerned.

Weekly changes in audience size for Series 1-7a (2005-12)

The top chart opposite plots the cumulative change in each episode's viewer numbers from the previous episode, with the initial episode normalised to zero. The immediate observation is that Series 2 (2006) was the only one to build on its debut audience the next week. Because season openers tend to get a higher rating than later episodes thanks to all the launch publicity, to build on this for the second episode is impressive. Note, however, that this series had the lowest audience for a debut episode, at 8.6m viewers, until 2012's Series 7a (8.3m). However, it was also one of only two seasons to later rise significantly above its initial audience, thanks to the return of the Cybermen in episode five; Series 4's surprise regeneration at the end of episode 12 led to the concluding episode gaining almost two million extra viewers, almost 1.5m above the season's opening episode.

Conversely, Series 1 (2005) had the biggest fall from its opening episode, although this did score a record high of 10.8m viewers owing to anticipation around the return of *Doctor Who* to our screens, a figure not beaten within any other 21st Century season (only by special episodes). The general trend for most of these Series is gradually to dip around the middle before picking up again towards the season finale. Series 3 (2007) bucked this trend the most, with a relatively light dip early on (surprisingly the return of the Daleks gained the second-lowest audience that year) but then a more steady rise to a finale almost as widely seen as its debut. Only Series 1 and 5 (2010) had an overall downward trend, closing with 3-4m viewers fewer than they started with. They had the greatest drop-offs after their opening episodes, however, and each was a new experience for viewers — Series 1 being the first for over 15 years, of course, and Series 5 being the first headed by Steven Moffat and starring Matt Smith.

The bottom graph shows the same cumulative changes, but normalised to each year's second episode, to take out the impact of the opening episodes' typically higher audiences. The relative evenness of Series 3 is clearer here, hovering around the zero line, as are the two halves of Series 6 (2011). Series 1's decline is also seen to be less severe without the huge opening audience, dipping by only a million or so towards the end. Being the only year to raise its audience after the first episode, Series 2's line moves down here, highlighting its mid-season dip.

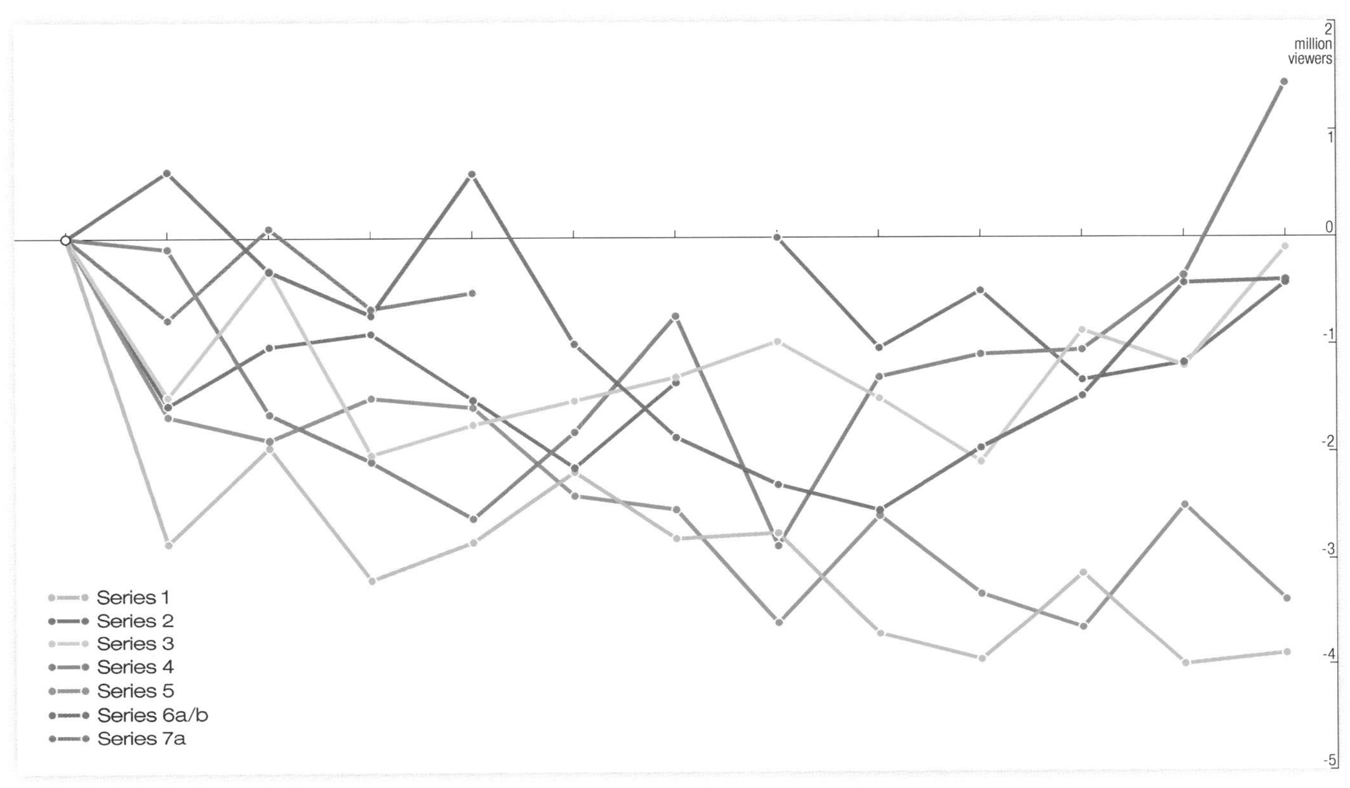

2
million
viewers
1
0
-1
-2
-3
-4
-5
Series 1
Series 2
Series 3
Series 4
Series 5
Series 6a/b
Series 7a

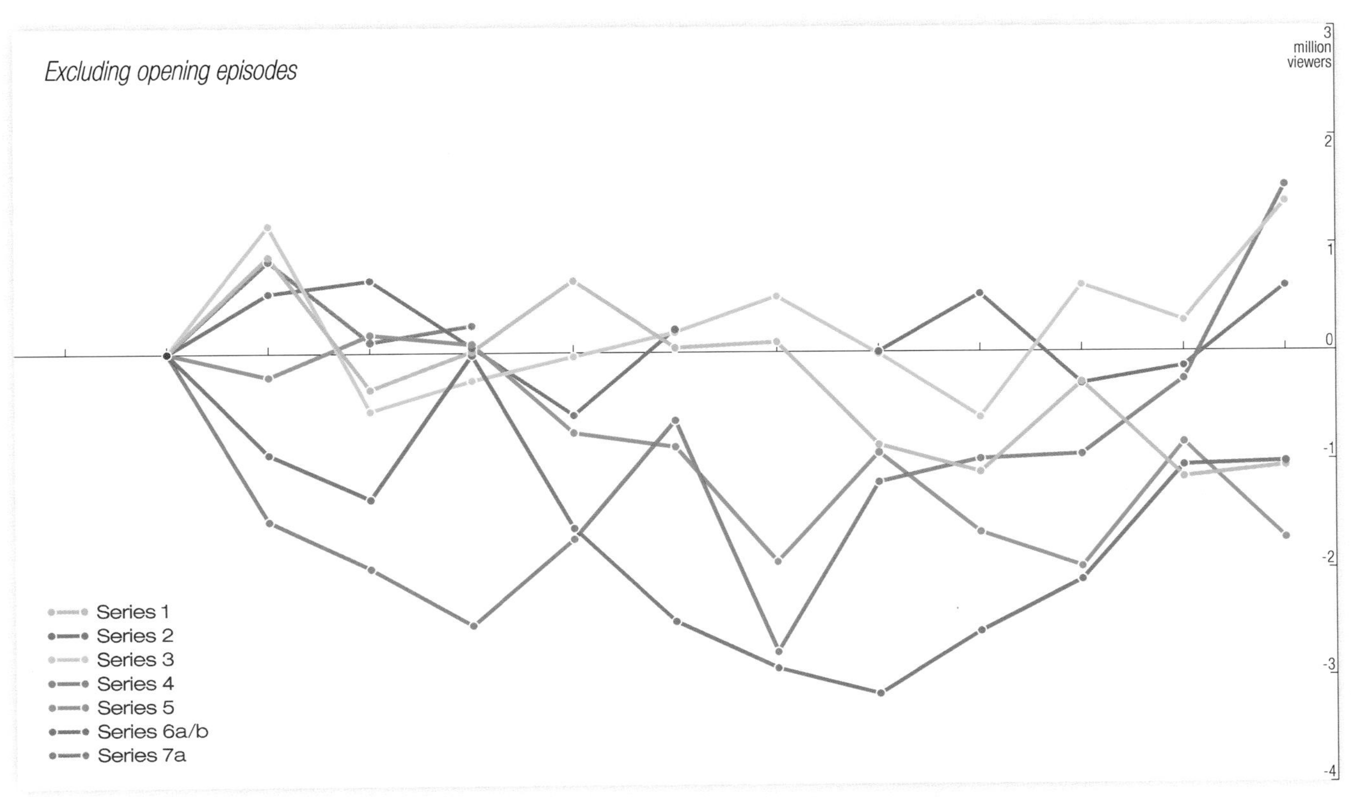

Excluding opening episodes
3
million
viewers
2
1
0
-1
-2
-3
-4
Series 1
Series 2
Series 3
Series 4
Series 5
Series 6a/b
Series 7a

Weekly changes in audience size for Seasons 7-16 (1970-79)

Over the Third Doctor's five years, the seasons got progressively higher ratings on average, but the top chart below shows the variation within that trend. Only two finished above their opening audience, Seasons 8 (1971) and 11 (1973-74), but the former was more consistent, only once dropping below its initial number of viewers. The others gradually declined after early fluctuations, Season 10 (1973) picking up in the middle with the return of the Daleks. The early years of the Fourth Doctor's era show much greater fluctuation, suggesting that while audience sizes were higher overall there were many casual viewers who didn't necessarily watch every week. Season 12 (1975) followed a similar path to the preceding years, but from Season 13 the series moved from a January to an autumn start, which seems to have led to rising audiences as the winter nights drew in. By 1978 things had settled down, with Season 16's figures hovering much closer to its starting audience, although "The Power of Kroll" part 2 picked up 6m viewers on New Year's Eve.

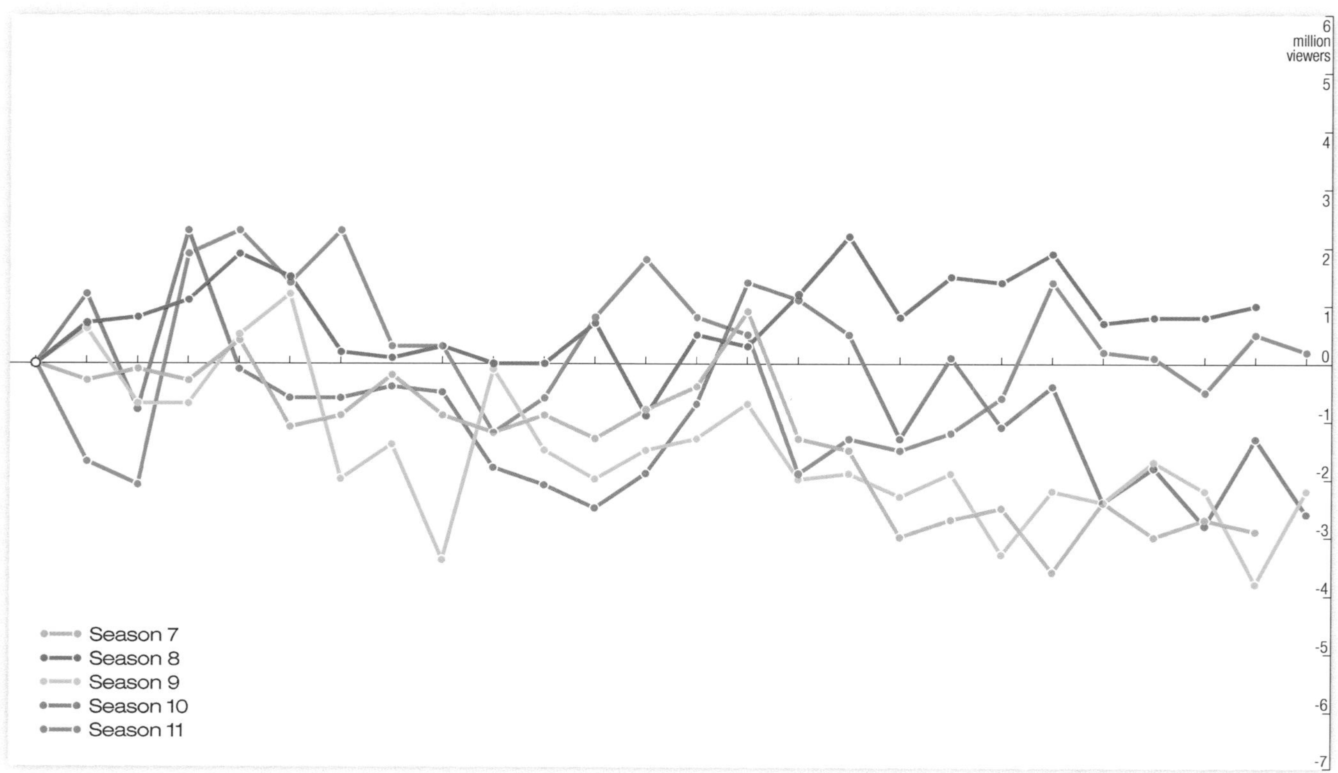

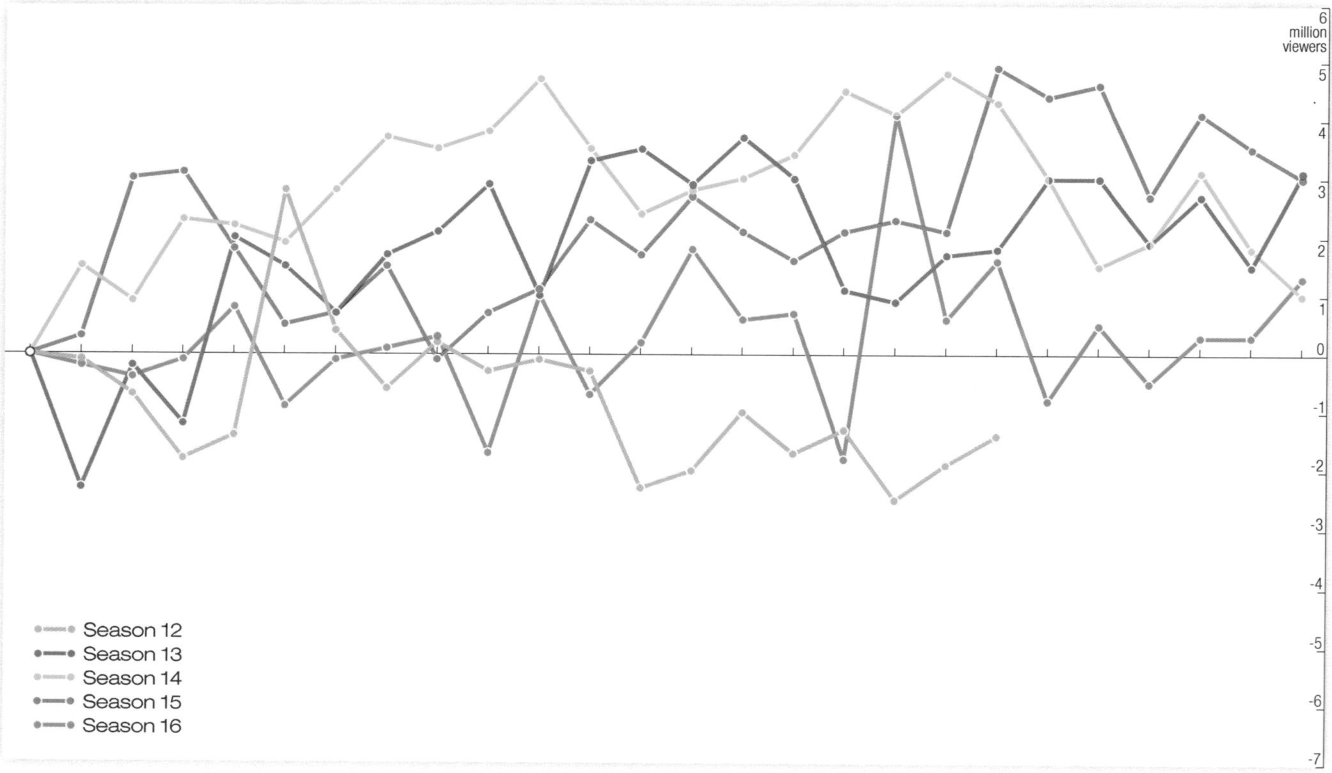

Weekly changes in audience size for Seasons 17-26 (1979-89)

The 1980s saw several changes to the broadcast of *Doctor Who*. While Season 17 (1979-80) initially benefitted from an ITV strike, this just highlights the fall off when ITV programmes returned. "The Horns of Nimon" part 1, shown a few days before Christmas Day, suffered as was seen the previous year. Seasons 19-21 saw the show broadcast two days a week, creating a sawtooth pattern as one day got more viewers than the other. Season 20 (1983) shows this most notably, with episodes on Wednesdays consistently getting more viewers than those on Tuesdays. This is also the most consistent year, the through line only dropping below zero towards the end, as do the figures for the two seasons either side. From 1985 the seasons had fewer episodes. While Season 22 dipped the most, publicity around the threatened cancellation of the series seemed to revive viewers' interest. The post-hiatus seasons were the most consistent of all, suggesting the smaller audience was more dedicated. Season 26 was the only one to see a steady rise throughout.

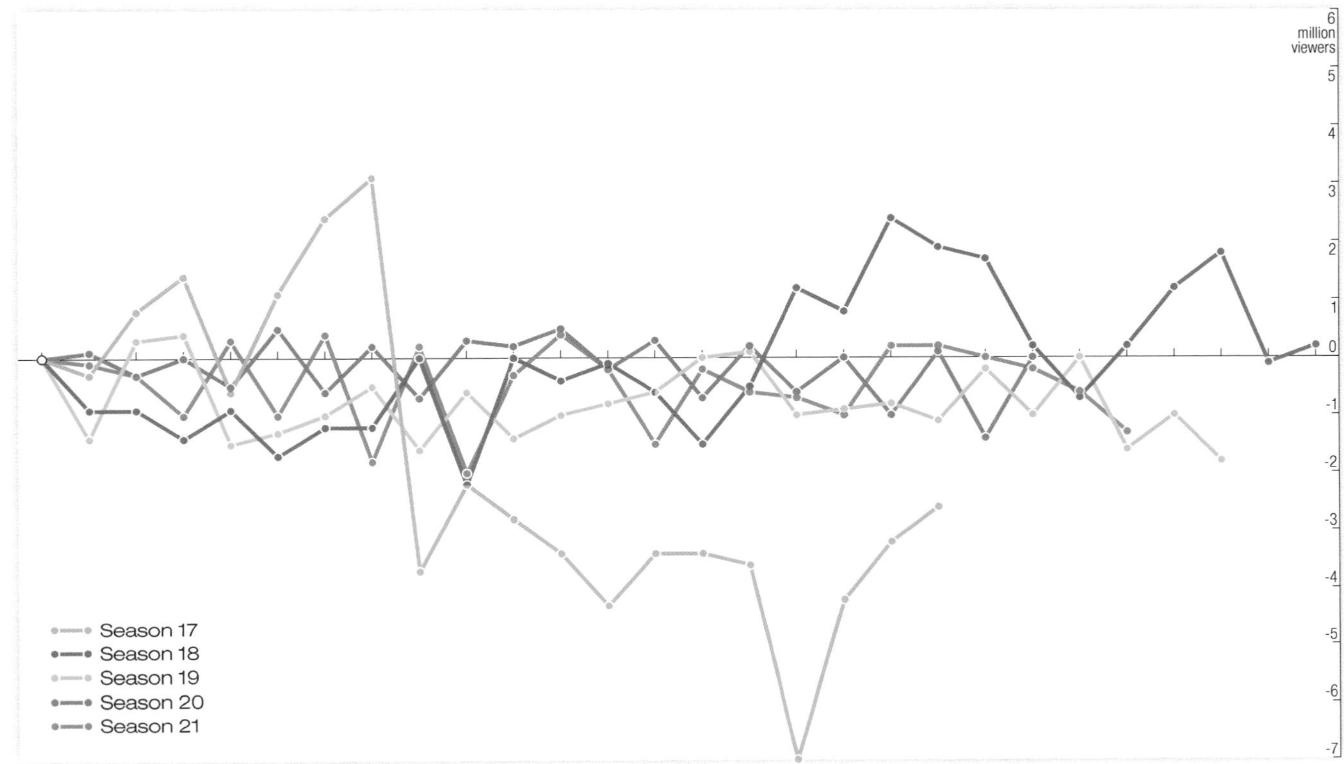

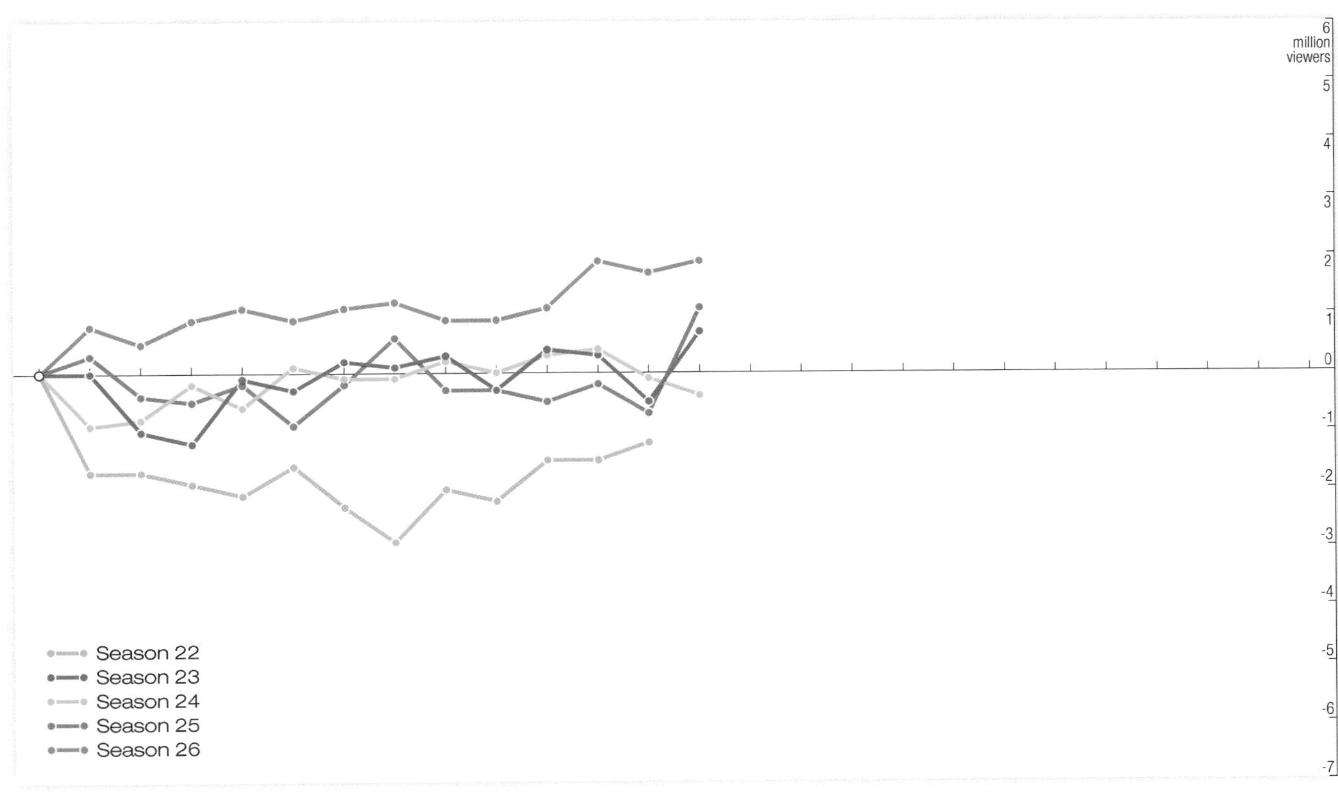

Weekly changes in audience size for Seasons 1-6 (1963-69), aligned by episode number *(top)*

Doctor Who got off to an auspicious start, with viewer numbers rising fast even before the arrival of the Daleks. They were an instant hit, however, and the series held on to its new audience well, only dropping when summer arrived, but even then staying consistent. Season 2 followed a similar pattern, with some of the largest audiences the show ever had, although viewers seemed to tire of antics on "The Web Planet". 1966 saw average audience size drop by a third, and this is clear from the figures for Season 3, losing 3m viewers after "The Daleks' Master Plan" concluded. Season 4 (1966-67) rose more rapidly but from a low start, the First Doctor's regeneration sandwiched between the introduction of the Cybermen and the return of the Daleks seeming to be a popular combination. The rest of that year and Seasons 5 (1967-68) and 6 (1968-69) were more consistent, the former only once dipping below its opening audience size, and the latter only doing so towards the end as the epic ten-part "The War Games" played out over the summer months.

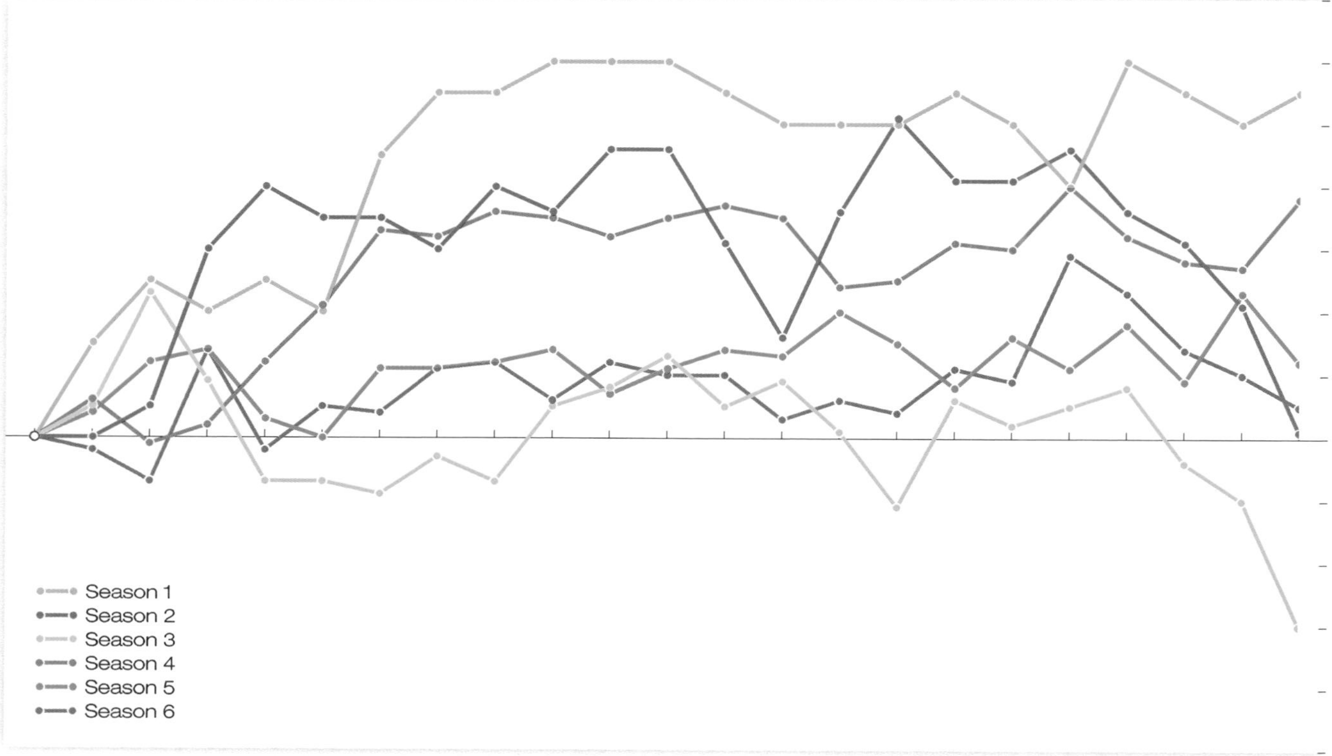

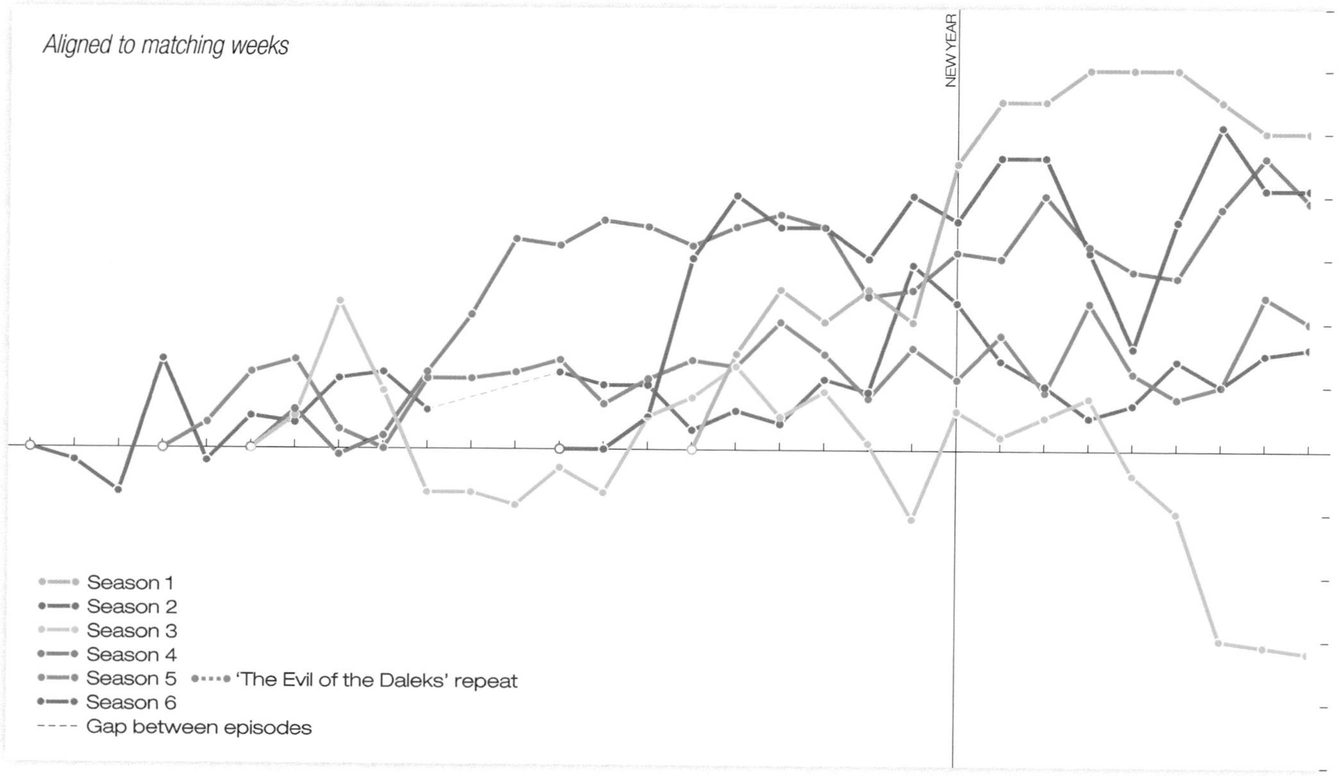

Weekly changes in audience size for Seasons 1-6 (1963-69), aligned by starting week *(bottom)*

Realigning the figures so they match to the week of the year each episode was shown allows for any seasonal variations to become more apparent. The pick-up in Season 4 around the regeneration is seen to come at a time when audiences were otherwise relatively static. Indeed, Seasons 3 and 4, although starting from different levels, go in almost opposite directions throughout their runs, suggesting the introduction of the Second Doctor was a welcome tonic for the programme. Season 2 shows a dip around the end of January most prominently, but it's now clear this is usual for all seasons except the first, riding high on the Dalek effect. Season 6 was the only one to see viewer numbers fall immediately after its debut, but did start earlier than usual, presumably so the two-week break for coverage of the Mexico Olympic Games fell between stories. The repeat of "The Evil of the Daleks" straight after Season 5 saw the audience dip little more than new episodes shown at that time of year, although not helped by a fortnight's break in the middle.

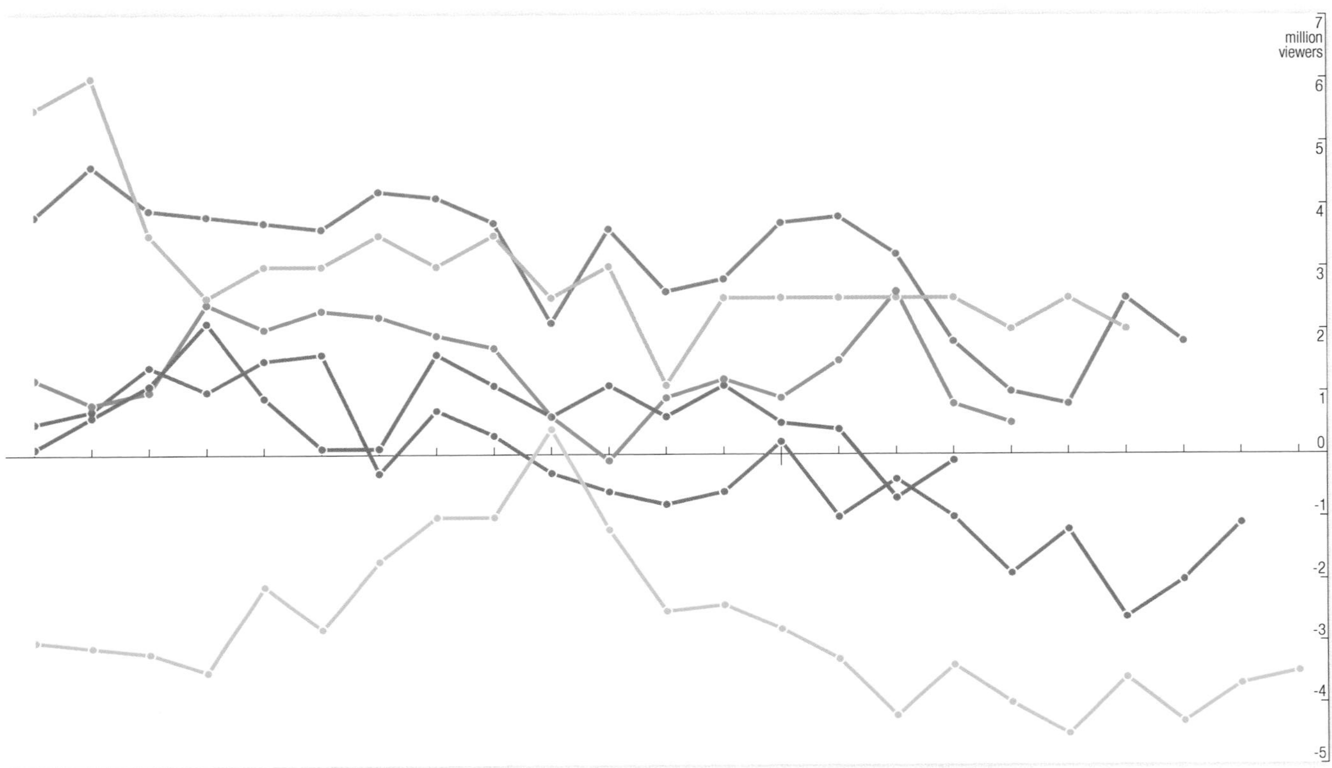

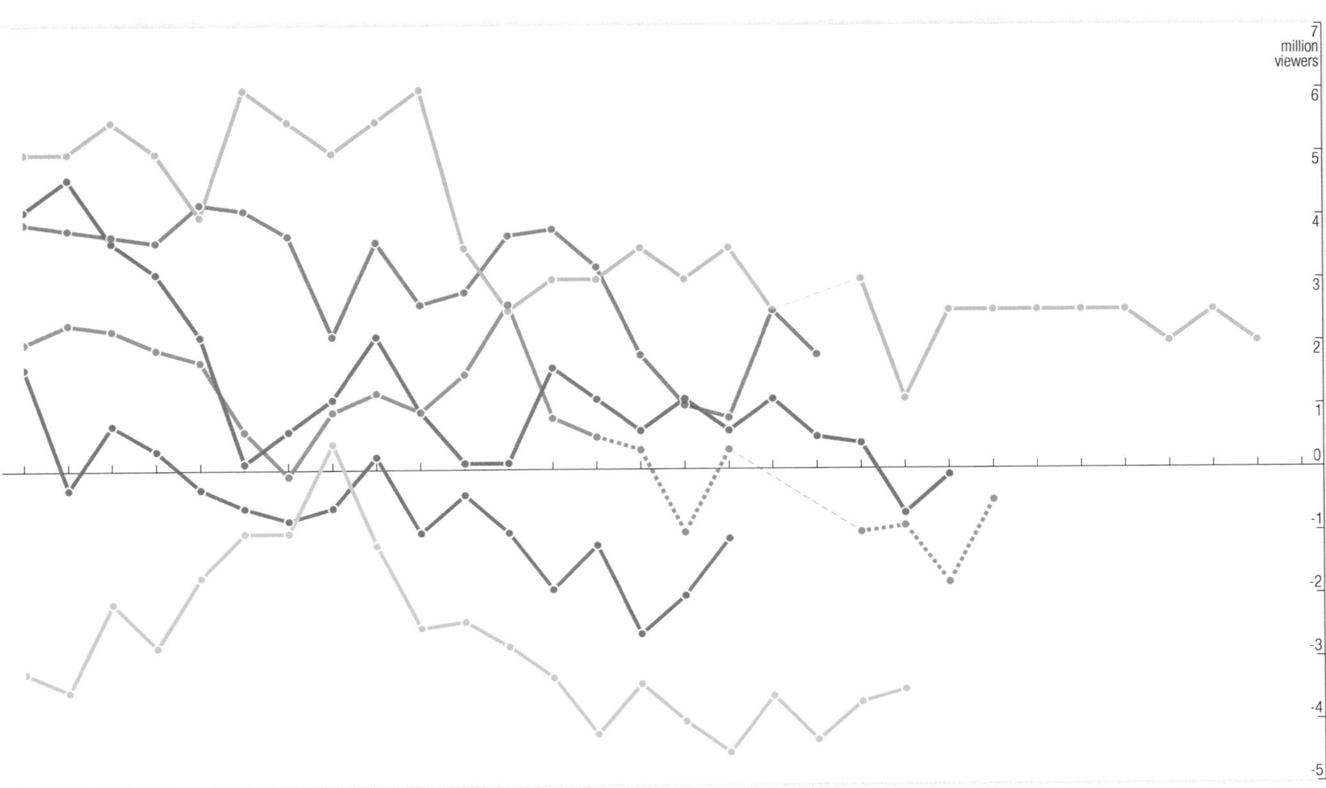

THE HAPPINESS PATROL

Audience appreciation relative to seasonally adjusted viewing figures of 1960s stories, by story type

Viewing figures only tell you how many people watched a programme (or at least were in the room while it was on), not whether they enjoyed what they were seeing. Over time this might become apparent as, obviously, if a majority of viewers dislike a programme the audience size will fall. But even a show with a small audience can be considered successful if those viewers really love it. For this reason the BBC, as well as measuring audience sizes, invites samples of its viewers to fill in more subjective questionnaires about their reactions to programmes, to create an 'audience appreciation index'.

Methods of calculating the index from people's opinions have varied over the years, so figures for the current series of *Doctor Who* aren't directly comparable to those from the original series, but a show's final score is a figure between 0 and 100 (whether expressed as a number or a percentage), so the higher the index, the more the audience enjoyed the programme. Audience appreciation figures weren't recorded for every *Doctor Who* serial, but scores for all the 1960s stories — from Seasons 1 to 6 — are available. As this was the period when, arguably, the programme was at its most inventive, exploring ways of involving the Doctor in different types of story in the days before the audience had a clear idea of what constituted a 'typical' *Doctor Who* adventure, the appreciation scores allow us to see if the 1960s audience had any preference for where the Doctor took them.

In this chart each of the first six seasons' stories has been given an overall 'popularity' score by multiplying the average of its episodes' individual appreciation scores by its average number of viewers. As we have seen, audience sizes vary throughout the year due to factors beyond the perceived quality of programmes, so to even out any seasonal bias each story's total was divided by the average audience size for the month in which it was shown (taken just from *Doctor Who* stories broadcast in the 1960s, so different from the overall monthly averages presented earlier). Where a serial was broadcast across two or more months, this monthly average was calculated in proportion to the number of episodes shown during each month. So a story scores higher if it had a large audience who rated it highly enjoyable, but those shown in the winter months are reduced more than those broadcast in the summer when audiences are generally smaller across all programmes.

The resulting scores were then grouped according to the type of story. This is inevitably a slightly subjective generalisation, although in the early years of the show the production teams deliberately tried to alternate between futuristic science stories and Earth-based historical adventures. The latter are clearest as they occur in defined periods and often feature genuine people from history. "The Time Meddler" has been included among these as it's the historical setting that's key to the story and the science-fiction elements (the Monk's having a TARDIS) are directly related to the time period. On the other hand, "An Unearthly Child" hasn't because, while set in the past after the first episode (although this is not specified on screen), at heart it's about the time-travellers' ability to work together to survive a hostile environment rather than dealing with specific factors of the period they're in.

To categorise the remaining science adventures, they have been split between 'Futuristic', which focus on an advanced setting (whether on an alien planet or in Earth's future), and 'Monster', where the attention is more on the creatures being fought than the situation they're encountered in. This latter therefore includes stories where the 'selling point' is the reappearance of a popular monster, primarily return matches with the Daleks and Cybermen. Those creatures' first appearances, however, are included in the futuristic category as initially they were presented as extensions of the themes of their debut stories.

Finally there are some stories that simply won't be defined. Some, like "The Celestial Toymaker" and "The Mind Robber", occur in imaginary dimensions, whereas "The War Games" begins as though it's a historical but quickly becomes more of a futuristic tale. Beginning with "The War Machines", stories set on contemporary Earth but with a futuristic or alien element became more common. Again these aren't futuristic as such, even if they slightly exaggerate the technology of the time, but don't feature generic monsters.

So was there any preference among 1960s audiences for one type of story over another? As we've seen, the peak in *Doctor Who*'s audience during that decade was its second year, and the stories from this season appear high in each category. However, the huge viewing figures in the months following the return of the Daleks in "The Dalek Invasion of Earth" boost some poorly received stories, such as "The Web Planet", which had an average appreciation index of just 50.2, the second worst of the season. This perhaps explains some of the three million drop-off in viewers for the next serial, "The Crusade". While "The Chase" two stories later had a similarly low audience (relatively — still 9.4m viewers), this was in May/June when the average audience was at its lowest, while its appreciation score was back to an above-average 55.8, making it the third most popular story overall.

There's no doubt that monster and futuristic stories were generally more popular — perhaps not surprising in a series about a time-travelling, face-changing alien. Their average popularity scores differ by only 0.37 points, but are 2.86 points ahead of the Historical category, which itself beats the Other group by 3.98 points (despite the latter having higher maximum and minimum scores). Indeed, the historicals are the most consistently scored for their top two-thirds, and it's only some poor viewing figures and audience appreciation for the late-Season 3 and Season 4 stories — when the programme as a whole was at its lowest ebb in the 1960s — that bring down the category averages. Most stories from this period are in the lower halves of their respective categories, except where popular returning monsters show up again. So perhaps the production team at the time was justified in dropping the historicals in favour of more monster-focused adventures, as evidenced by the consistently scoring stories from the Second Doctor's seasons that make up the bulk of the Monster category. While this has led to the general assumption for the rest of the show's history that it's all about the Doctor fighting monstrous creatures, originally there was much more diversity.

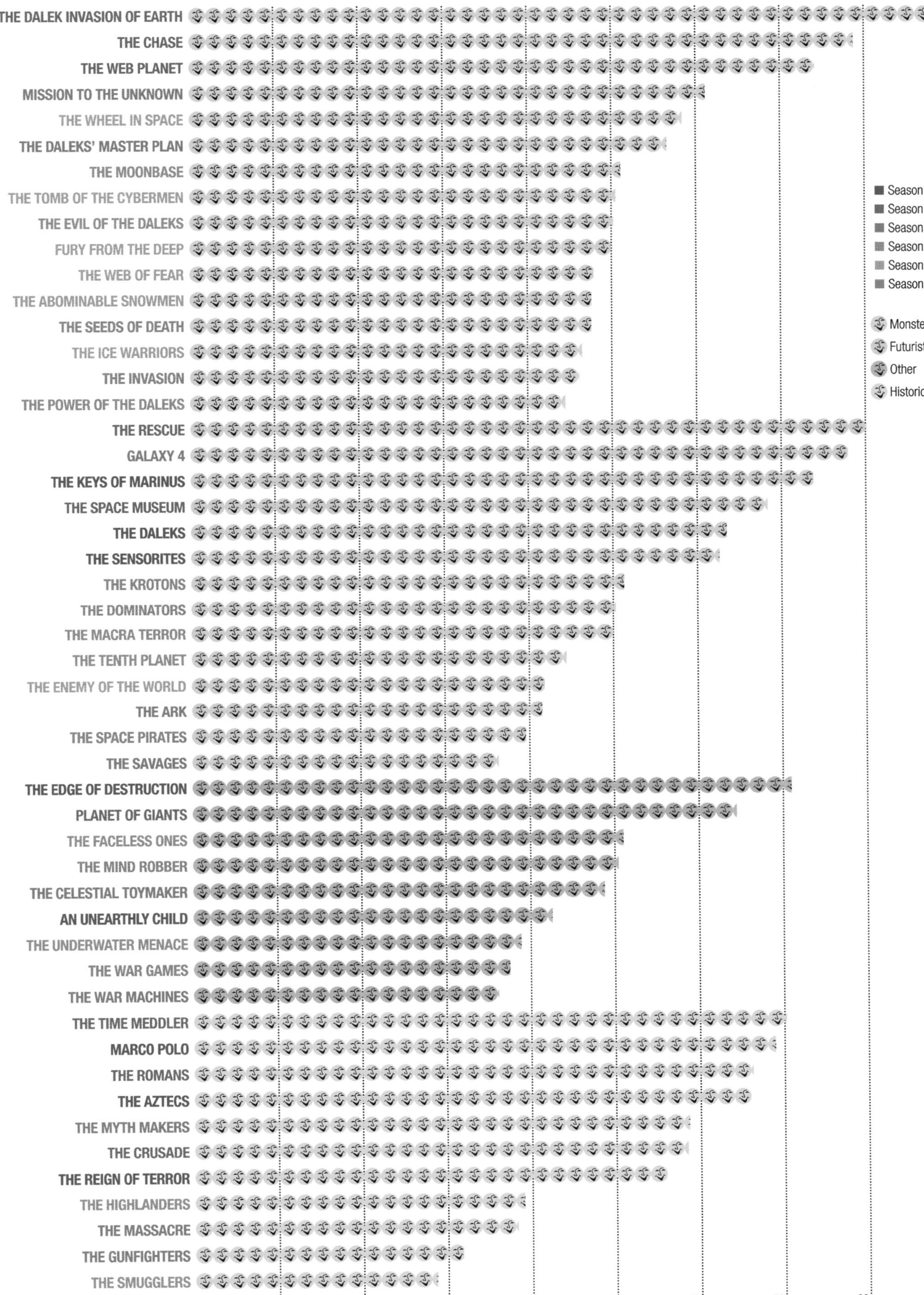

THE DALEK INVASION OF EARTH
THE CHASE
THE WEB PLANET
MISSION TO THE UNKNOWN
THE WHEEL IN SPACE
THE DALEKS' MASTER PLAN
THE MOONBASE
THE TOMB OF THE CYBERMEN
THE EVIL OF THE DALEKS
FURY FROM THE DEEP
THE WEB OF FEAR
THE ABOMINABLE SNOWMEN
THE SEEDS OF DEATH
THE ICE WARRIORS
THE INVASION
THE POWER OF THE DALEKS
THE RESCUE
GALAXY 4
THE KEYS OF MARINUS
THE SPACE MUSEUM
THE DALEKS
THE SENSORITES
THE KROTONS
THE DOMINATORS
THE MACRA TERROR
THE TENTH PLANET
THE ENEMY OF THE WORLD
THE ARK
THE SPACE PIRATES
THE SAVAGES
THE EDGE OF DESTRUCTION
PLANET OF GIANTS
THE FACELESS ONES
THE MIND ROBBER
THE CELESTIAL TOYMAKER
AN UNEARTHLY CHILD
THE UNDERWATER MENACE
THE WAR GAMES
THE WAR MACHINES
THE TIME MEDDLER
MARCO POLO
THE ROMANS
THE AZTECS
THE MYTH MAKERS
THE CRUSADE
THE REIGN OF TERROR
THE HIGHLANDERS
THE MASSACRE
THE GUNFIGHTERS
THE SMUGGLERS
Season 1
Season 2
Season 3
Season 4
Season 5
Season 6
Monster
Futuristic
Other
Historical
10
20
30
40
50
60
70
80

Original audience size versus popularity rating by fans

When gauging the popularity of any particular *Doctor Who* story there are two available measures: the number of people who chose to watch it when it was first broadcast, and the subsequent opinion of dedicated fans. (A third measure would be the audience appreciation index, but these figures aren't available for all episodes.) As we have seen, there are many factors affecting the number of people who decide to sit down and watch an episode of *Doctor Who* at any given showing. So audience size is a very broad guide to how much people like the programme, perhaps better applied to longer timescales than individual serials, but it's the best indicator of the general popularity of the series we have. Fans, on the other hand, like nothing more than debating the pros and cons of stories and scoring them relative to each other. There have been many surveys of story popularity over the years and, while finding two fans who agree on how good a story is is pretty close to impossible, the bigger the survey sample the more accurately an overall opinion can be divined. For this chart, the scores from the Doctor Who Dynamic Rankings site at dewhurstdesigns.co.uk/dynamic were used. This hosts an ongoing survey of fan opinion, with more than 7,300 voters to date. The scores used here were those as of 23 November 2012.

Plotting each story on an axis of average number of viewers versus overall fan rating shows the spread of the programme's popularity. A diagonal joining the minimum and maximum figures on each axis gives a line that can be said to represent agreement between general viewers and fans about their liking of a story, with results above and to the left of this line indicating the audience liked them more than fans do, while those below and to the right are stories fans like more than the public did. An imaginary line moving perpendicular to this would connect stories of equal overall regard, with greater concord between the two audiences the closer the story is to the diagonal.

Not unexpectedly, more stories fall below the diagonal, indicating they're more highly appreciated by fans than their original broadcast audience size suggests they were by the general public. This is clearly demonstrated by the fans' highest rated story (by some margin), 2007's "Blink", which was originally seen by a below-average 6.62m viewers on broadcast. 1965's "The Web Planet" (closest to the upper left corner of the chart), on the other hand, was seen by an impressive 12.5m people when first shown but is the 12th lowest rated story by fans, with a score of 4.71 out of 10. Conversely, only 4.63m people chose to watch 1987's "Time and the Rani" when it was shown, a story now ranked second worst by fans, making it the least loved story from all of *Doctor Who*. Most loved is 1979's "City of Death", ranked 10th by fans and viewed on broadcast by 14.5m people. This was helped by a strike blanking out ITV at the time, but it's still comforting to fans to know that one of their most respected stories was seen by so many people. More balanced is the result for 1977's "The Robots of Death", the next most loved story and much closer to the diagonal, viewed by 12.73m people and ranked 18th by fans with a score of 7.94. Close behind, but slipping into the 'preferred by fans' side of the chart, is 1976's "The Deadly Assassin", ranked slightly higher by fans at 17th with a score of 7.95 but seen by 12.18m people on broadcast.

Other stories sitting on or very close to the diagonal are, from top right to bottom left: 1982's "The Visitation" (9.78m viewers/6.6 fan score); 1972's "Day of the Daleks" (9.6m/6.66); 2008's "Partners in Crime" (9.14m/6.36); 1977's "The Sun Makers" (8.83m/6.25); 1967's "The Macra Terror" (8.2m/5.87); 1985's "Attack of the Cybermen" (8.05m/5.86); 2005's "The Long Game" (8.01m/5.87); the same year's "Aliens of London/World War Three" (7.81m/5.73); 2007's "The Lazarus Experiment" (7.19m/5.48); 1983's "Arc of Infinity" (7.15m/5.31); 2007's "Daleks in Manhattan/Evolution of the Daleks" (6.83m/5.25); 1983's "The King's Demons" (6.5m/4.99); 1966's "The Gunfighters" (6.25m/5.0); and 1987's "Delta and the Bannermen" (5.27m/4.45).

Assessing the results by Doctor, while all have most of their stories falling on the 'preferred by fans' side, the First and Fourth are most evenly split either side of the diagonal (although widely spread), corresponding to the two periods of the programme when viewing figures were at their highest. Most closely clustered along the diagonal are the Third, Fifth and Sixth Doctors. The Third Doctor only has one result straying far from the consensus line, 1970's "Inferno", which is rated highly by fans with a score of 7.99 (ranked 14th) but was seen on broadcast by just 5.57m viewers. The Fifth Doctor has a similar fan favourite in 1984's "The Caves of Androzani" — ranked third with a fan score of 8.42 but with viewing figures in line with the rest of the stories that year — but also a story that's way over into the 'preferred by audience' side: 1982's "Time-Flight" was seen by 9m viewers on broadcast but is generally disliked by fans, scoring just 4.26, putting it fifth from the bottom of their rankings. The Second, Ninth and Eleventh Doctors' stories all fall very close to each other, largely clustered in the region between 7m and 9m viewers with fan scores of 6-8. Of the two last, only season openers and Christmas specials fall significantly outside this area.

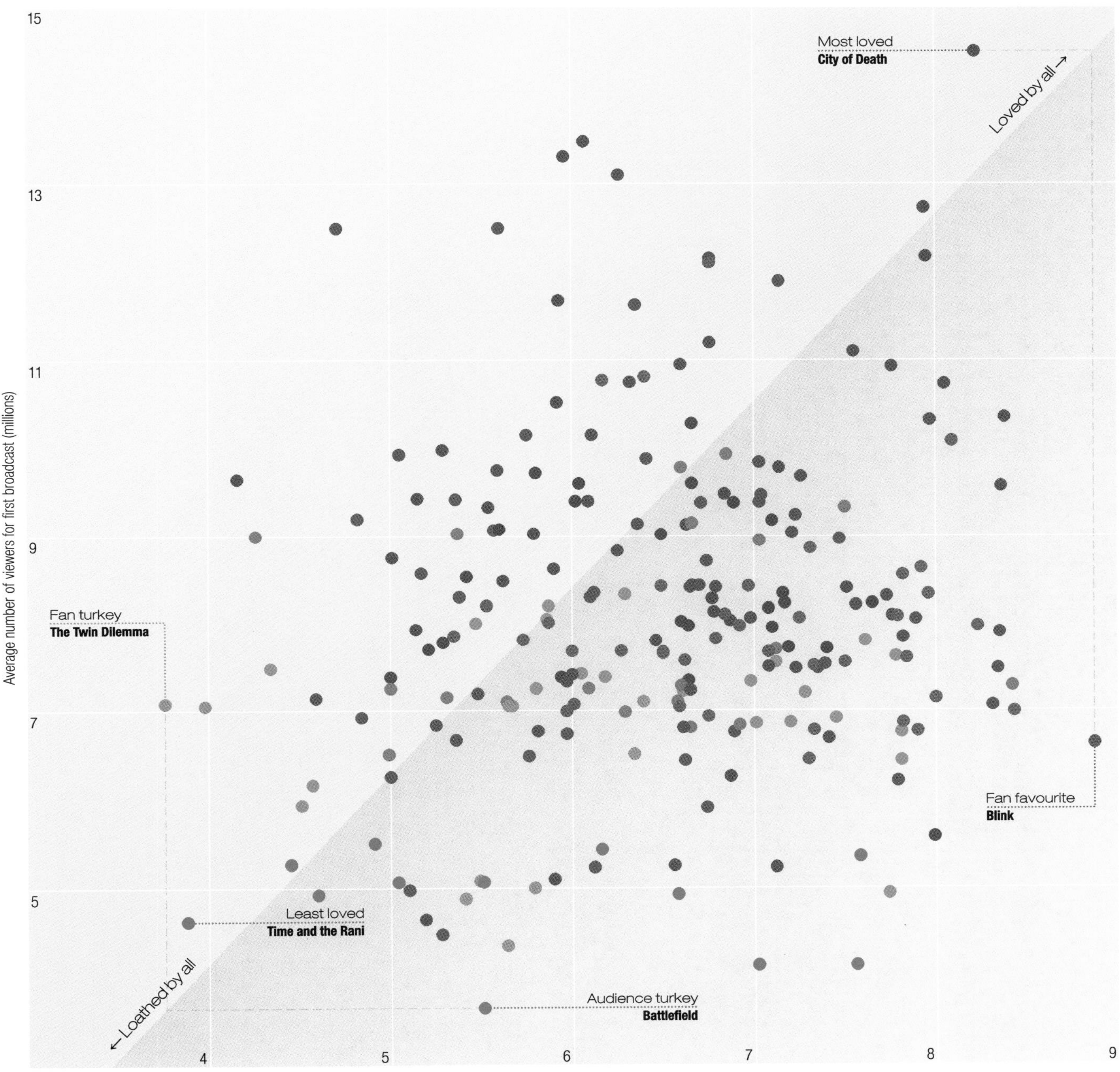

Most loved
City of Death
Loved by all
Fan turkey
The Twin Dilemma
Fan favourite
Blink
Least loved
Time and the Rani
Loathed by all
Audience turkey
Battlefield
Average number of viewers for first broadcast (millions)
15
13
11
9
7
5
4
5
6
7
8
9
Score from online Dynamic Rankings (out of 10)
General audience liked more than fans
Fans like more than general audience
First Doctor
Second Doctor
Third Doctor
Fourth Doctor
Fifth Doctor
Sixth Doctor
Seventh Doctor
Eighth Doctor
Ninth Doctor
Tenth Doctor
Eleventh Doctor

REITERATION

THE RETURN

Average ratings for repeat broadcasts of *Doctor Who* episodes on BBC1 and BBC2, by year and number of stories

In contrast to today's television landscape, where 24-hour schedules are cheaply filled with repeats of past shows, in the 1960s and 1970s when there were only three or four channels, reshowings of even popular programmes were a rarity. Not only did repeats require extra payments from the broadcasters to the people who appeared in them (as actors' union Equity feared they might do its members out of new work), they were often criticised by viewers, who felt they should be getting new programmes to watch. The culture at the time was that if you wanted to see a particular show you had better catch it on broadcast as it was likely never to be seen again.

Doctor Who fans were more accepting of repeats; indeed, they welcomed them. Another chance to see an adventure you only half-remembered from a recent season — or worse, had unavoidably missed an episode of — was a thrilling event that didn't occur often enough. In fact, *Doctor Who*'s earliest repeated episode was its first. The BBC decided that as the show had launched amid the turmoil following US President John F Kennedy's assassination the day before, plus being hit by a widespread power outage (another more common feature of the 1960s and 1970s), it didn't get the attention they had hoped for and so "An Unearthly Child" part 1 was repeated ahead of the second episode, "The Cave of Skulls". It gained 1.6m more viewers than the initial broadcast the week before.

Another repeat wasn't forthcoming for five years, however. In the mid-1960s Dalek creator Terry Nation withdrew the BBC's rights to use the creatures as he tried to launch them in their own series in the US. "The Evil of the Daleks" broadcast at the end of Season 4 in May-July 1967 was therefore presented as the final Dalek story, with their seeming destruction from civil war (engineered by the Doctor, of course). So that the following season wouldn't be completely Dalek-less, however, the serial was chosen to be repeated during the gap between Seasons 5 and 6. This move was so unusual that the showing was actually tied into the narrative of the preceding story. At the end of "The Wheel in Space", the Doctor warns Zoe, who has stowed away aboard the TARDIS, of the dangers she might face by presenting his "thought patterns" on a screen — that is, the video of "The Evil of the Daleks". The following week, the repeat of episode one began with an extra voiceover by the Doctor and Zoe to explain the opening scene, and Season 6's first story, "The Dominators", began the week after the Dalek serial concluded with the Doctor tired from his mental efforts.

With the boom in popularity of *Doctor Who* during the 1970s, it became common practice to repeat a few episodes between seasons, often at Christmas. The first was a repeat of the Third Doctor's opening story, "Spearhead from Space", a couple of weeks after the close of Season 8, followed at Christmas by a reshowing of that season's concluding story, "The Dæmons", edited from five episodes into a 90-minute omnibus edition. This became a regular feature, with omnibus versions of "The Sea Devils", "The Green Death", "Planet of the Spiders" and "Genesis of the Daleks" shown in the weeks between Christmas and New Year of 1972-75 respectively. Also slotted in were a late-summer 1973 omnibus repeat of "Day of the Daleks", a further unscheduled repeat of the "Sea Devils" omnibus in 1974 (when cricket coverage was hit by industrial action), and an omnibus of "The Ark in Space" ahead of the launch of Season 13 in 1975.

From 1976 it was usual to repeat a story or two from the previous run in the summer gap between seasons, either with the episodes edited together into a 'feature' length but not cut, or individually as originally shown. In the case of the "Five Doctors" repeat in 1984, the original 90-minute special was shown in four parts as it had been overseas. These repeats only ceased after *Doctor Who* was suspended in 1985.

The biggest chance to see old episodes on television again came in autumn 1981 when producer John Nathan-Turner secured a five-week run on BBC2 to bridge the longer than usual gap between Seasons 18 and 19. Billed as "The Five Faces of Doctor Who", this was the first time past Doctors' stories had been reshown, and a rare outing for black-and-white episodes ten years after the introduction of colour. Limited to four-part stories (from what was then available in the archive) and wanting to feature all the Doctors, Nathan-Turner chose "An Unearthly Child", "The Krotons", "Carnival of Monsters", "The Three Doctors" and "Logopolis" for broadcast. With good publicity and a teatime slot, this was a popular outing, as the rise of home video was beginning to make audiences appreciate the ability to revisit past programmes. It was such a success that the following summer more space was given to 'out-of-time' *Doctor Who* repeats, with omnibus editions of "The Curse of Peladon", "Genesis of the Daleks" and "Earthshock".

With no new *Doctor Who* after 1989's Season 26, the next batch of repeats on BBC2 were a welcome relief from the drought. Kicked off with a specially made half-hour documentary, *Resistance is Useless*, these again presented one story from each Doctor: "The Time Meddler", "The Mind Robber" and "The Sea Devils" in early 1992, and "Genesis of the Daleks" (again!), "The Caves of Androzani", "Revelation of the Daleks" and "Battlefield" in early 1993. The series' anniversary in 1992 was celebrated with a showing of the freshly recolourised "The Dæmons", and its 30th birthday the year after saw a return to BBC1 with a repeat of "Planet of the Daleks", each episode preceded by a five-minute look at different aspects of the show.

With the release of stories on home video ramping up in the 1990s, and satellite television channels showing old programmes, *Doctor Who* fans had more chances than ever to see past adventures. The American-made TV Movie didn't lead to a series but got a repeat on BBC2 in November 1999 as part of *Doctor Who Night*. It was intended to follow this with a full run of colour story repeats at weekday teatimes, beginning with "Spearhead from Space". Sadly audiences were poor and after "The Silurians" the run skipped ahead to "Genesis of the Daleks", but this failed to drum up extra viewers. Full audience figures for these last two aren't available so in the chart they are represented by the average of the episodes that do have figures.

These days, with multiple channels and online catch-up services, missing an episode of *Doctor Who* seems impossible and repeats on BBC3 are numerous (at least of New Series episodes). As such, repeats on BBC1 are afforded only to special episodes. The 2007 Christmas special, "Voyage of the Damned" starring Kylie Minogue, was shown again in the New Year, while the high audience for the Series 4 finale led to a speedy repeat of its two episodes. Further repeats have been restricted to Christmas specials, including all of those to date following the 2010 special "A Christmas Carol".

The chart shows the average audience for repeat showings for each year they were shown, in chronological order. The width of the bars is proportional to the total number of episodes repeated that year, with omnibus editions counted as one episode.

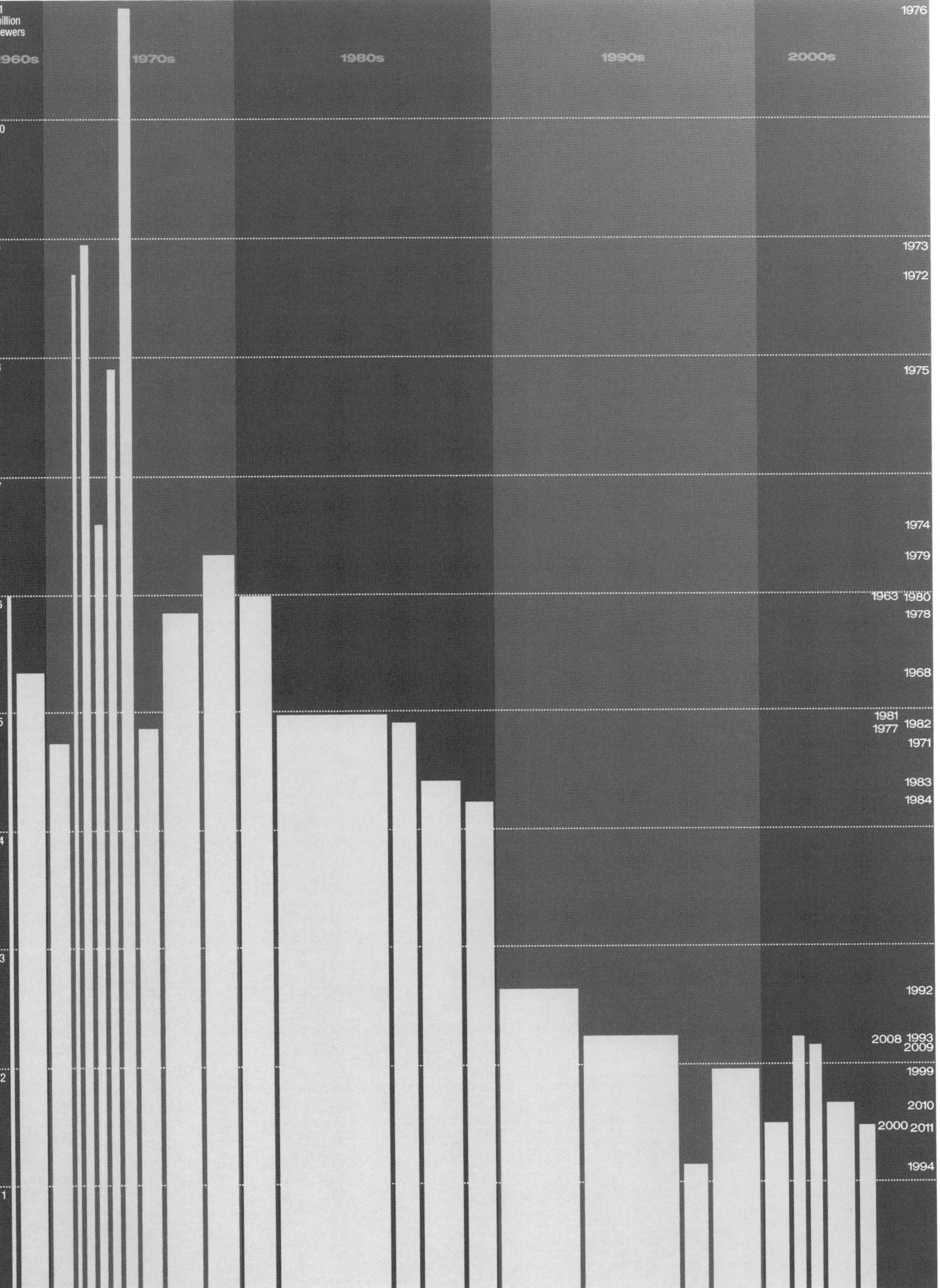

11
million
viewers
1960s
1970s
1980s
1990s
2000s
10
9
8
7
6
5
4
3
2
1
1976
1973
1972
1975
1974
1979
1963 1980
1978
1968
1981
1977 1982
1971
1983
1984
1992
2008 1993
2009
1999
2010
2000 2011
1994

THE EXPLODING PLANET

Countries that broadcast *Doctor Who* in the 20th Century, by number of stories shown

While repeats of *Doctor Who* on UK television were few and far between in the pre-digital age, the series was re-broadcast around the world in more than 70 countries. By the time *Doctor Who* started, the BBC was commonly selling its programmes to overseas broadcasters, either directly through its Television Enterprises department (later BBC Enterprises, now BBC Worldwide) in London or subsidiary offices in Toronto and Sydney, or via regional distributors such as Television International Enterprises, which supplied broadcasters in Africa, the Middle East and the Caribbean; Time Life Films/ Television, which marketed programmes to the Americas; and Overseas Rediffusion, whose clients included South-East Asian broadcasters.

Because different countries used different television systems of varying levels of technical sophistication, it was simpler, cheaper and more reliable to supply programmes on film rather than videotape. For this reason BBC Enterprises regularly 'telerecorded' programmes, whereby the picture was shown on a special large, flat monitor to which was synched a film camera. *Doctor Who* was telerecorded onto 16mm black-and-white film from the start until near the end of the Third Doctor's era, by which time providing overseas broadcasters with colour videotape was much more viable. Positive copies of the telerecorded film negatives would then be sent to countries that bought the rights to show the programme and, after an agreed time or number of broadcasts, were destroyed, returned to BBC Enterprises or passed on to another country that had negotiated to transmit the show. This meant Enterprises didn't necessarily have to strike a new print for every broadcaster that bought the show but could reuse copies already in circulation or which had previously been returned. So although "An Unearthly Child", for example, was sold to 34 countries in the ten years after its UK broadcast, it's unlikely anywhere near that number of copies were made. Then again, larger countries such as Australia may have been sent or made their own duplicate copies for distribution to regional television stations. Without full records, it's impossible to know how many copies of each story there were.

Australia was one of the earliest and most consistent buyers of *Doctor Who*, first showing the series from January 1965 and going on to broadcast all but two of the original series stories. This was actually key to the programme's showing in Asia and New Zealand as a major broadcaster like ABC in Australia could afford the initial clearance fees necessary to show the episodes. These were generally applied to a region rather than one country, so once ABC had bought a serial other broadcasters in the same region could purchase it at a much lower price. This meant if the Australian broadcaster rejected a story, it was effectively unavailable to the rest of the region as other broadcasters were unable or unwilling to pay the full clearance fees. Nonetheless, the first overseas broadcaster to show *Doctor Who* was NZBC in New Zealand, which bought the first three stories and showed them from September 1964. These were given a 'Y' rating by the country's television censors, which meant they couldn't be shown before 7.30pm; subsequently NZBC decided it preferred to show the programme earlier (and maybe wasn't keen on paying the initial clearance fees) and so didn't buy any more until the late-1960s, by which time Australia had bought and shown later stories, making them cheaper for NZBC to purchase. Even then it only broadcast those which received a 'G' rating, which meant many serials were omitted if they couldn't be suitably cut. Australia's censors also required occasional cuts to make the programme suitable for a young audience, and ironically the removed material was kept long after the episodes themselves had been destroyed, making these short snippets all that survives from many 1960s episodes.

The other major buyers of *Doctor Who* were Canada and the US, although they didn't pick up the programme until the 1970s and only later showed the earlier stories. (Canada had bought the first seven stories in 1965 but dropped the series after showing only five.) Other countries that had significant periods of showing *Doctor Who* were Gibraltar, the Arab Emirates of Abu Dhabi and Dubai, Hong Kong and Singapore.

This map shows which countries broadcast original-series episodes of *Doctor Who* before 2000. The size of each disc is relative to the number of stories shown, and the colouring indicates which Doctors' eras these covered. Note that these bands are sized relative to the radius of the disc, not its area, with the least-shown Doctors in the centre and the most-shown at the edge. Visually this favours those Doctors who had more episodes shown in the country to highlight which are most likely to be remembered by viewers. As Australia, Canada, New Zealand and the US showed most (surviving) episodes from all eight 20th Century Doctors, their discs have not been colour coded. Although BBC Enterprises sales records have been examined by various researchers over the years, they are not always complete nor even consistent. The broken circles indicate where there is some evidence the country bought *Doctor Who* but either it's inconclusive or searches of local newspaper listings have given no proof the episodes were actually shown.

The two main periods of overseas sales — the early First Doctor and Fourth Doctor stories — are clear (also see next chart, overleaf). The former are predominantly in the Caribbean, Africa and the Middle East, plus Hong Kong, Singapore and Thailand in the Far East. The later sale of Fourth Doctor stories to American broadcasters through Time Life also opened up markets in Central and South America, as well as Brunei and the United Arab Emirates. The cluster of European countries showing Fourth Doctor stories, plus Saudi Arabia and South Korea, came later after the BBC's surviving archive of episodes had been collated and offered for sale in the mid-1980s. The Second Doctor got most exposure in parts of Africa plus Hong Kong and Singapore, whereas the Third Doctor's appearances in Guam, the Philippines and Saudi Arabia were probably off the back of Time Life's deal with US television stations, which also supplied US Air Force bases. The 1980s Doctors had far less distribution, the Fifth only showing in the Netherlands and ever-faithful Gibraltar, plus later in the UAE, while the sale of the Seventh Doctor stories to Germany led to it later showing the Sixth Doctor's era.

For comprehensive information on the sale of Doctor Who *overseas, visit broadwcast.org, from which data used here was derived*

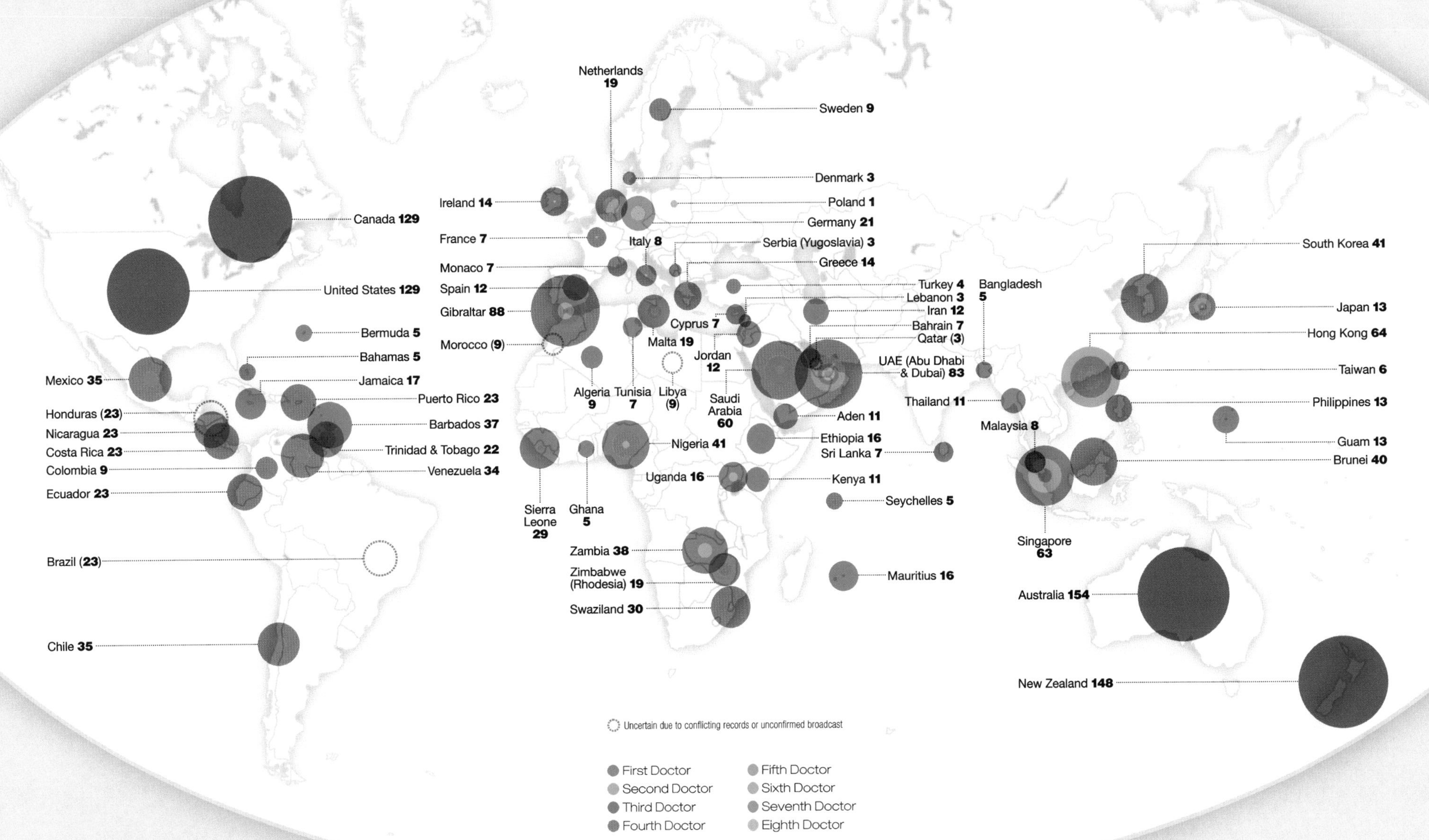

Netherlands 19
Sweden 9
Denmark 3
Poland 1
Germany 21
Serbia (Yugoslavia) 3
Greece 14
Canada 129
Ireland 14
France 7
Italy 8
Monaco 7
Spain 12
Gibraltar 88
Morocco (9)
United States 129
Bermuda 5
Bahamas 5
Mexico 35
Jamaica 17
Puerto Rico 23
Honduras (23)
Barbados 37
Nicaragua 23
Costa Rica 23
Trinidad & Tobago 22
Colombia 9
Venezuela 34
Ecuador 23
Brazil (23)
Chile 35
Turkey 4
Lebanon 3
Iran 12
Cyprus 7
Bahrain 7
Qatar (3)
Malta 19
Jordan 12
UAE (Abu Dhabi & Dubai) 83
Algeria 9
Tunisia 7
Libya (9)
Saudi Arabia 60
Aden 11
Ethiopia 16
Sri Lanka 7
Nigeria 41
Uganda 16
Kenya 11
Seychelles 5
Sierra Leone 29
Ghana 5
Zambia 38
Zimbabwe (Rhodesia) 19
Swaziland 30
Mauritius 16
Bangladesh 5
Thailand 11
Malaysia 8
Singapore 63
South Korea 41
Japan 13
Hong Kong 64
Taiwan 6
Philippines 13
Guam 13
Brunei 40
Australia 154
New Zealand 148
Uncertain due to conflicting records or unconfirmed broadcast
First Doctor
Second Doctor
Third Doctor
Fourth Doctor
Fifth Doctor
Sixth Doctor
Seventh Doctor
Eighth Doctor

A HOLIDAY FOR THE DOCTOR

Number of countries each *Doctor Who* story was broadcast in during the 20th Century, by region

We've looked at where around the world *Doctor Who* was shown, but which Doctors and stories were most widely seen? This chart lists each 20th Century story with a dot for every country in which it was broadcast. These are coloured by region, with the four key markets — Australia, Canada, New Zealand and the US — getting their own colours, while other countries are grouped into the six main territories in which the series was sold. Solid dots represent overseas showings during the episodes' original sales period (usually within five or ten years of their original offering by BBC Television Enterprises), while rings indicate countries that bought the stories when they were offered again after the BBC's archive holdings of the series were first collated in the early 1980s. For stories originally broadcast in the UK after around 1984, a ring indicates a country that has bought the story as 'back catalogue', having already shown later stories. Filled paler rings denote a country that documents suggest probably showed *Doctor Who* but for which corroboratory evidence, such as contemporary programme listings in local newspapers, has not yet been found.

Most immediately obvious are the two periods when the series was most widely sold: the early First Doctor stories and the early Fourth Doctor stories. The colouring also makes it easy to see where these showings were: in the former case, predominantly African countries, along with the Caribbean and the Middle East, while the latter's sales were initially to Central and South American countries (although exactly how many is unclear), boosted by further sales in Europe in the late-1980s. Conversely, the Third Doctor era saw most sales to Asia, alongside the US's first purchases of the series.

Some of the variations in early overseas sales of *Doctor Who* can be tied to the batches in which episodes were offered, although a buyer didn't have to take all the episodes in a batch. For example, the first batch consisted of the opening three stories and, presumably as it was a new series, this was shown in full by all the countries that bought it. The next few batches covering "Marco Polo" to "The Chase" were less consistent, however, with some African, Middle Eastern and South American countries not showing all stories. The reason for this is to do with how the programme was dubbed for non-English-speaking audiences. BBC Enterprises was happy to sell to foreign-language broadcasters and would supply them with the usual film prints (with English soundtrack) plus a tape of just music and sound effects (that is, no dialogue [and often different music from that used in the original episodes]) with which the buyer could mix their own recording of the dialogue in their local language. One early such market was the Spanish-speaking countries of Central and South America, and in 1966 one of the first here to show interest was Radio Caracas Televisión (RCTV) in Venezuela. This was the first broadcaster in the region to show *Doctor Who* and, it seems, the one to arrange for a batch of early serials to be dubbed into Spanish. However, for reasons unknown, RCTV chose not to re-dub the historical stories — except for "The Aztecs", which had obvious relevance to its audience. Records show it cancelled its purchase of "Marco Polo" and "The Reign of Terror" from the first season, presumably after viewing the film prints and deciding adventures in 13th Century China and Revolutionary France wouldn't interest Venezuelans (or at least not as much as voyages to Marinus and the Sense-Sphere). The BBC would only have created music-and-effects tracks for the serials Venezuela ultimately bought, so when other countries such as Mexico and Chile purchased the series they were only offered those stories that had already been re-dubbed. Equally, when broadcasters in Arabic-speaking countries in the Middle East and North Africa were considering buying *Doctor Who* in late-1967, they were only offered those same non-historical serials for which music-and-effects tracks had already been made, to which they could add new Arabic dialogue.

The effect of this is clear from the chart. Of the first 17 stories, the ones set in Earth's past — "Marco Polo", "The Reign of Terror", "The Romans", "The Crusade" and "The Time Meddler" — sold significantly less, all because RCTV decided it didn't want those historicals (only "The Aztecs"). The African countries that showed all these stories were English-speaking ones like Sierra Leone and Uganda, whereas only nine of the serials up to "The Rescue" were dubbed into Arabic. The fall in sales with the loss of those African and Middle Eastern buyers is striking (not helped by Hong Kong and Thailand dropping the series at this point too), followed by the South American broadcasters after "The Chase".

For the remainder of the First Doctor's time, Barbados, Sierra Leone, Singapore and Zambia were the main buyers alongside Australia and New Zealand, while the Second Doctor stories were mainly bought by Australia, Hong Kong, Singapore and, latterly, Gibraltar. It's these less-widely sold stories that are now largely missing from the BBC archives, but that doesn't necessarily imply a direct causal link. Indeed, research has shown most of these episodes survived undiscovered in Sierra Leone until the 1990s when they were destroyed during civil war. Conversely, even perversely, three episodes survive from "The Daleks' Master Plan", which with its prequel "Mission to the Unknown" are the only stories never to have been broadcast abroad. Australian censors rated some episodes as too adult for the ABC's preferred transmission time so it decided not to show them rather than make extensive cuts, which left them too expensive for other broadcasters to acquire. ("Invasion of the Dinosaurs" almost suffered the same fate as it too was initially rejected by the ABC and the original transmission tapes were subsequently marked for erasure surprisingly soon after UK broadcast. Fortunately all but episode 1 evaded the wiping process and the serial was later sold to the four key markets during the 1980s.)

While the early Fourth Doctor seasons were ultimately seen in more countries than even the early First Doctor stories, their distribution was slower. Initially only Australia, Hong Kong, the Netherlands, New Zealand and the United Arab Emirates showed Fourth Doctor stories within two or three years of their UK transmission. It was only after American distributor Time Life bought Seasons 12-15 in 1978 that the programme gained wider showings in Central and South America (dubbed into Spanish), boosted later by sales in Asia, the Caribbean and Europe from the mid-1980s onwards. While these episodes established a dedicated audience for *Doctor Who* in the US, which went on to buy the rest of the series and as much of its back catalogue as then survived, few of the other countries stuck with it, only Brunei, Gibraltar and the UAE showing most of the remainder of the Fourth Doctor era. For the rest of the original series the four key markets were almost the sole buyers, with other countries occasionally showing sporadic blocks of episodes: Gibraltar's once-consistent broadcasts ended with Season 19; the Netherlands showed nine stories from Seasons 19 and 20; Japan bought Season 24 but no more, whereas Germany's transmission of the Seventh Doctor stories were popular enough that it later showed the Sixth Doctor's.

For comprehensive information on the sale of Doctor Who *overseas, visit broadwcast.org, from which data used here was derived*

An Unearthly Child
The Daleks
The Edge of Destruction
Marco Polo
The Keys of Marinus
The Aztecs
The Sensorites
The Reign of Terror
Planet of Giants
The Dalek Invasion of Earth
The Rescue
The Romans
The Web Planet
The Crusade
The Space Museum
The Chase
The Time Meddler
Galaxy 4
Mission to the Unknown
The Myth Makers
The Daleks' Master Plan
The Massacre
The Ark
The Celestial Toymaker
The Gunfighters
The Savages
The War Machines
The Smugglers
The Tenth Planet
The Power of the Daleks
The Highlanders
The Underwater Menace
The Moonbase
The Macra Terror
The Faceless Ones
The Evil of the Daleks
The Tomb of the Cybermen
The Abominable Snowmen
The Ice Warriors
The Enemy of the World
The Web of Fear
Fury from the Deep
The Wheel in Space
The Dominators
The Mind Robber
The Invasion
The Krotons
The Seeds of Death
The Space Pirates
The War Games
Spearhead from Space
The Silurians
The Ambassadors of Death
Inferno
Terror of the Autons
The Mind of Evil
The Claws of Axos
Colony in Space
The Dæmons
Day of the Daleks
The Curse of Peladon
The Sea Devils
The Mutants
The Time Monster
The Three Doctors
Carnival of Monsters
Frontier in Space
Planet of the Daleks
The Green Death
The Time Warrior
Invasion of the Dinosaurs
Death to the Daleks
The Monster of Peladon
Planet of the Spiders
Robot
The Ark in Space
The Sontaran Experiment
Genesis of the Daleks

10 20 30

Revenge of the Cybermen
Terror of the Zygons
Planet of Evil
Pyramids of Mars
The Android Invasion
The Brain of Morbius
The Seeds of Doom
The Masque of Mandragora
The Hand of Fear
The Deadly Assassin
The Face of Evil
The Robots of Death
The Talons of Weng-Chiang
Horror of Fang Rock
The Invisible Enemy
Image of the Fendahl
The Sun Makers
Underworld
The Invasion of Time
The Ribos Operation
The Pirate Planet
The Stones of Blood
The Androids of Tara
The Power of Kroll
The Armageddon Factor
Destiny of the Daleks
City of Death
The Creature from the Pit
Nightmare of Eden
The Horns of Nimon
The Leisure Hive
Meglos
Full Circle
State of Decay
Warriors' Gate
The Keeper of Traken
Logopolis
Castrovalva
Four to Doomsday
Kinda
The Visitation
Black Orchid
Earthshock
Time-Flight
Arc of Infinity
Snakedance
Mawdryn Undead
Terminus
Enlightenment
The King's Demons
The Five Doctors
Warriors of the Deep
The Awakening
Frontios
Resurrection of the Daleks
Planet of Fire
The Caves of Androzani
The Twin Dilemma
Attack of the Cybermen
Vengeance on Varos
The Mark of the Rani
The Two Doctors
Timelash
Revelation of the Daleks
The Trial of a Time Lord
Time and the Rani
Paradise Towers
Delta and the Bannermen
Dragonfire
Remembrance of the Daleks
The Happiness Patrol
Silver Nemesis
The Greatest Show in the Galaxy
Battlefield
Ghost Light
The Curse of Fenric
Survival
The TV Movie *Also on cable across Caribbean and South/Central America*

10 20 30

AUSTRALIA · NEW ZEALAND · CANADA · UNITED STATES · AFRICA · ASIA · CARIBBEAN · EUROPE · MIDDLE EAST · SOUTH/CENTRAL AMERICA · Post-archive sale · Unconfirmed

A CHANGE OF IDENTITY

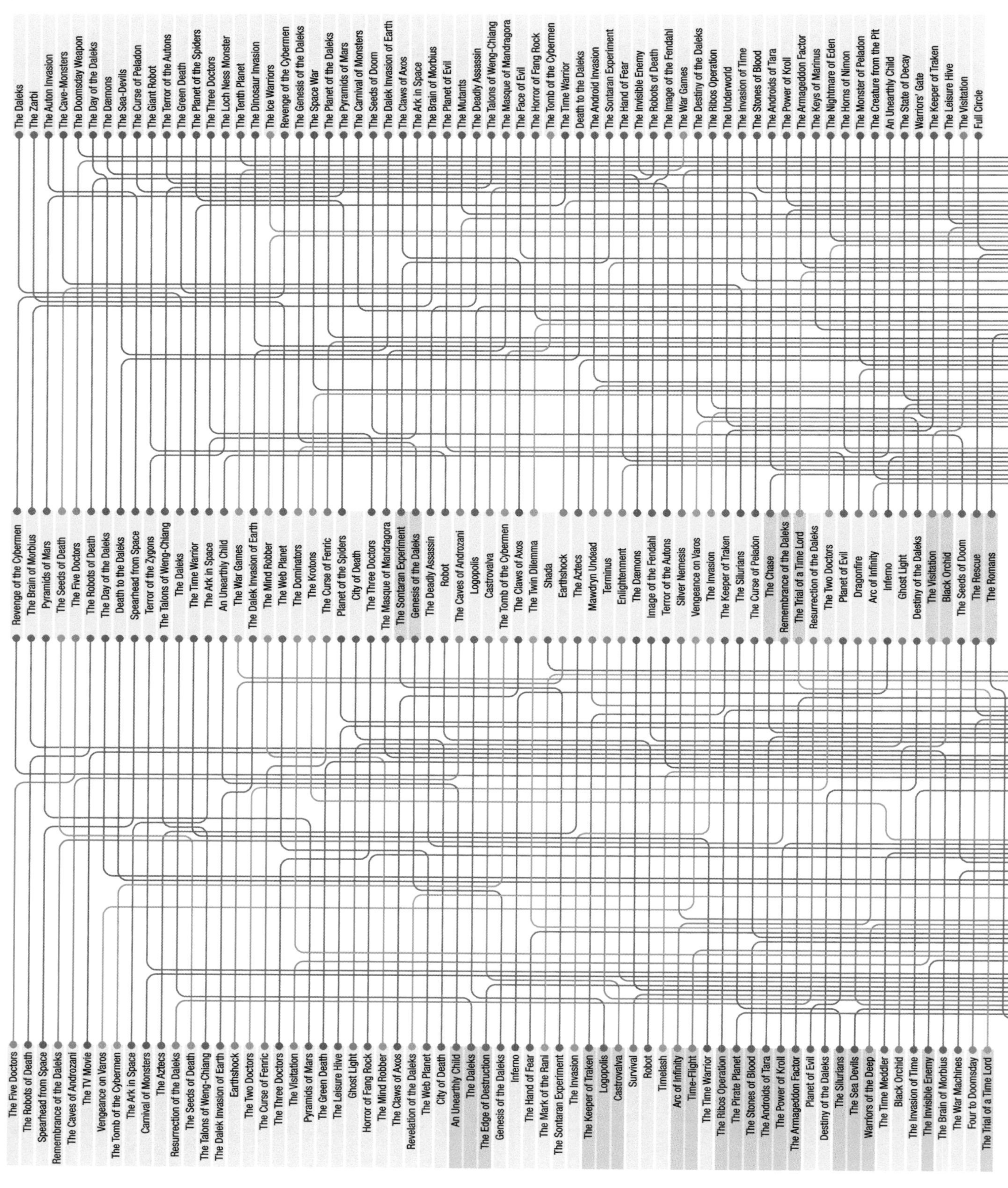

Comparison of initial UK release orders of *Doctor Who* Target books, BBC videos and BBC DVDs

Unlike most TV series, *Doctor Who* has never been issued on other media in the order of its broadcast, starting with the first story and working through to the most recent. The book range from the Target imprint of WH Allen & Co began while the original show was still on air, but although it launched with three First Doctor stories that had previously been released in the 1960s, these weren't the first three stories broadcast. It then skipped to stories featuring the then-current Third Doctor, moving onto the Fourth, Fifth, Sixth and Seventh as they came along, but interspersing their stories with unreleased ones from the programme's past. When *Doctor Who* came to be released on VHS and then DVD, the order became even more random, to offer a more even spread of stories from each Doctor's era. Note the list of books omits those for missing stories, while some stories were never novelised.

Target book | BBC VHS | Released in box set | BBC DVD | Released in box set

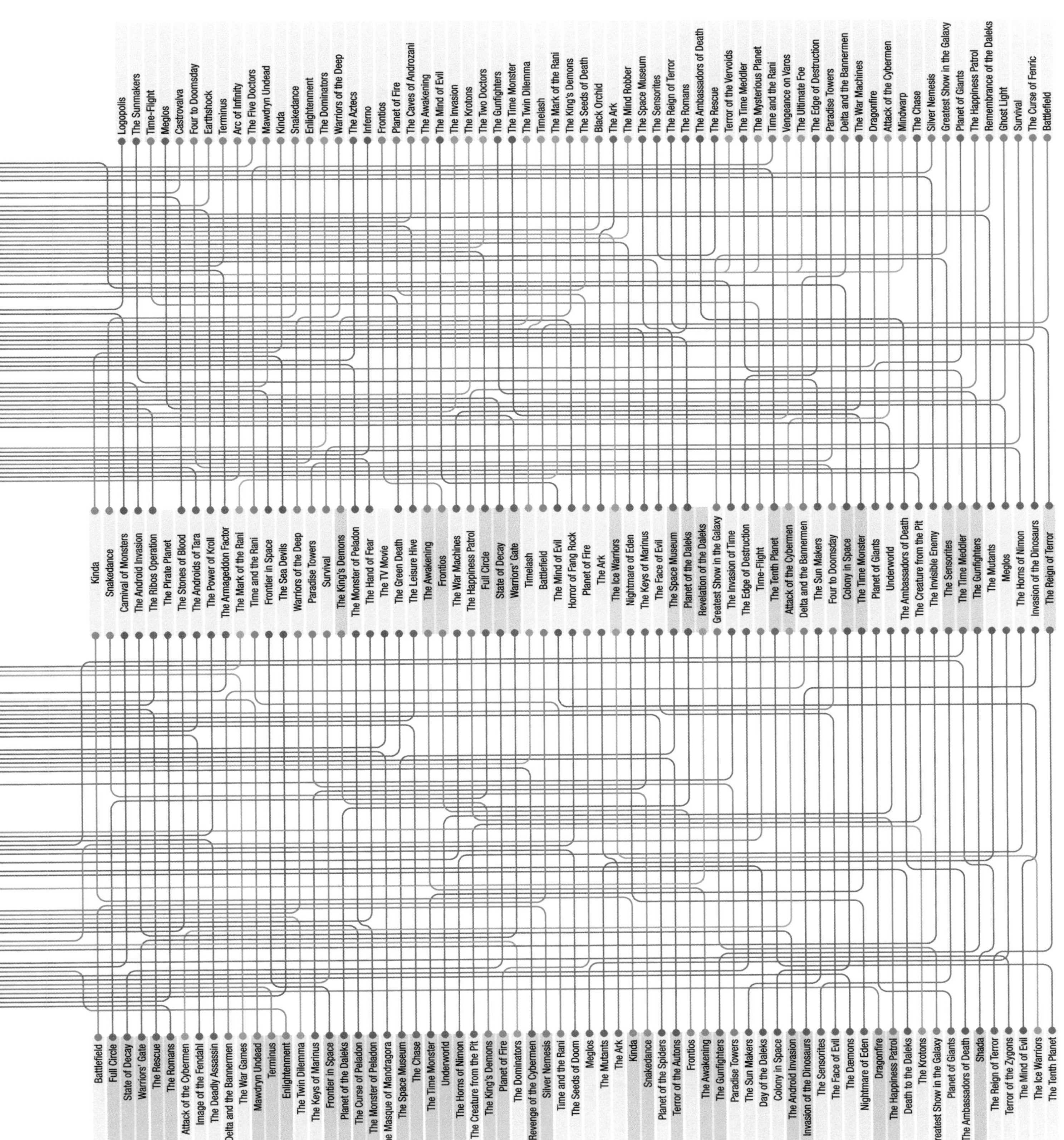

SILENCE IN THE LIBRARY

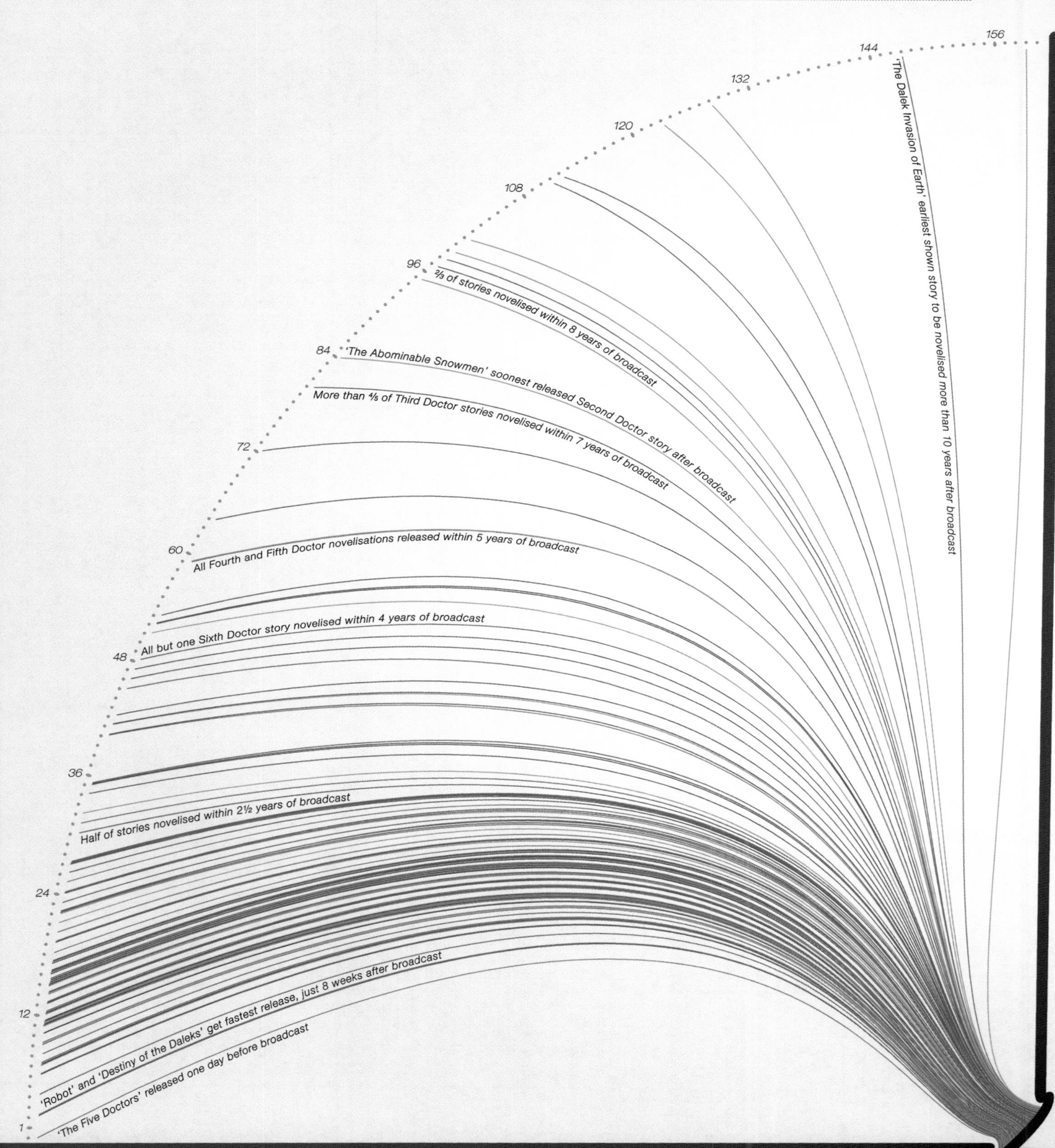

156
144
132
120
108
96
84
72
60
48
36
24
12
1
'The Dalek Invasion of Earth' earliest shown story to be novelised more than 10 years after broadcast
⅔ of stories novelised within 8 years of broadcast
'The Abominable Snowmen' soonest released Second Doctor story after broadcast
More than ⅘ of Third Doctor stories novelised within 7 years of broadcast
All Fourth and Fifth Doctor novelisations released within 5 years of broadcast
All but one Sixth Doctor story novelised within 4 years of broadcast
Half of stories novelised within 2½ years of broadcast
'Robot' and 'Destiny of the Daleks' get fastest release, just 8 weeks after broadcast
'The Five Doctors' released one day before broadcast

Time difference in months between Classic *Doctor Who* stories' broadcast and their release as Target books

The Target books range didn't get going until ten years after *Doctor Who* began and, despite publishing half a dozen or more books a year, took just over 20 years to novelise all but a handful of original-series stories (just four broadcast stories were never novelised). This means the biggest gap between a story being shown and its book being released was close to 27 years. Most were released much sooner after broadcast, of course, particularly for then-current Doctors — most within five years of broadcast, and all of the Seventh Doctor's within two years. The longest gaps were for First and Second Doctor stories, most of which didn't get novelised until the later years of the range, by which time they were 20 or more years past broadcast. The quickest to be published was "The Five Doctors", which was actually released in the UK the day before the story was shown on television.

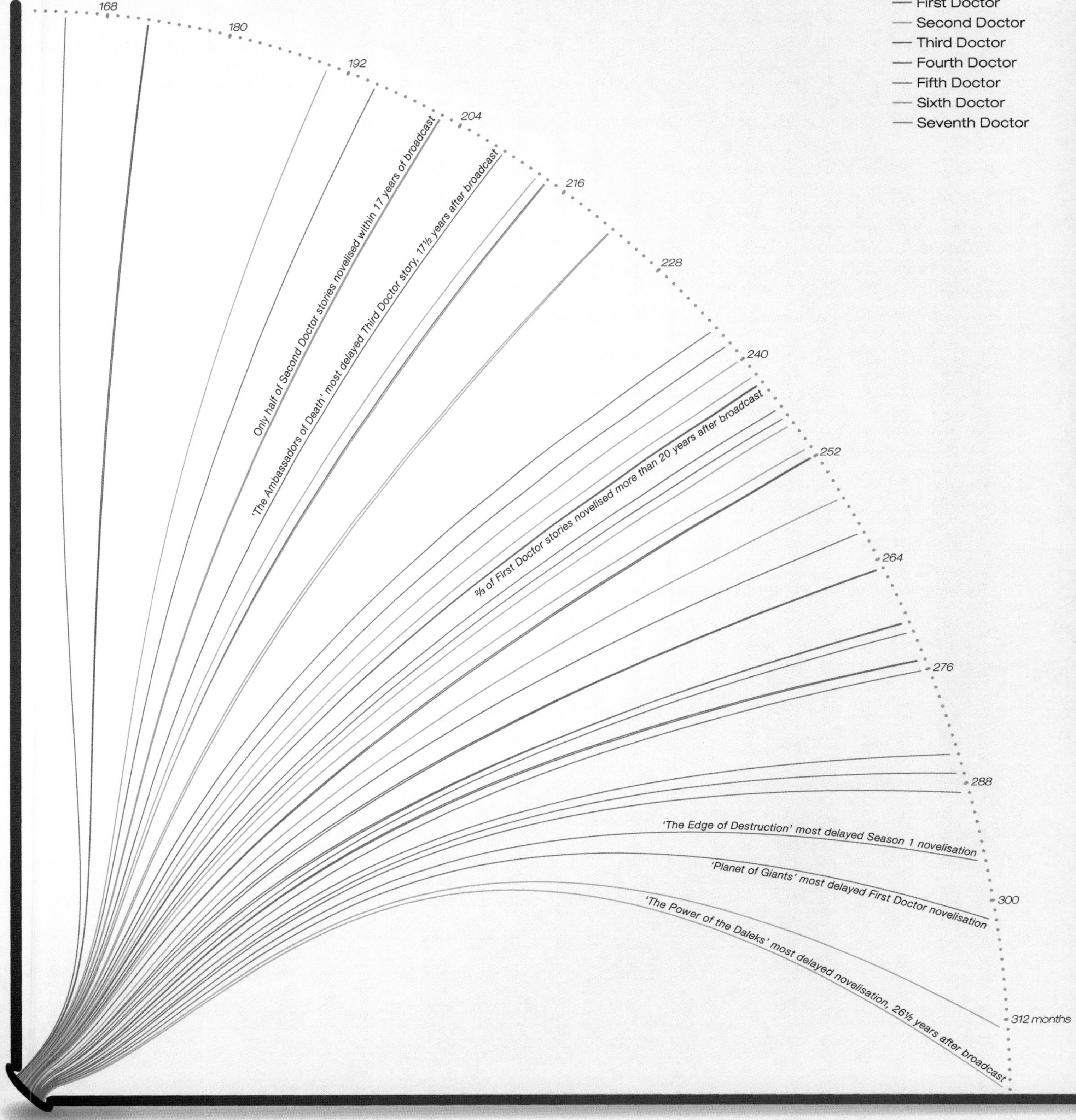

THE SHAKESPEARE CODE

Relative contributions of authors and artists to the Target range of *Doctor Who* novelisations

For many years, until the take-off of sell-through videos in the mid-1980s, the Target books were a *Doctor Who* fan's only way to relive the television adventures. Three books had been published in 1965 by Frederick Muller, based on "The Daleks", "The Crusade" (both written by original story editor David Whitaker) and "The Web Planet" (adapted by the TV serial's writer Bill Strutton). These were long out of print when, in 1972, Universal-Tandem was looking for ideas for its new children's imprint, Target. It bought the rights to those original three novelisations and approached the BBC for permission to publish further books based on the television scripts. Keen to write these was Terrance Dicks, the show's script editor at the time, who shortly afterwards left the programme to become a freelance writer and for whom the Target books became a steady source of work.

Initially Dicks handled the bulk of the writing duties, helped occasionally by a few of his *Doctor Who* colleagues, such as Gerry Davis, Brian Hayles, Philip Hinchcliffe, Malcolm Hulke, Barry Letts and Ian Marter. It wasn't until the 1980s that greater moves were made to invite the television serials' writers to adapt their own scripts for print. Despite this, Dicks continued to pen many of the novelisations that script writers turned down or from the series' still available back catalogue, and is by far the most prolific writer in the range, with 41.3% of titles published under his name. In contrast, the next most frequent author, Ian Marter, wrote only 5.8% of *Doctor Who* novelisations, and Malcolm Hulke just 4.5%. As the bookshelf opposite shows, most other writers contributed only a handful of titles to the range, with just over one in nine of the Target books being written by a one-off author. These were: Ben Aaronovitch, Alison Bingeman, Kevin Clarke, Barbara Clegg, Graeme Curry, William Emms, Paul Erickson, Robert Holmes, Glyn Jones, Malcolm Kohll, Barry Letts, Peter Ling, Glen McCoy, Rona Munro, Victor Pemberton, Eric Pringle, Andrew Smith and Bill Strutton.

The first cover artist for the *Doctor Who* books was Chris Achilleos, whose unique style quickly became synonymous with the range and is still considered the classic look for the novelisations. He illustrated all but four covers over the first four years of the range, producing an impressive 28 paintings. Beating his tally, however, was Andrew Skilleter, who painted covers throughout the 1980s. He just topped Achilleos for first-run covers, with 34, but also did eight further covers for reprints (all but one replacing previous Achilleos covers), taking his tally to just under a quarter (24.3%) of all Target covers. Alister Pearson painted all but two of his 23 Target covers within just three years, including all but one of the Seventh Doctor novelisations. The last two, in 1993, were for "The Power of the Daleks" and "The Evil of the Daleks", which were published by the Target brand's inheritor Virgin Publishing. It also re-issued many out-of-print *Doctor Who* titles with new covers, for which Pearson provided 48 new paintings, while a further 13 used artwork he had originally done for the video range, making him by far the most prolific cover artist overall.

While 16 other artists each produced a handful of covers, they account for two-fifths of the range (including reprints). Briefly in the early 1980s, Target switched to photographic covers instead of painted artwork in a bid to freshen the range alongside the introduction of the Fifth Doctor on television. Nine stories from Seasons 19 and 20 were published with photo covers before the costs of using actors' likenesses forced a return to artwork. All but two of these — "Time-Flight" and "Terminus" — later received painted covers by Alister Pearson among Virgin's reissues. One last photo cover was used on "Time and the Rani" in 1988 when a problem with the commissioned artwork required a quick replacement: a model shot of the Tetraps' cave.

For the full story behind the Target range of Doctor Who *novelisations, read 'The Target Book' (David J Howe and Tim Neil, Telos Publishing, 2007)*

TERRANCE DICKS
IAN MARTER
MALCOLM HULKE
GERRY DAVIS
JOHN PEEL
PIP AND JANE BAKER
NIGEL ROBINSON
CHRISTOPHER H. BIDMEAD
IAN STUART BLACK
PETER GRIMWADE
DONALD COTTON
PHILIP HINCHCLIFFE
JOHN LUCAROTTI
ERIC SAWARD
IAN BRIGGS
TERENCE DUDLEY
DAVID FISHER
BRIAN HAYLES
JOHN LYDECKER
PHILIP MARTIN
MARC PLATT
STEPHEN WYATT
DAVID WHITAKER
ONE-OFF AUTHORS

1988 was the only year to have a new book published each month

More than 2 out of every 5 Target books were written by Terrance Dicks

65

All but 2 of Malcolm Hulke's books used different titles to the TV stories

9 7 5 4 3 2 18

42 DOCTOR WHO
Andrew Skilleter

28 DOCTOR WHO
Chris Achilleos

10 Target books were issued with photo covers, 2 of which were never rejacketed

23 Doctor WHO
Alister Pearson

Alister Pearson painted a further 48 covers when Virgin reissued the Target books

David McAllister

10
Jeff Cummins

Tony Masero

Graham Potts
Graeme Way
1
Colin Howard
Ian Burgess

Tony Clark
2

Steve Kyte
3
Alun Hood

Alun Hood is the only artist not to provide a first-edition cover, just for reprints

Nick Spender
Bill Donohoe
4
Mike Little
Peter Brookes

Roy Knipe
6
John Geary

LOGOPOLIS

THE DALEKS	DAVID WHITAKER
THE ZARBI	BILL STRUTTON
THE CRUSADERS	DAVID WHITAKER
THE AUTON INVASION	TERRANCE DICKS
THE CAVE-MONSTERS	MALCOLM HULKE
THE DOOMSDAY WEAPON	MALCOLM HULKE
THE DAY OF THE DALEKS	TERRANCE DICKS
THE DÆMONS	BARRY LETTS
THE SEA-DEVILS	MALCOLM HULKE
THE ABOMINABLE SNOWMEN	TERRANCE DICKS
THE CURSE OF PELADON	BRIAN HAYLES
THE CYBERMEN	GERRY DAVIS
THE GIANT ROBOT	TERRANCE DICKS
THE TERROR OF THE AUTONS	TERRANCE DICKS
THE GREEN DEATH	MALCOLM HULKE
THE PLANET OF THE SPIDERS	TERRANCE DICKS
THE THREE DOCTORS	TERRANCE DICKS
THE LOCH NESS MONSTER	TERRANCE DICKS
THE TENTH PLANET	GERRY DAVIS
THE DINOSAUR INVASION	MALCOLM HULKE
THE ICE WARRIORS	BRIAN HAYLES
THE REVENGE OF THE CYBERMEN	TERRANCE DICKS
THE GENESIS OF THE DALEKS	TERRANCE DICKS
THE WEB OF FEAR	TERRANCE DICKS
THE SPACE WAR	MALCOLM HULKE
THE PLANET OF THE DALEKS	TERRANCE DICKS
THE PYRAMIDS OF MARS	TERRANCE DICKS
THE CARNIVAL OF MONSTERS	TERRANCE DICKS
THE SEEDS OF DOOM	PHILIP HINCHCLIFFE
THE DALEK INVASION OF EARTH	TERRANCE DICKS
THE CLAWS OF AXOS	TERRANCE DICKS
THE ARK IN SPACE	IAN MARTER
THE BRAIN OF MORBIUS	TERRANCE DICKS
THE PLANET OF EVIL	TERRANCE DICKS
THE MUTANTS	TERRANCE DICKS
THE DEADLY ASSASSIN	TERRANCE DICKS
THE TALONS OF WENG-CHIANG	TERRANCE DICKS
THE MASQUE OF MANDRAGORA	PHILIP HINCHCLIFFE

1973 1974 1975 1976 1977

Word counts for Target *Doctor Who* novelisations in order of publication

This chart shows the variation in word counts of the Target books over time. Written primarily for children, they were not intended to be exhausting reads, but their crisp language made them an influential part of many young would-be writers' lives. As one might expect the length of the final book to depend on the number of television episodes it was adapting, the base of each tower shows the average word count per 25-minute episode or equivalent — so "The Five Doctors" is counted as four episodes and the 45-minute episodes of the Sixth Doctor's time as two. "Planet of Giants" is treated as four episodes as the book was based on the full script before the programme was cut down to three parts. John Peel's 'Mission to the Unknown' covers seven episodes: "Mission to the Unknown" and the first six parts of "The Daleks' Master Plan"; while 'The Mutation of Time' covers parts 7-12. The two Dalek novelisations published in 1993 are excluded as their inflated word counts would constrict the rest of the chart. *[continued overleaf]*

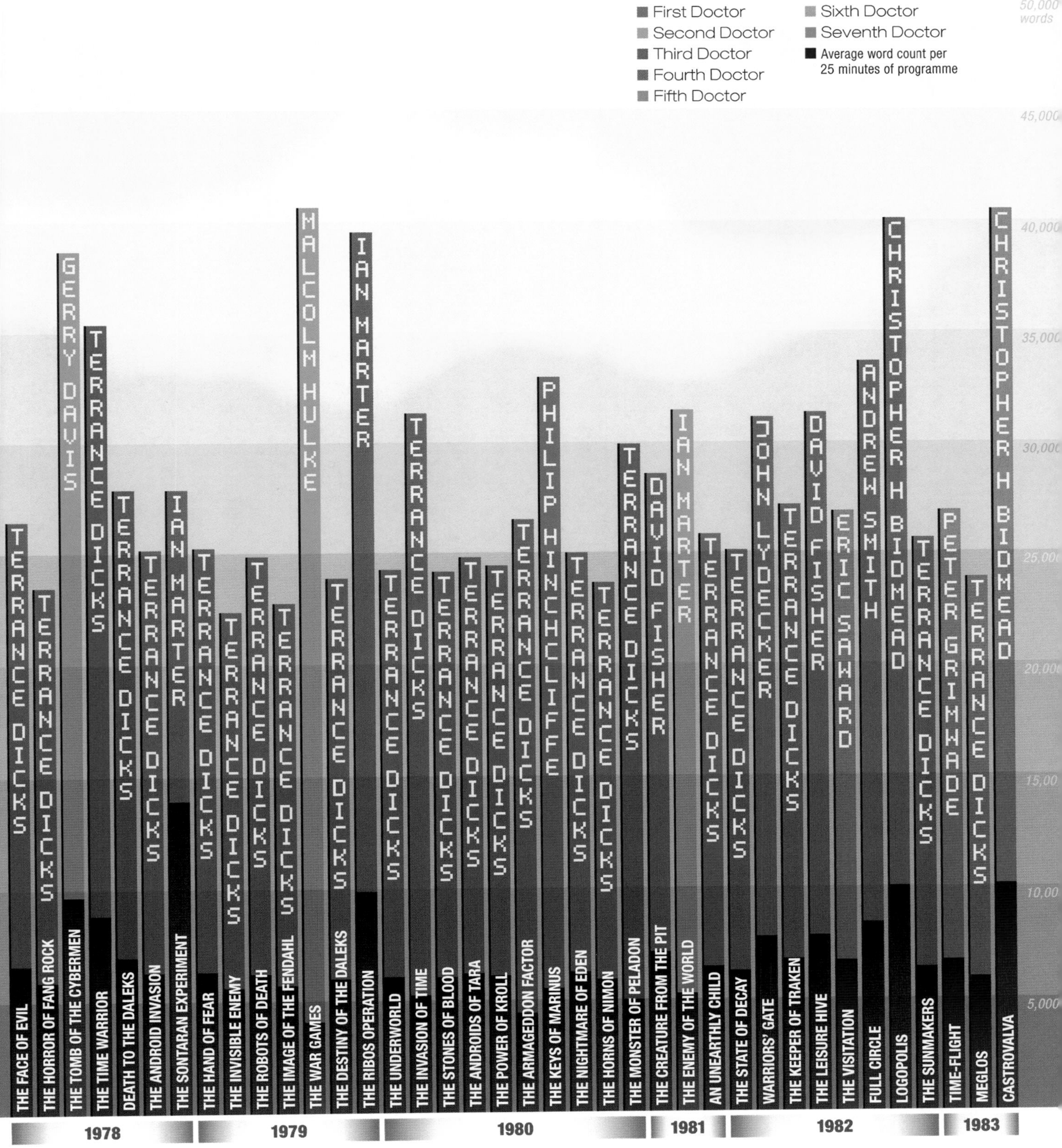

After some initial 40-50,000-word books in line with the three repurposed from the 1960s, the length of the Target books soon fell to 25-30,000 once Terrance Dicks settled into writing the bulk of them. This is no comment on his diligence, merely a reflection of the increasing rate of releases: he wrote three of those published in 1974, but nine of 1977's output. As more writers began adapting their own scripts during the 1980s, the average word count gradually rose as they looked to expand their original ideas. Victor Pemberton's novelisation of "Fury from the Deep" is notable here as the first book to top 50,000 words despite efforts by him and his editor to cut it down. A significant drop in the average length occurred in 1987/88 when several of the less well-remembered 1960s stories were published — including three two-parters as well as three books in the staccato style of Pip and Jane Baker — before rising again as the Seventh Doctor era writers adapted their own scripts, which had frequently been heavily cut to fit the allotted time on television.

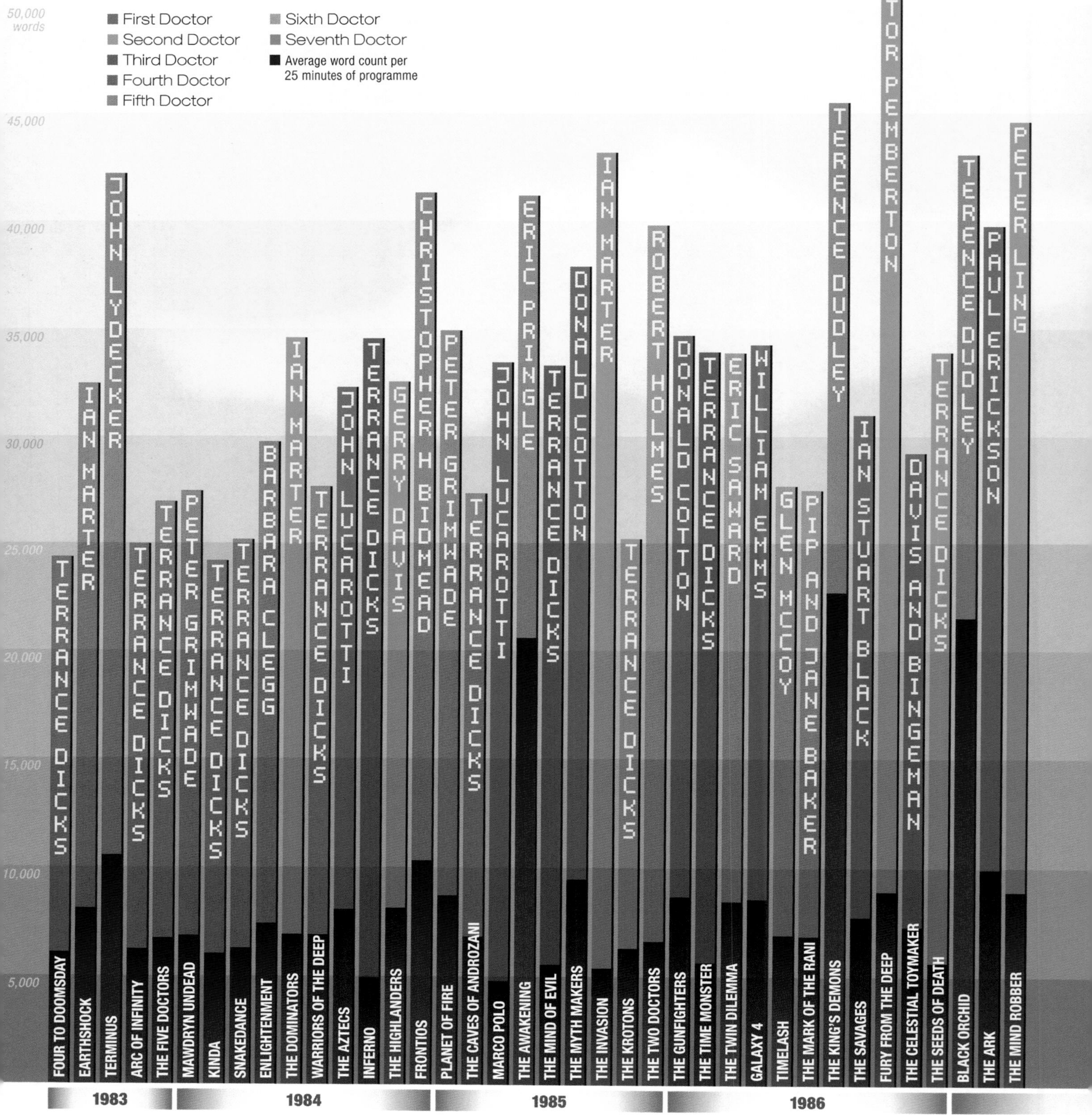

In theory, the average words per episode should be more even, as they represent an equivalent amount of screen time. However, there is still much variation. Most notably, the two-part stories seem to have inspired their adapters to greatly expand on what was seen on television. After adding much to "The Sontaran Experiment", Ian Marter later went further for "The Rescue", getting close to 20,000 words from each episode. Most impressive are Eric Pringle's and Terence Dudley's efforts, producing some of the longest books from their 50 minutes of script. Conversely, at the other end of the scale, those books that barely get 5,000 words from each episode are mainly stories originally of six parts or more. Terrance Dicks is a repeat offender, with books like "The Ambassadors of Death", "The Planet of the Daleks", "The Armageddon Factor" and "The Space Pirates", but John Lucarotti heavily condenses the seven episodes of "Marco Polo" while Philip Hinchcliffe wrings just 4,300 words from each of the six parts of "The Seeds of Doom".

Thanks to Paul Scoones for the word counts

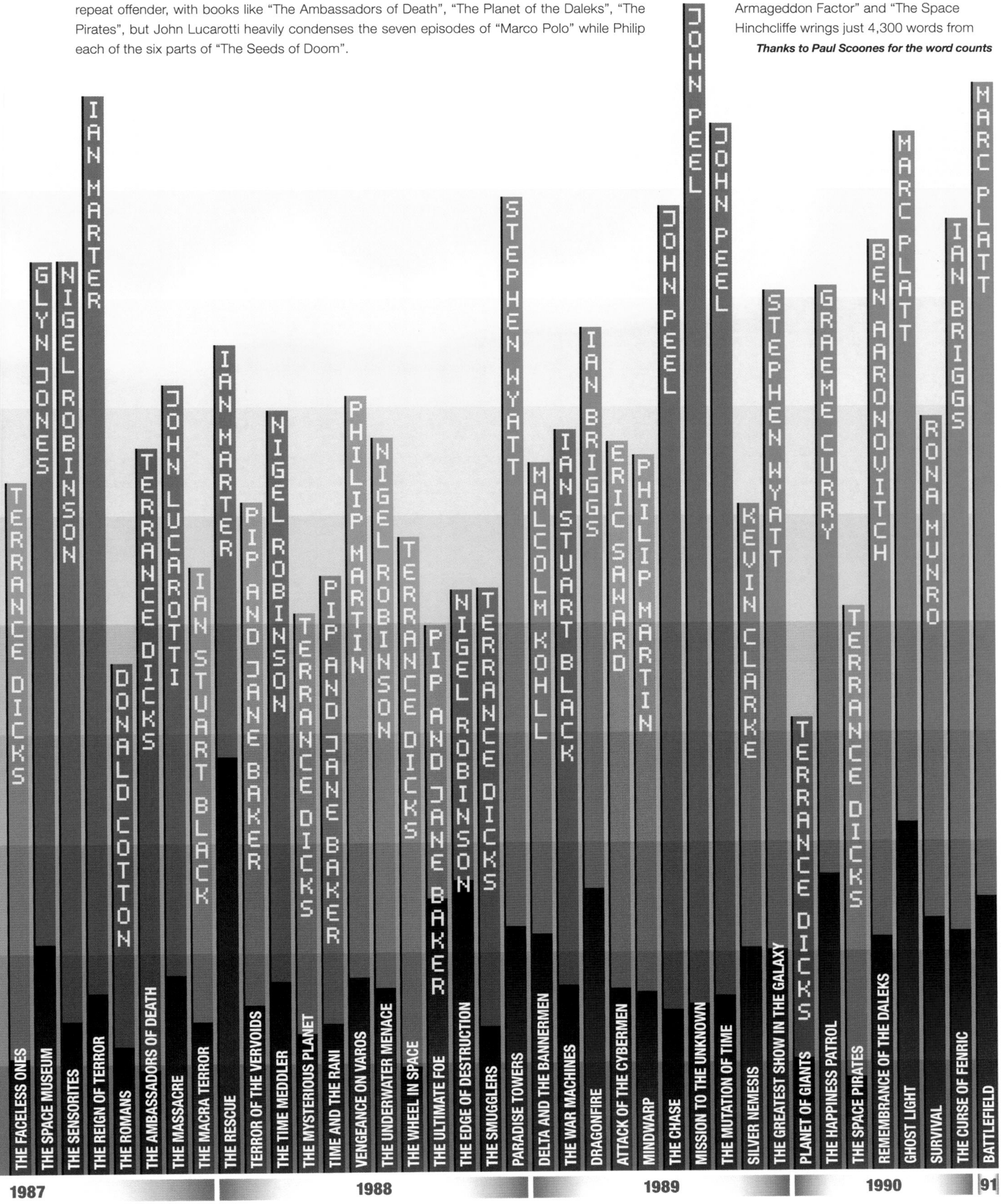

THE FACELESS ONES — TERRANCE DICKS
THE SPACE MUSEUM — GLYN JONES
THE SENSORITES — NIGEL ROBINSON
THE REIGN OF TERROR — IAN MARTER
THE ROMANS — DONALD COTTON
THE AMBASSADORS OF DEATH — TERRANCE DICKS
THE MASSACRE — JOHN LUCAROTTI
THE MACRA TERROR — IAN STUART BLACK
THE RESCUE — IAN MARTER
TERROR OF THE VERVOIDS — PIP AND JANE BAKER
THE TIME MEDDLER — NIGEL ROBINSON
THE MYSTERIOUS PLANET — TERRANCE DICKS
TIME AND THE RANI — PIP AND JANE BAKER
VENGEANCE ON VAROS — PHILIP MARTIN
THE UNDERWATER MENACE — NIGEL ROBINSON
THE WHEEL IN SPACE — TERRANCE DICKS
THE ULTIMATE FOE — PIP AND JANE BAKER
THE EDGE OF DESTRUCTION — NIGEL ROBINSON
THE SMUGGLERS — TERRANCE DICKS
PARADISE TOWERS — STEPHEN WYATT
DELTA AND THE BANNERMEN — MALCOLM KOHLL
THE WAR MACHINES — IAN STUART BLACK
DRAGONFIRE — IAN BRIGGS
ATTACK OF THE CYBERMEN — ERIC SAWARD
MINDWARP — PHILIP MARTIN
THE CHASE — JOHN PEEL
MISSION TO THE UNKNOWN — JOHN PEEL
THE MUTATION OF TIME — JOHN PEEL
SILVER NEMESIS — KEVIN CLARKE
THE GREATEST SHOW IN THE GALAXY — STEPHEN WYATT
PLANET OF GIANTS — TERRANCE DICKS
THE HAPPINESS PATROL — GRAEME CURRY
THE SPACE PIRATES — TERRANCE DICKS
REMEMBRANCE OF THE DALEKS — BEN AARONOVITCH
GHOST LIGHT — MARC PLATT
SURVIVAL — RONA MUNRO
THE CURSE OF FENRIC — IAN BRIGGS
BATTLEFIELD — MARC PLATT

1987 1988 1989 1990

THE REIGN OF TERRY

Share of Terrance Dicks books featuring each Doctor

With the Target range being launched towards the end of the Third Doctor's era and Terrance Dicks being the most prolific novel writer throughout the Fourth Doctor's, it's no surprise that most of the 64 Target books he wrote feature these two Doctors, almost half of his output being Fourth Doctor tales. With seven books apiece from the Second and Fifth Doctors' eras, they each account for 10.9% of his novelisations. By the time the majority of the First Doctor stories were being adapted, Target's policy was to approach the original script writers first, many of whom were glad to revisit and revise stories they'd written some 20 years previously, and which often hadn't yet been released on video. This left fewer pickings for Dicks, whose four First Doctor books are "An Unearthly Child", "Planet of Giants", "The Dalek Invasion of Earth" and "The Smugglers". He wrote only one Sixth Doctor story — the late Robert Holmes' 'The Mysterious Planet' (parts 1-4 of "The Trial of a Time Lord") — and no Seventh Doctor books, all but one of which were by their original script writers.

Share of each Doctor's books written by Terrance Dicks

Looking at Dicks' books in relation to the total number of novelisations for each Doctor gives a rather different picture. While just under half of his books featured the Fourth Doctor, these accounted for seven-tenths of that incarnation's stories, highlighting just how prolific Dicks was during that era of the programme. Similarly he adapted two-thirds of the Third Doctor's stories — a sensible choice given he was script editor for that period of the show's history. Again, with a similar number of stories each in total, the share of Second and Fifth Doctor stories adapted by Dicks is roughly equal at around a third. Even his one book for the Sixth Doctor accounts for 9.1% of all Sixth Doctor stories as there were only 11 to be adapted. Of the 5,242,181 words in the entire Target range, Dicks wrote 1,814,202 — just over 35%. In comparison, the next most prolific writer, Ian Marter, wrote just 6.25% of the total word count.

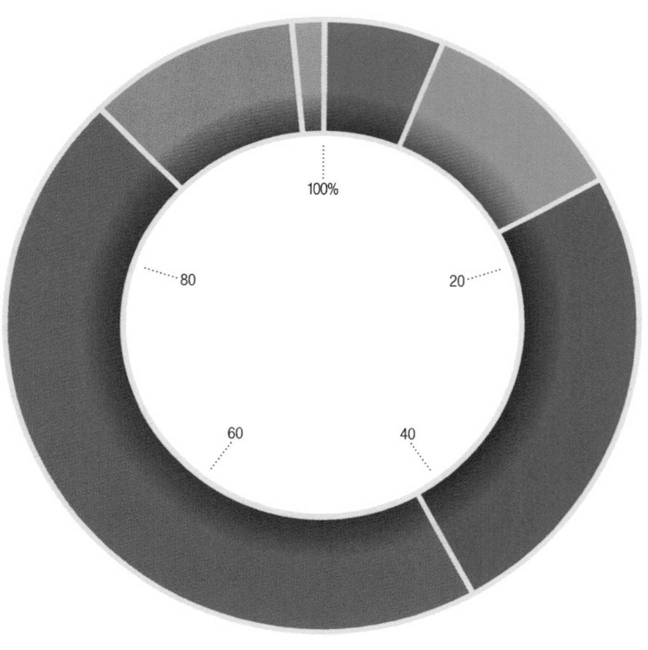

Average word counts by author

Dicks may have written the most Target *Doctor Who* novelisations, but they're by no means the longest. In terms of the average word count per book for each author to have written more than one, Dicks comes second to last, just above the terse writings of Pip and Jane Baker. John Peel's position excludes his adaptations of "The Power of the Daleks" and "The Evil of the Daleks", which at 79,222 and 93,600 words respectively are far above the standard allowed during the main run of Target books and would give him an overall per-book average of 62,711. As such, Marc Platt's near-50,000-word adaptations of "Ghost Light" and "Battlefield" place him top. The overall average word count across all books is 33,350 words, to which John Lucarotti comes closest on average, in spite (or perhaps because) of his novelisation of "Marco Polo" having one of the lowest average words per episode of the range.

Thanks to Paul Scoones for the word counts

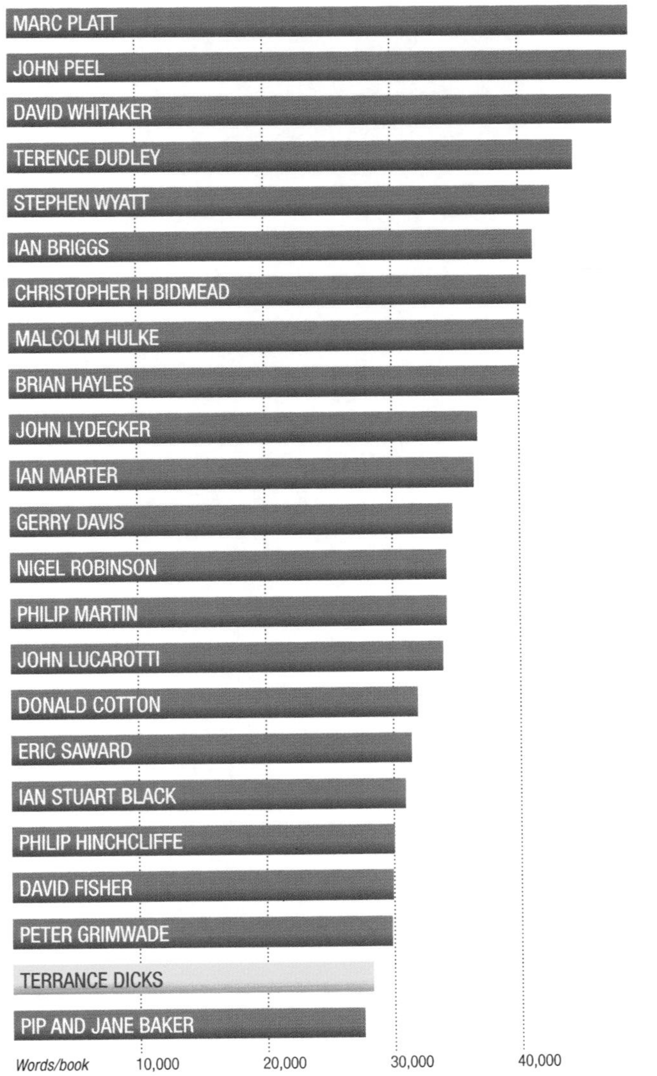

Share of novelisations by original TV writers

Even though the Target range increasingly moved towards having the television serials' original writers adapt them for print, the sheer number taken on by Terrance Dicks means that overall more than half of all the books were written by different authors to the original scripts. Dicks' coverage of other writers' work is highlighted by the fact that although he adapted all of the television scripts he penned alone — including "The Brain of Morbius" but not "The War Games" (nor "The Seeds of Death" for which as story editor he totally rewrote most of Brian Hayles' scripts) — because this was only five stories the vast majority of his work for Target was in novelising other people's work. This becomes even clearer when looking at just those books published between 1973 and 1980 inclusive (inner ring), of which just over a quarter were by their original script writers whereas three-fifths were Dicks adapting others' serials.

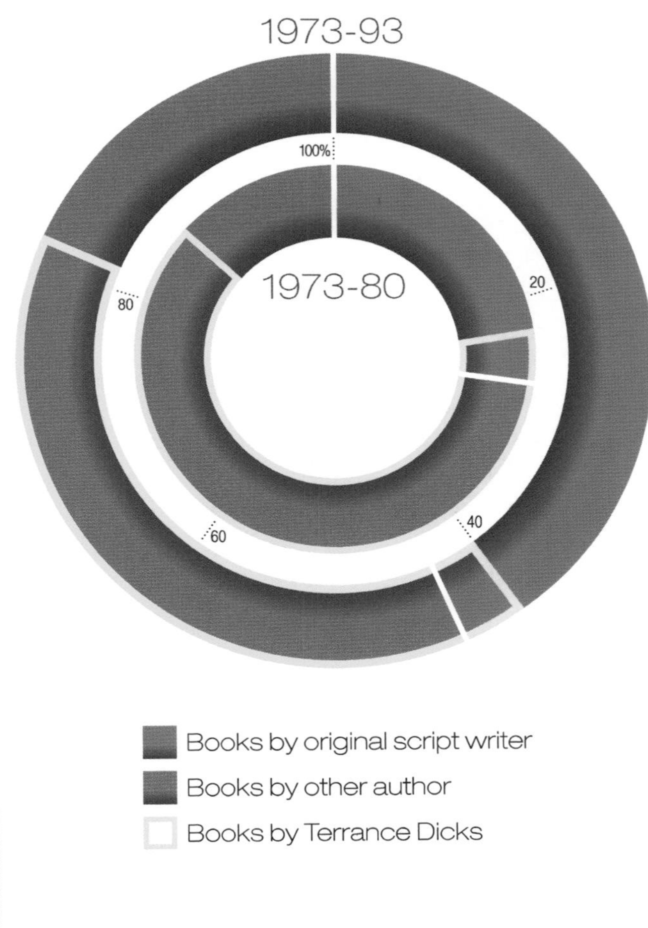

THE WHEEL OF FORTUNE

Time difference in months between Classic *Doctor Who* stories' releases on VHS and DVD

As we saw earlier, the release orders for *Doctor Who* on both video and DVD have been pretty random, in part owing to the changing priorities of the people at BBC Worldwide who control the schedule, but mainly because there really is no set order for watching the programme. Rather than an ongoing narrative, *Doctor Who* has been more like an anthology series with a couple of continuing characters, as the TARDIS deposits its inhabitants in a new location every four weeks or so. Throughout most of the original series, there was little to link one story to the next beyond some subtle character development for the regular companions (sometimes not even that) and the occasional back reference.

So when it comes to releasing the series for home viewing, there is little imperative to present it in its original broadcast order. For one thing, many of the early serials are missing from the BBC's archive or are incomplete, so some jumps would be necessary anyway. Then there's the fact that not all viewers like every era of *Doctor Who*. The show's unique ability to regularly recast its leading man and frequent changes of production team (as with any long-running series) mean the style of storytelling has changed many times over the years, as has the whole process of television programme making. So to release the series in strict order would not only depress the Seventh Doctor fans who would have to wait years to see their favourite stories, but limiting buyers to fans of a particular era for any length of time could have made the range uncommercial.

Following on from the almost-as-erratic story-based release order of the Target books, to which fans were already accustomed, it was entirely reasonable for the BBC, when it came to issuing *Doctor Who* on VHS, to take a similar approach and offer stories from across the show's rich history to appeal to as much of the potential audience as possible. The range started slowly and expensively, as toes were dipped into the relatively new home video market, but by the 1990s its commercial viability was proven and releases quickly rose to around one a month.

The move to DVD began in earnest towards the end of 2000, overlapping with the tail end of the video releases (although "The Five Doctors" had been included among BBC Worldwide's first water-testing DVD issue in November 1999). As such it might be expected that the earliest stories to be sold on video would be prime choices for DVD. Indeed, if the DVDs had followed the same schedule as the videos, the rings in this chart would be much more even, although gradually shortening owing to the faster release rate of the DVDs overall. In fact, many of the earliest VHS releases took the longest time to make it onto DVD, notably "Revenge of the Cybermen", the very first story on video but a relative latecomer to DVD almost 27 years later.

The shortest gap between video and DVD releases is for the TV Movie, first released shortly after broadcast in 1996, then on disc in 2003, when a story from each Doctor was issued to celebrate the show's 30th anniversary. "The Time Meddler" has the same 63-month gap, being one of the last stories to come out on video but reaching DVD mid range in 2008. No story has been released on DVD less than five years after its video release, therefore, with the average gap across the range being 13 years and 1 month, which at least is less than half the full span of releases, from the first video in October 1983 to the last DVD, scheduled for October 2013 at the time of writing.

To aid in reading the chart, the VHS release order is given below. This excludes stories that are missing the majority of their episodes and so didn't get their own video, instead having their surviving episodes released either alongside complete stories or combined in sets.

VHS release order

1983
- Revenge of the Cybermen

1984
- The Brain of Morbius

1985
- Pyramids of Mars
- The Seeds of Death
- The Five Doctors

1986
- The Robots of Death
- The Day of the Daleks

1987
- Death to the Daleks

1988
- Spearhead from Space
- Terror of the Zygons
- The Talons of Weng-Chiang

1989
- The Daleks
- The Time Warrior
- The Ark in Space

1990
- An Unearthly Child
- The War Games
- The Dalek Invasion of Earth
- The Mind Robber
- The Web Planet
- The Dominators

1991
- The Krotons
- The Curse of Fenric
- Planet of the Spiders
- City of Death
- The Three Doctors
- The Masque of Mandragora
- The Sontaran Experiment
- Genesis of the Daleks
- The Deadly Assassin

1992
- Robot
- The Caves of Androzani
- Logopolis
- Castrovalva
- The Tomb of the Cybermen
- The Claws of Axos
- The Twin Dilemma
- Shada
- Earthshock
- The Aztecs
- Mawdryn Undead

1993
- Terminus
- Enlightenment
- The Dæmons
- Image of the Fendahl
- Terror of the Autons
- Silver Nemesis
- Vengeance on Varos
- The Invasion
- The Keeper of Traken
- The Silurians
- The Curse of Peladon
- The Chase
- Remembrance of the Daleks
- The Trial of a Time Lord
- Resurrection of the Daleks
- The Two Doctors
- Planet of Evil
- Dragonfire

1994
- Arc of Infinity
- Inferno
- Ghost Light
- Destiny of the Daleks
- The Visitation
- Black Orchid
- The Seeds of Doom
- The Rescue
- The Romans
- Kinda
- Snakedance

1995
- Carnival of Monsters
- The Android Invasion
- The Ribos Operation
- The Pirate Planet
- The Stones of Blood
- The Androids of Tara
- The Power of Kroll
- The Armageddon Factor
- The Mark of the Rani
- Time and the Rani
- Frontier in Space
- The Sea Devils
- Warriors of the Deep
- Paradise Towers
- Survival
- The King's Demons
- The Monster of Peladon

1996
- The Hand of Fear
- The TV Movie
- The Green Death

1997
- The Leisure Hive
- The Awakening
- Frontios
- The War Machines
- The Happiness Patrol
- Full Circle
- State of Decay
- Warriors' Gate

1998
- Timelash
- Battlefield
- The Mind of Evil
- Horror of Fang Rock
- Planet of Fire
- The Ark
- The Ice Warriors

1999
- Nightmare of Eden
- The Keys of Marinus
- The Face of Evil
- The Space Museum
- Planet of the Daleks
- Revelation of the Daleks

2000
- The Greatest Show in the Galaxy
- The Invasion of Time
- The Edge of Destruction
- Time-Flight
- The Tenth Planet
- Attack of the Cybermen

2001
- Delta and the Bannermen
- The Sun Makers
- Four to Doomsday
- Colony in Space
- The Time Monster

2002
- Planet of Giants
- Underworld
- The Ambassadors of Death
- The Creature from the Pit
- The Invisible Enemy
- The Sensorites
- The Time Meddler
- The Gunfighters

2003
- The Mutants
- Meglos
- The Horns of Nimon
- Invasion of the Dinosaurs
- The Reign of Terror

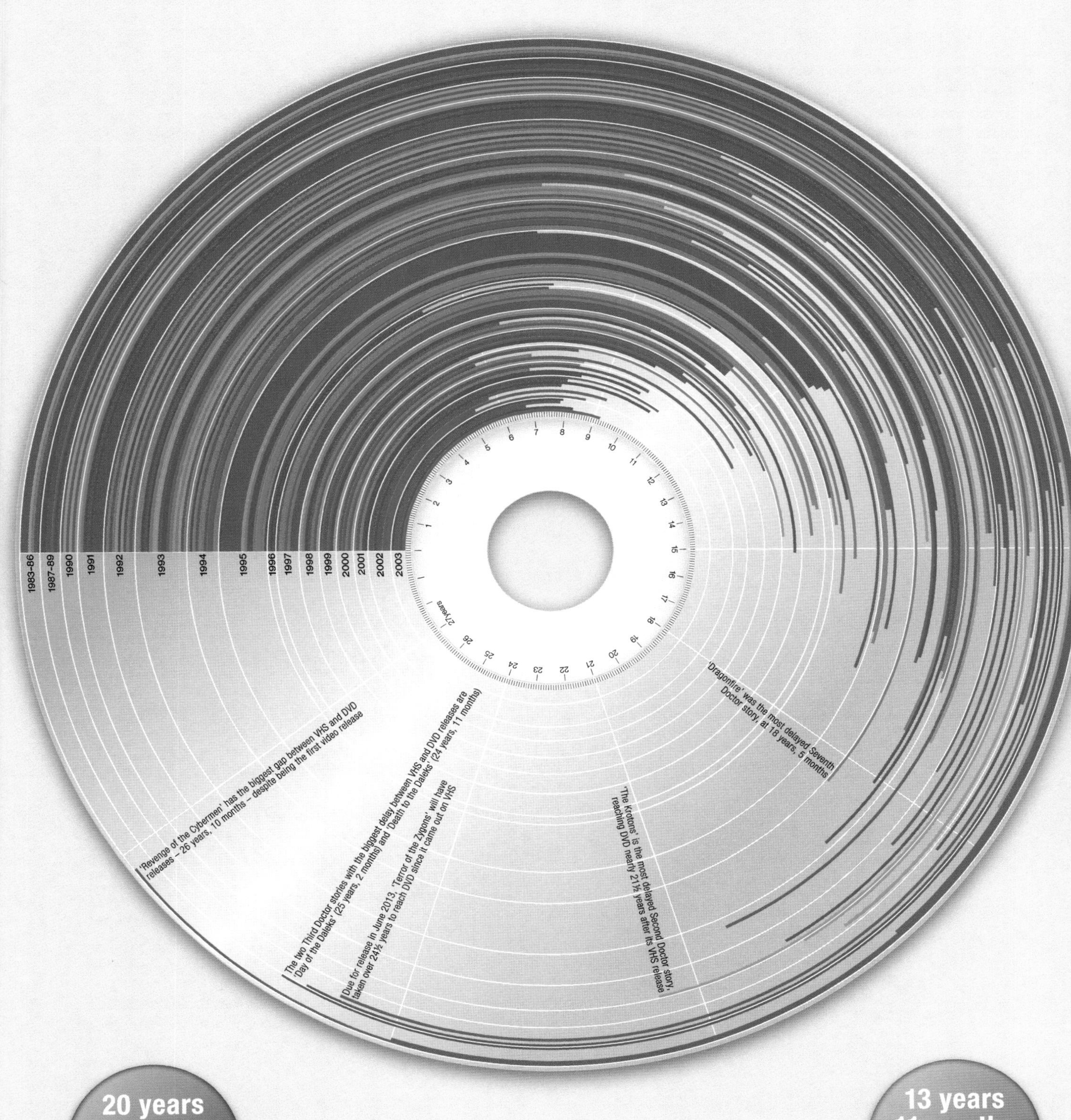

1983-86
1987-89
1990
1991
1992
1993
1994
1995
1996
1997
1998
1999
2000
2001
2002
2003
27 years
'Revenge of the Cybermen' has the biggest gap between VHS and DVD releases – 26 years, 10 months – despite being the first video release
The two Third Doctor stories with the biggest delay between VHS and DVD releases are 'Day of the Daleks' (25 years, 2 months) and 'Death to the Daleks' (24 years, 11 months)
Due for release in June 2013, 'Terror of the Zygons' will have taken over 24½ years to reach DVD since it came out on VHS
'The Krotons' is the most delayed Second Doctor story, reaching DVD nearly 21½ years after its VHS release
'Dragonfire' was the most delayed Seventh Doctor story, at 18 years, 5 months

20 years 1 month
Time to release all stories on VHS

- First Doctor
- Second Doctor
- Third Doctor
- Fourth Doctor
- Fifth Doctor
- Sixth Doctor
- Seventh Doctor
- Eighth Doctor

13 years 11 months
Time to release all stories on DVD

THE LONG GAME

Rate of Classic *Doctor Who* DVD releases by Doctor

The previous chart showed that, assuming all releasable stories are available by November 2013, the DVD range will have taken six years less to be completed than the same stories took to be released on VHS. However, it will still have been 14 years, and as many fans moved straight from collecting the series on video to upgrading to DVD, they could have been buying these stories for just over 30 years. (If you add the span of Target book releases before that, the *Doctor Who* serials have been made available in various media for closing in on 40 years.)

It's little wonder, then, that the approaching end of the DVD range is being seen as a form of liberation by some avid collectors (although there are hints that further releases of some sort will continue). But could their collections have been completed any quicker? With 134 stories from the first eight Doctors available for release, issuing them at a rate of one a month would still have taken 11 years and 2 months, shortening the schedule by just three years. Fortunately the later years of the DVD schedule have included box sets of two or three stories, speeding up the rate, but barely compensating for the early years of the range when six or fewer discs a year was the norm.

The chart opposite shows these two phases of the schedule clearly. Taking the DVD range proper as starting in November 2000 with the release of "The Robots of Death", it shows each release over time cumulatively for each Doctor (excluding the sole Eighth Doctor release in August 2001 and any reissues of stories already available on DVD). Splitting the time scale in two halves for clarity coincidentally highlights the significant increase in the release rate from around that mid-point of the schedule. Prior to 2007 stories were released only every two or three months, with each Doctor seeing releases at a similar rate — although it was nearly two years into the releases before a First Doctor story was seen. Although Fourth Doctor serials were pulling ahead towards the end of 2006 — an inevitable requirement given there are significantly more stories from his record reign — by the start of 2007 only 36 stories were available — barely a quarter of the total. At that rate the range would have taken more than 24 years to be completed.

Plotting a line from the first release for each Doctor to their last indicates what a steady rate for each would be, had the end point been known at the outset (that for the Fifth Doctor is taken from his first 'proper' release in June 2001). It's clear that by halfway through the schedule all but the Second Doctor were way behind, although the First Doctor was briefly on track thanks to the release of his first three stories in the box set 'The Beginning'. Most never catch up until their final releases, as the second half of the schedule demonstrates. Boosted by the release of the Key to Time season as a single box set, the Fourth Doctor finally catches up in 2009 with the 'E-Space Trilogy' set and then maintains steady releases slightly above the average line. The First Doctor catches up with his ideal line in March 2010 and then stays just below it, while the Third Doctor only does so for his last few releases. The others only catch up with their averages thanks to last-minute pushes towards the end of their releases. Only the Second Doctor — with just eight stories available for standalone release anyway — maintains a steady release rate across his span.

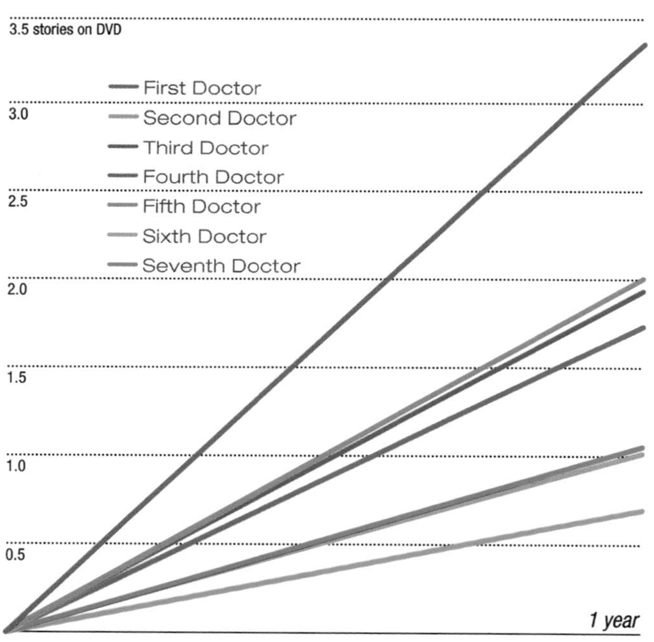

Looking at each Doctor's average number of releases per year (left) reflects the relative number of stories available featuring each. Had all Doctors been rotated evenly from the outset, then obviously the Second and Sixth Doctors, with eight stories apiece, would have been completed way ahead of the Fourth with 42 stories. That they have all been spread across almost the full time span of the range means those with fewer stories have had a correspondingly lower average number of releases per year. Yet only the Second Doctor falls below one release a year, mainly because his last available story, "The Ice Warriors", is scheduled for the end of the range. The Sixth Doctor escapes a similar fate by having his era completed first, with its final release in September 2009, just eight years after its first. The First, Third and Fifth Doctors achieve close yearly averages thanks to a similar number of stories, although the Fifth's would drop to just below the First's if taken from the early release of "The Five Doctors" instead. With the most stories spread over only the longest number of months, the Fourth Doctor achieves the highest annual release rate at close to three and a half stories on DVD per year.

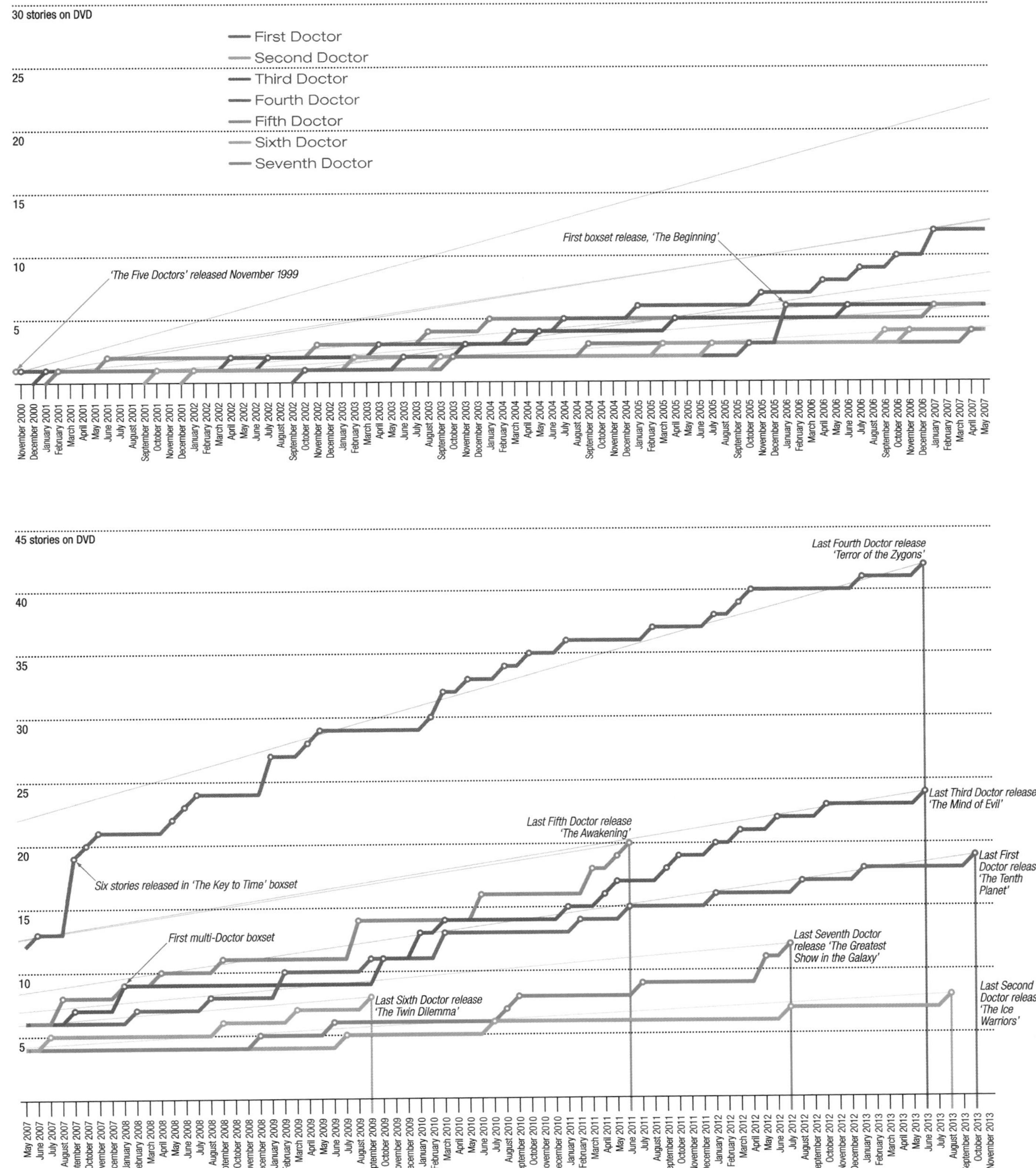

30 stories on DVD
First Doctor
Second Doctor
Third Doctor
Fourth Doctor
Fifth Doctor
Sixth Doctor
Seventh Doctor
25
20
15
10
5
First boxset release, 'The Beginning'
'The Five Doctors' released November 1999
45 stories on DVD
Last Fourth Doctor release 'Terror of the Zygons'
40
35
30
25
20
15
10
5
Last Third Doctor release 'The Mind of Evil'
Last Fifth Doctor release 'The Awakening'
Last First Doctor release 'The Tenth Planet'
Six stories released in 'The Key to Time' boxset
First multi-Doctor boxset
Last Seventh Doctor release 'The Greatest Show in the Galaxy'
Last Second Doctor release 'The Ice Warriors'
Last Sixth Doctor release 'The Twin Dilemma'

OPERATION GOLDEN AGE

50th events in the 50-year history of *Doctor Who*

This chart highlights some of the half-centenaries for various aspects of *Doctor Who* over the last 50 years, based on the topics covered in this book. But how rare is it for a television programme to reach its 50th anniversary and what does that mean for its place in the nation's consciousness?

While *Doctor Who* isn't the only show to keep going for 50 years, of course, it is in rare company. (Although it hasn't been on television for all that time, even during the 15 years it was off our screens it persisted in other media. And this wasn't just niche markets for dedicated fans — books, videos and other merchandise were on the shelves of major high-street stores, new stories were transmitted on BBC Radio and online, and even on television there were four noteworthy retrospectives: *Resistance is Useless* in 1992, kicking off a run of repeats; more repeats, the documentary *30 Years in the TARDIS* and *Dimensions in Time*, a 3D mini-adventure starring all five surviving Doctors (and featured on the cover of *Radio Times*) to celebrate the programme's 30th anniversary in 1993; *Doctor Who Night* took over BBC2s evening schedule on 13 November 1999 (and gained another *Radio Times* cover); and for its 40th birthday in 2003 there were not one but four *Radio Times* covers, forming one long image, followed by *The Story of Doctor Who* in December, this time on BBC1 thanks to the announcement a few months before of the show's return. Plus, of course, the brand new TV Movie in 1996. Not bad for a series that hadn't been in regular production since 1989.)

Certainly among UK television drama serials it's unique, its nearest rival being children's drama *Grange Hill*, which ran for 30 years from 1978 (thus beating *Doctor Who*'s initial run). Of current ongoing dramas, BBC stalwart *Casualty* is still going strong after 26 years. The real long-runners among drama series are the soaps, of course, headed on UK television by ITV's *Coronation Street*, which celebrated its own half-century at the end of 2010. The nearest BBC rival is the Welsh-language soap *Pobol y Cwm*, which has been telling stories about life in the Valleys since 1974. But for real soap longevity you need to look to radio, where that "everyday story of country folk" *The Archers* has been on air for over 60 years, since 1951.

What about beyond drama? Some form of daily evening News has been broadcast almost since the start of television, and on radio before that, of course. As for specific programmes, *Newsnight* has been analysing the day's top stories since 1980, but is beaten by that innovation of presenting news to children without talking down to them — *Newsround* — first fronted by John Craven in 1972. Outdoing both, however, is *Panorama*, which has been broadcasting since 1953 and is the world's longest running public affairs programme, and the oldest of all BBC television programmes.

Quiz shows can last a long time, too. *University Challenge* began testing UK students' breadth of knowledge in 1962 and is still doing so today, although on a different channel and with Jeremy Paxman proving an even sterner question master than Bamber Gascoigne. But a seven-year absence from 1987 to 1994 knocks it back to 43 years on air. The oldest quiz show on UK television is *A Question of Sport*, kicking off in 1968 and playing regularly ever since. But to top that half-century we must turn again to radio, where *Brain of Britain* has been quizzing our country's very brightest since 1953, making it the longest running quiz programme in the world.

The most long-lived programme in all of British broadcasting, and worldwide if you exclude news, is BBC Radio's *Desert Island Discs*, created by Roy Plomley in 1942 and hosted by him for its first 43 years. It has now been on air for 71 years and there's no reason why it should ever run out of people to select their eight most indispensable music tracks. Just five years behind is *Gardeners' Question Time*, which emerged from the wartime push for people to grow their own produce and whose longevity proves the Brits' love of their gardens. And if we allow *Doctor Who* it's off-screen break and revival suitably modernised, me must credit *Come Dancing* not just for its 46 years from 1949 to 1995 but also its 21st Century reincarnation as *Strictly Come Dancing*, taking it to 63 years and counting since it began. Music has also kept *Top of the Pops* on our screens for 49 years, appearing weekly from 1964 to 2006 and as occasional specials since. Two other notable series topping the 50-year mark are more closely related to *Doctor Who*. *The Sky at Night* has been charting the Doctor's playground since 1957, all but one edition presented by the esteemed Patrick Moore until his sad passing in December 2012. The other is *Blue Peter*, a long-time advocate of *Doctor Who*, featuring many items on the programme in its 54 years.

What all these programmes have in common is not necessarily their popularity keeping them going — *Doctor Who* isn't the only one to have had periods when audience sizes were in decline — but that they have, often quite quickly, become part of the national consciousness. Like Big Ben or The Beatles, they're instantly familiar to everyone, even if they haven't actively watched or listened in a while, if ever. Whether they last because they're loved, or they're loved because they've been around for decades, some programmes get to the point where to take them off air would seem a tragedy, that some part of our essential Britishness had been lost. This was notable when the BBC first tried to cancel *Doctor Who* in 1985 and felt the full strength of the support it had not just from a legion of fans but from the general public too. And while it did eventually succeed in taking the programme off air, it was always with the desire, if not the drive, to bring it back refreshed and recuperated. It took a while, but the huge success of the revived series has proven it never left the British public's heart and that even if it's not on for another 50 years solid, there'll always be a place for *Doctor Who*.

50TH LINE OF DIALOGUE
"John Smith is the stage name of the Honourable Aubrey Waites." Ian Chesterton, 'An Unearthly Child' 1

50TH CREDITED CHARACTER
Cameca, 'The Aztecs'

50TH EPISODE
'The Dalek Invasion of Earth' 5

50TH HIGHEST AUDIENCE
'The Crusade'

50TH STORY
'The War Games'

50TH MAJOR VILLAIN
Brigade Leader, 'Inferno'

50TH DUDLEY SIMPSON SCORE
'Underworld'

50TH FOUR-PARTER
'The Ribos Operation'

100TH STORY
'The Stones of Blood'

50TH NOVELISATION
'The War Games'

50TH ALIEN WORLD
Argolis, 'The Leisure Hive'

50TH DIRECTOR
Michael Owen Morris, 'The Awakening'

50TH TERRANCE DICKS NOVELISATION
'Snakedance'

50TH STORY WRITER
Philip Martin, 'Vengeance on Varos'

150TH STORY
'Silver Nemesis'

50TH MONSTER SPECIES
Cheetahs, 'Survival'

50TH STORY ON VHS
'The Silurians'

50TH REPEAT
'Spearhead from Space'

50TH STORY ON DVD
'The Pirate Planet'

200TH STORY
'The Next Doctor'

50TH MURRAY GOLD SCORE
'Victory of the Daleks'

50TH MOST POPULAR STORY AMONG FANS*
'A Good Man Goes to War' *according to Doctor Who Dynamic Rankings as of 23 November 2012

50TH TYPE OF ROBOT
Handbots, 'The Girl Who Waited'

November 1963
November 1964
November 1965
November 1966
November 1967
November 1968
November 1969
November 1970
November 1971
November 1972
November 1973
November 1974
November 1975
November 1976
November 1977
November 1978
November 1979
November 1980
November 1981
November 1982
November 1983
November 1984
November 1985
November 1986
November 1987
November 1988
November 1989
November 1990
November 1991
November 1992
November 1993
November 1994
November 1995
November 1996
November 1997
November 1998
November 1999
November 2000
November 2001
November 2002
November 2003
November 2004
November 2005
November 2006
November 2007
November 2008
November 2009
November 2010
November 2011
November 2012
November 2013

25784274R00067

Made in the USA
Lexington, KY
04 September 2013